CONSTITUTIONAL PARIAH

Landmark Cases in Canadian Law

Since Confederation, Canada's highest court – first the Judicial Committee of the Privy Council in England and then the Supreme Court of Canada – has issued a series of often contentious decisions that have fundamentally shaped the nation. Both cheered and jeered, these judgments have impacted every aspect of Canadian society, setting legal precedents and provoking social change. The issues in the judgments range from Aboriginal title, gender equality, and freedom of expression to Quebec secession and intellectual property. This series offers comprehensive, book-length examinations of high court cases that have had a major impact on Canadian law, politics, and society.

Other books in the series are:

The Tenth Justice: Judicial Appointments, Marc Nadon, and the Supreme Court Act Reference by Carissima Mathen and Michael Plaxton

From Wardship to Rights: The Guerin *Case and Aboriginal Law* by Jim Reynolds

Privacy in Peril: Hunter v Southam *and the Drift from Reasonable Search Protections* by Richard Jochelson and David Ireland

Flawed Precedent: The St. Catherine's *Case and Aboriginal Title* by Kent McNeil

For a list of other titles,
see www.ubcpress.ca/landmark-cases-in-canadian-law.

**LANDMARK CASES
IN CANADIAN LAW**

CONSTITUTIONAL PARIAH

Reference re Senate Reform
and the Future of Parliament

Emmett Macfarlane

UBCPress · Vancouver · Toronto

30 29 28 27 26 25 24 23 22 21   5 4 3 2

Printed in Canada on FSC-certified ancient-forest-free paper (100% post-consumer recycled) that is processed chlorine- and acid-free.

Library and Archives Canada Cataloguing in Publication

Title: Constitutional pariah : reference re Senate reform and the
   future of Parliament / Emmett Macfarlane.
Names: Macfarlane, Emmett, author.
Series: Landmark cases in Canadian law.
Description: Series statement: Landmark cases in Canadian law |
   Includes bibliographical references and index.
Identifiers: Canadiana (print) 20200400657 | Canadiana (ebook)
   20200400711 | ISBN 9780774866217 (hardcover) |
   ISBN 9780774866224 (paperback) | ISBN 9780774866231 (PDF) |
   ISBN 9780774866248 (EPUB)
Subjects: LCSH: Canada. Parliament. Senate—Reform. | LCSH: Canada.
   Supreme Court. | CSH: Canada—Politics and
   government—2006–2015.
Classification: LCC JL155 .M125 2021 | DDC 328.71/071—dc23

Canadä

UBC Press gratefully acknowledges the financial support for our publishing program of the Government of Canada (through the Canada Book Fund), the Canada Council for the Arts, and the British Columbia Arts Council.

This book has been published with the help of a grant from the Canadian Federation for the Humanities and Social Sciences, through the Awards to Scholarly Publications Program, using funds provided by the Social Sciences and Humanities Research Council of Canada.

UBC Press
The University of British Columbia
2029 West Mall
Vancouver, BC V6T 1Z2
www.ubcpress.ca

In memory of

ALAN CAIRNS,

*one of Canada's foremost scholars of Canadian politics,
federalism, and the Constitution,
and a source of incredible kindness and inspiration*

Contents

Acknowledgments

I never thought I'd write a book about the Senate. I came to this project by way of my interest in the role of the Supreme Court of Canada, and as part of a more recent research focus on constitutional change. I am indebted to Richard Albert, who has repeatedly demonstrated his generosity by inviting me to conferences and to write on different aspects of constitutional change. The first such invite was to a colloquium at McGill University in 2014, focusing on *Reference re Senate Reform.* That event was the genesis of extensive thinking about institutional reform of Parliament and constitutional amendment.

I have benefitted from casual discussions or formal feedback in these areas from a large number of people, all of whom, whether they know it or not, contributed to the intellectual development of this book (and some of whom will disagree with the arguments herein). My thanks to Richard Albert, Dennis Baker, Patrick Baud, Kate Glover Berger, the late Alan Cairns, Jamie Cameron, Andrew Coyne, Erin Crandall, Paul Daly, Elizabeth Goodyear-Grant, Kyle Hanniman, Matt Hennigar, the late Peter Hogg, Mark Jarvis, Phil Lagassé, Robert Leckey, Mary Liston, Carissima Mathen, Dwight Newman, Benjamin Oliphant, Mike Pal, Alexander Pless, Kate Puddister, Troy Riddell, Leslie Seidle, Léonid Sirota, Dale Smith, David E. Smith, Dave Snow, and Paul G. Thomas.

My thanks as well to the public servants and parliamentarians who agreed to not-for-attribution interviews, as well as those senators who granted on-the-record interviews: Joseph A. Day, Peter Harder, Yonah Martin, and Yuen Pau Woo.

Chapter 4 is a revised and expanded version of arguments made in "Unsteady Architecture: Ambiguity, the Senate Reference, and the

Future of Constitutional Amendment in Canada" (2015) 60:4 McGill LJ 883. Chapter 5 is an updated and expanded version of "The Renewed Canadian Senate: Organizational Challenges and Relations with the Government" (IRPP Study 71, May 2019). My thanks to the Institute for Research on Public Policy for authorizing the use of this material.

This is my second book with UBC Press. I am very grateful to have worked with Randy Schmidt, who so expertly guided the book through the review process and who is unfailingly helpful and generous with his time. My thanks as well to all of the other UBC Press staff. I am also grateful to the anonymous peer reviewers for their helpful comments and suggestions.

I am fortunate to have the support of many friends and colleagues. My thanks to those who have been particularly supportive during this project, including Christopher Bennett, Andrea Collins, Shelby Davies, Anna Esselment, Aaron Ettinger, Dan Henstra, Jasmin Habib, Rachael Johnstone, Mariam Mufti, and Heather Whiteside. My parents, Don and Eileen Macfarlane, my sister, Aingeal Macfarlane, and my in-laws, Peter and Karolyn Drake, are a constant source of support. As always, none of this would be possible without the care and encouragement of my wife, Anna, and the minimal amount of toleration from our daughter, Thea, who is far too young to know what the Senate is but wise enough to know that politics sounds "silly."

CONSTITUTIONAL PARIAH

INTRODUCTION

The Making of a Landmark Case

IN *REFERENCE RE SENATE REFORM*, the Supreme Court of Canada
ruled out major unilateral reform of the Senate of Canada by
Parliament. The federal government, headed by Prime Minister
Stephen Harper's Conservative Party of Canada, had sought to enact
consultative elections and senatorial term limits for the upper house.
The Senate was enmeshed in a scandal over expenses, and the public
overwhelmingly favoured reform or abolition of the deeply unpopular
institution. The court's 2014 decision might have stood as a simple
story of the country's apex court acting, as it occasionally does, as a veto
player via constitutional interpretation. If left at that, the reference
could be regarded as just one of a string of constitutional defeats for
the government of the day,[1] or analogized to the many times the court
has adjudicated disputes between the two orders of government throughout the country's history.[2] Yet two factors make the decision stand out:
first, within a very short period of time, the decision contributed to the
most significant reform of the Senate – arguably even Parliament – in
Canadian history; second, it marked the Supreme Court's first comprehensive foray into articulating the boundaries between key procedures
in the constitutional amending formula since its entrenchment in 1982.

This book examines *Reference re Senate Reform* as a landmark case
in Canadian constitutional law. With an analysis of the decision at its
centre, the book undertakes a study of the Senate in light of the changes

implemented after 2014. It also assesses the decision's implications for the future prospects of constitutional change in Canada more broadly.

As a study of the Senate, the book first sets the context by exploring the various roles of Parliament's upper house, how its performance in fulfilling them has evolved, and historical efforts at reform. The Senate's critics view the institution as an anachronism in a modern democracy, with some advocating reform to make it an elected body and others wishing it were abolished altogether. These are far from new ideas as they relate to the upper house – it has long been the pariah of Canada's governing institutions. Such displeasure with the Senate, however, runs headlong into a constitutional framework and intergovernmental political context that makes reform notoriously difficult to achieve. The Harper government thought it had found a way to effect reform of the Senate without recourse to formal constitutional amendment. *Reference re Senate Reform* is, in part, the story of how the Supreme Court put an end to that aspiration but – perhaps ironically – paved the way for informal change to the Senate appointments process that may have lasting effects on Parliament and the legislative process for decades to come.

As a study of constitutional reform, this book explores the potentially far-reaching effects *Reference re Senate Reform* has for the future of constitutional change in Canada. Despite the changes to the Senate appointments process, the Supreme Court's arguably nebulous approach to assessing the requirements of the amending formula may ultimately hinder future constitutional change in other contexts. This is significant because the Canadian Constitution is already one of the most difficult to amend in the world.[3] This book will specifically examine the implications of the decision for future attempts at reform, not just with respect to formal amendment but also in relation to informal constitutional change.

The Senate's status as the black sheep of Canada's governing institutions plays a pivotal role in the narrative presented in these pages. Historically, when the Senate of Canada has not been generally ignored, it has been an object of derision or controversy. This was no less true in the lead-up to the 2014 reference, as the Senate found itself mired in an ongoing scandal over improper expenses. The scandal only exacerbated the general public's long-standing dissatisfaction with an unelected and arguably ineffective upper chamber. The political stakes should then be quite apparent: How does a governing party deal with the constitutional pariah that is the Senate without becoming tainted by mere association? In the lead-up to the reference, the Harper government itself became implicated by the expenses scandal, not only by having appointed a number of the senators most directly associated with dubious expenses but also in dealing with the fallout when it was revealed that the prime minister's chief of staff personally cut a cheque to assist one of those senators in reimbursing his expenses. By the time the Supreme Court ruled on the Conservatives' long-delayed reform proposals, the government had little appetite for dealing with the Senate at all – to the point of announcing a constitutionally dubious policy of non-appointment to the upper chamber.

When the Liberals took power under Prime Minister Justin Trudeau in 2015, they were seemingly left with a single option: If major reform or abolition was off the table, would it be possible to repair the institution's reputation by improving its performance? The proposal, a new "merit-based, non-partisan" appointments process, had the twin virtues of good policy and good politics. The Liberals sought to eliminate patronage and partisanship as the main criteria for appointment, installing an independent advisory body to nominate lists of candidates for consideration on the basis of merit, including criteria such as an exemplary record of public service. As a matter of policy, the proposal had the appeal of addressing what might be the most cynical view of the Senate: that it was little more than a halfway house for party hacks. As a matter of politics, the Liberals could insulate themselves from the Senate by emphasizing its renewed independence from the government of the day, thereby making it less likely they could become associated with future senatorial scandal.

The Senate itself has been the object of increasing academic scrutiny in the twenty-first century. From 1867 through 2000, only four book-length studies focusing on the upper house were published.[4] In the last twenty years, this number has more than doubled, in addition to edited collections and myriad articles focusing especially on the topic of Senate reform.[5] The most important modern academic contribution in this vein is David E. Smith's *The Canadian Senate in Bicameral Perspective*, and the present study stands directly on the shoulders of Smith's and other previous works. Like many (though certainly not all) of these works, this book is written from the perspective of someone who believes an appointed Senate can serve a useful, if modest, function in the context of the broader democratic parliamentary system. This is especially true in light of the reforms that followed *Reference re Senate Reform*.

One of the unique aspects of the court's decision as a landmark case in Canadian law is its status as a reference. References, or "advisory opinions," are notable in the Canadian context in part because countries with similar systems of government (such as Australia) or courts comparably empowered with judicial review (such as the United States) do not permit the use of the reference procedure. Indeed, in the US context, advisory opinions are not permitted because the constitution limits federal courts to resolving cases and controversies (advisory opinions are technically not considered cases, although for reasons described in the next paragraph I do not consider "landmark case" a misnomer in this context). In Canada, references typically pertain to constitutional matters, but they can involve any area of law. Until recently, the legacy of the reference power was relatively understudied in Canada, but two books, one by legal scholar Carissima Mathen and another by political scientist Kate Puddister, shed important light on the dynamics around references and their general impact on doctrine and government decision making.[6]

One of the most notable features of references in the Canadian experience is that, as Mathen emphasizes, they contain all the trappings of regular cases. Technically nonbinding, they are treated as every bit as authoritative as any judicial decision, not only by governments that consistently adhere to the decisions but also by the courts themselves (Mathen notes, for example, the tendency of judges to apply them via *stare decisis* as they would normal cases, or even apply remedies).[7] This is backed up by interview-based research where Supreme Court justices view references as a serious component of their work and an opportunity to provide clarity to other branches of government on issues of import-ance.[8] And it is clear that references are among some of the most notable judicial decisions in Canadian legal history, ranging from landmarks like the *Patriation Reference*[9] or the constitutionality of Quebec secession[10] to some of the leading federalism and Charter cases.[11] As Puddister notes, references also routinely result in the invalidation or rejection of legislation and policy (in more than a third of all such cases). They also feature a high third-party intervener participation rate – indeed, *Reference re Senate Reform* is among the highest of such cases, with seventeen interveners (twelve of them governments).[12]

Yet what distinguishes references is the ability of governments to choose to defer a degree of authority over policy-making to courts, and to frame the questions about legal (and often fundamentally political) issues in often broad and calculated ways. As Puddister writes, there is considerable evidence of a strategic dimension to the decision to initiate references, including using them as a method for dealing with hot-potato political issues, freezing the politics around an issue for a time, or even forcing negotiations between governments. Governments might be seeking assurance, not only about the constitutionality of their position or policy proposals but also to get courts to effect the political legitimization of those policies.[13]

The fact that many references take place in the context of abstract review (rather than dealing with a concrete case involving litigants directly affected by a law or policy) also structures how the Supreme Court deals with the issues before it, especially as it relates to highly salient constitutional references like the Quebec secession decision or *Reference re Senate Reform*. Mathen points out that institutional references like these involve "highly contested disputes that were inescapably political."[14] This is a feature of many constitutional cases, but the abstract nature of certain references effectively invites creativity on the part of the court. In the secession reference, the court famously articulated a novel duty to negotiate but then disavowed any direct oversight of a process that might result in negotiations over secession, something Mathen points out perhaps "signaled the Court's awareness that it was on less-than-solid constitutional ground."[15]

Reference re Senate Reform similarly has the Supreme Court drawing principles from the abstract. The court explicitly bases its decision on an approach that requires recourse to the nebulous concept of the constitutional "architecture." Changes to the basic structure of the Constitution, the court argues, require provincial consent. This approach obliges the court itself to correctly identify and describe the animating core features of the institutions, processes, and values comprising the Constitution and then determine whether they are essential or not. It is a recipe for uncertainty, unintended consequences, and the creation of virtually unlimited judicial discretion over the acceptability of future constitutional reform proposals. In this respect, the analysis of this landmark case extends well beyond its immediate impact on the Senate.

This book consists of six chapters. In Chapter 1, I examine the various roles of the Senate, including its roles as an independent chamber of sober second thought, as a defender of regional interests, as a protector of property rights, and as a defender of minority rights. These roles emanate from the Confederation debates and the essential purposes of the upper house, but they have evolved over time. The Senate's record in fulfilling any one of these roles is mixed at best, and that mediocre-to-poor performance has contributed to the various reform proposals that have emerged, particularly over the last half-century. Yet it is also worth noting the ways in which these roles can sometimes come into tension, if not outright contradiction. An understanding of the Senate's disparate roles is important because changes to them that are viewed by the court as essential – even ones that seem relatively minor on their face – now trigger a requirement for provincial consent under the constitutional amending formula.

Chapter 2 explores historical reform proposals with an analysis of why these efforts have continuously failed. Critics of the Senate have generally been divided between those supporting various efforts to improve the institution along different dimensions and those in favour of abolishing the upper house altogether. Should provinces have a say in appointments, such that the Senate's role as a defender of regional interests can be strengthened? Should the Senate be elected, to satisfy those who view it as a vestige of an undemocratic tradition? Any of these changes would likely have profound implications for other aspects of the Senate's functioning, including its independence or its role as a complementary chamber of sober second thought. The perennial failure of these reform efforts in part reflects the fact that certain reforms were at cross-purposes with what other Senate critics disliked about the institution and wanted to see changed. This lack of consensus among the Senate's fiercest critics persists to this day. The chapter concludes with a brief examination of more modest or informal proposals for reform.

The events leading up to *Reference re Senate Reform* are presented in Chapter 3. The chapter examines the Conservative government's legislative initiatives to introduce term limits for senators and consultative elections for senatorial selection. A series of difficulties, ranging from the government's minority status from 2006 to 2011, followed shortly by the explosive scandal over Senate expenses, contributed to delays in getting various bills to third reading in the House of Commons. The chapter then explores the lead-up to the reference itself, including an analysis of the reference first posed by the Quebec government to its own court of appeal. The combined effects of the scandal over expenses and Quebec's legal maneuvering compelled the federal government to initiate its own reference, setting the stage for the Supreme Court's landmark decision.

The Supreme Court's decision in *Reference re Senate Reform* is analyzed in Chapter 4. In finding that the Harper government's proposed reforms required provincial consent under the general procedure of the constitutional amending formula, the court articulated its own view of the Senate's role, one that is arguably simplistic and incomplete. Moreover, although the court likely came to the correct conclusion regarding the introduction of consultative elections, the analysis in Chapter 4 reveals that its logic as it relates to the issue of term limits suffers from serious inconsistencies. Most importantly, the court's approach to assessing the requirements for the amending formula – premised in part on the idea that changes to the "constitutional architecture" require provincial consent – introduces considerable uncertainty for future constitutional change.

Chapter 5 undertakes a study of the reform to the Senate appointments process in 2016, and the operation of the renewed Senate in its aftermath. The chapter provides a bit of an insider's perspective on the reform, as I provided non-partisan, unpaid advice to the government in crafting the new advisory process for appointments. The chapter then turns to appraising the major effects of the turn towards a merit-based, non-partisan appointments process. The rise of independent senators created organizational difficulties and added considerably to the complexity of the legislative process, particularly from the government's perspective. Parliament also witnessed a spike in amendment activity from the upper house, as both the independent senators and the Conservative opposition demonstrated a growing willingness to propose changes to government bills. Yet the Senate avoided obstructionism. It neither blocked government legislation nor played ping-pong with the House of Commons over bills. Thus, the renewed Senate has so far served the role largely envisioned for it: active engagement to improve or safeguard legislation while avoiding conflict or competition with the elected chamber. Much remains to be seen, particularly with regard to how a non-partisan upper house will come to organize itself. Further, the analysis is limited to the duration of a single Parliament. It remains unclear how senators appointed under the new process will conduct themselves in the context of a government of a different stripe.

Chapter 6 begins with an explanation of why the 2016 reform to the appointments process was constitutional, with reference to the court's logic in *Reference re Senate Reform*. Yet the success of the 2016 reform may constitute an outlier. The chapter examines why the court's approach clouds what future reforms to the Senate might be possible under the amending formula. It then turns to broader constitutional change, noting that the reference threatens to exacerbate Canada's constitutional stasis. Even informal changes, or attempts to alter constitutional conventions, may be heavily implicated by the court's structural approach, to the detriment of the flexibility and appropriate evolution of the Constitution and the various institutions, processes, and values that comprise it.

The conclusion examines the two major legacies of *Reference re Senate Reform* – its impact on reform of the Senate itself and its implications for future constitutional change. First, many of the criticisms of the renewed Senate focus on the impact the changes have for senatorial independence and for the functioning of Parliament. From the perspective of some critics, the enhanced legitimacy conferred upon the Senate by the elimination of patronage and partisanship threatens to turn the Senate into an activist or obstructionist chamber. Other critics fear unintended and negative consequences stemming from the elimination of partisanship in the Senate. My analysis suggests that these criticisms suffer from a misguided or distorted conception of independence, which includes both the independence of the Senate at the institutional level and the independence of individual senators. Second, the conclusion briefly dissects the prospects for creative constitutional change in light of *Reference re Senate Reform*. Although there may be possibilities to replicate the sort of informal reform brought about for the Senate appointments process, I argue that such reforms are akin to walking on a tightrope. To one side lies constitutional stasis, to the other the danger of inventive but ultimately illegitimate attempts at constitutional change. Whatever transpires, the legacy of *Reference re Senate Reform* for both Parliament itself and the future of Canada's constitutional evolution will continue to play out for years to come.

1

The Senate's (Unfulfilled) Roles

A T THE TIME OF Confederation, the inclusion of an upper
house in the new Parliament was inevitable. As David E. Smith
notes, "it would have been inconceivable not to have followed
the model" of bicameralism,[1] both for the obvious favouritism shared
by most of Canada's constitutional framers towards the British exemplar
and for the basic fact of federalism. The key debates over the Senate,
which absorbed much of the 1864 Quebec Conference in the lead-up
to Confederation, concerned the extent of representation allotted to the
smaller provinces to compensate for the intention of a representation-
by-population basis for apportioning seats in the lower house. Yet while
the question of regional representation tends to dominate discussions
of the Senate's origins, the constitutional framers had a number of roles
in mind for the upper house. This includes the much-vaunted role of
the Senate as a chamber of "sober second thought," with the upper
house intended to act as an independent check on the worst impulses
of the popularly elected lower house, and especially the Cabinet. The
Senate is also regarded as a defender of minority rights and a protector
of private property.

This chapter examines the Senate's evolving history through its
disparate roles and its execution of them. It finds that the Senate's
performance on any of these fronts is subject to much debate and
disagreement. If the Senate acts with too much verve as an independent

check on the Commons or the executive, it is attacked as illegitimate. If it evinces too much deference, it is a useless rubber stamp. Whether viewed as an undemocratic thorn or a waste of resources, Canada's constitutional pariah can never seem to win. Its defenders, meanwhile, will consistently remind us that its valued sober second thought capacity extends beyond the brute force of its legislative powers. These disagreements are at the heart of the reform debates examined in Chapter 2. In relation to the Senate's roles, it may surprise some to learn of the sizable chasms between how we talk about the Senate's purpose and how it has evolved in practice. The Senate has never been a particularly strong defender of regional interests, a function of the relatively weak exercise of its powers coupled with the fact that it is appointed, and has historically organized itself, on a partisan basis. Its role as a defender of minority rights emerges infrequently and pales in comparison with the role of the courts in the period since the *Canadian Charter of Rights and Freedoms*. And its role as a protector of property has all but vanished from contemporary discourse.

This chapter thus serves as the broad historical and institutional foundation to a primary background question faced by the Supreme Court of Canada in the 2014 *Reference re Senate Reform:* What is the Senate for? The questions of what the constitutional framers intended, how the Senate operates in practice, and how it has evolved with respect to its various roles all seem relevant to identifying the institution's role. Given that the court's landmark reference opinion centred on whether that role would be altered by certain reform proposals, and whether the provinces have an interest in those changes, the analysis in this chapter provides a basis for understanding and critically examining the court's reasoning.

THE SENATE AS AN INDEPENDENT CHAMBER

Janet Ajzenstat writes that the theory of checks and balances as it relates to a parliamentary system "regards Cabinet ministers as potential tyrants, the ambitious leaders in the lower house as potential demagogues, and senators as potential oligarchs. When all is working as it should, when the branches are free to check each other, the system forestalls the three classic forms of despotism."[2] The expectation among framers was thus that the Senate would act as a fully independent body within Parliament. Most frequently quoted on this point among the framers is John A. Macdonald, in debate in the legislative assembly:

> [The Senate] would be of no value whatever if it were a mere Chamber for registering the decrees of the Lower House. It must be an independent House, having a free action of its own, for it is only valuable as being a regulating body, calmly considering the legislation initiated by the popular branch, and preventing any hasty or ill-considered legislation which may have come from that body, but which will never set itself in opposition to the deliberate and understood wishes of the people.[3]

Similarly, George Brown noted that the desire among framers "was to render the Upper House a thoroughly independent body, one that would be in the best position to canvass dispassionately the measures of this House, and stand up for the public interest in opposition to hasty or partisan legislation."[4]

The composition of the Senate differs from the British House of Lords in important respects, and the most immediately obvious one to the framers was the fact that the colonies lacked an aristocratic class. The Canadian Senate, therefore, would not come to represent the upper class (at least in a narrow sense) or protect it from unruly democratic decisions of those who represent the masses, but it would nonetheless embody a "deeply rooted conservatism" as the basis for the functioning of upper houses in modern times.[5] Thus in terms of its role, "the absence of feudal-aristocratic elements from the social environment made no difference in the expectations as to the substantive function of a second chamber."[6]

How could the Senate exercise this desired independence as an appointed body? Whatever influence the House of Lords may have had on the framers' intentions surrounding the Senate, the framers were not ignorant of the electoral option. The upper house of the Province of Canada, the Legislative Council, underwent reform to hold elections for new seats in 1856. This reform was in part due to complaints about obstructionism.[7] Yet the result was a Legislative Council emboldened by its elected status and that directly opposed legislation passed by the lower chamber (including a supply bill in 1859), raising the spectre of long-term deadlock.[8] This experience led representatives from Canada to favour an appointed upper chamber for the Senate, including Macdonald, who had been a supporter of elective reform in 1856.[9] In the Confederation debates, only Prince Edward Island advocated strongly for an elected Senate, while most founders opposed the proposition for fear of conflict between the two houses (although the Opposition in the Canadian legislative assembly argued that an appointive chamber was a retrograde step).[10] Brown argued that a system of appointments would ensure the independence of the upper house, as with the House of Lords, and that it should be "responsible to no one" and "thus no threat to the operation of responsible government."[11] The impact of an elected upper house on responsible government remains relevant to the ongoing reform debate, and is discussed in more depth below.

Any assessment of whether the Senate has fulfilled its role as a truly independent body is complicated, for several reasons. First, although the framers clearly desired an upper house with the capacity to stifle imprudent or hasty legislation emanating from the popularly elected house – short of introducing money bills, the Senate's formal powers are effectively equal to those of the House of Commons – they also anticipated that the Senate would never act as a legislative roadblock or in a way that would create deadlock between the two houses. This is reflected by Macdonald's statement that the Senate will "never set itself in opposition to the deliberate and understood wishes of the people."[12] This "democratic character" of the Senate was not sufficient to assuage the concern of the British secretary of state for the colonies, Henry Herbert, the Earl of Carnarvon, over the risk of collision between the two houses. Lord Carnarvon "insisted that some provision should be made in the *British North America Act* to overcome such a contingency, should it arise."[13] The result was section 26 of the act, a safety valve provision permitting the addition of four or eight senators (representing equally the various regions) to overcome deadlock. Section 26 would not be used for over century, and, as discussed below, has been used only once in Canadian history.

Second, the Senate's role in this regard, at least as represented by the degree of activity it has generated in proposed amendments to legislation, has evolved considerably over time. For example, in the period from 1867 to 1960, the Senate amended 20.4 percent of all bills coming from the House of Commons.[14] The Senate began to demonstrate considerable deference to the lower house in the modern era. For example, from 1963 to 1974, the percentage of bills amended by the Senate fell to only 3.5.[15] The outright veto rate of bills during these two periods also fell, from 2.4 percent from 1867 to 1960[16] to 1.2 percent from 1963 to 1974.[17] During a more recent period, the Senate's amendment rate settled a bit higher, at 8.3 percent from 1994 to 2011.[18] This evolution in the extent of the Senate's role and activity is reflected in existing scholarship, but it is somewhat remarkable that early studies of the Senate were every bit as interested in how often the *House* amended and rejected Senate bills as vice versa. The idea that the House "has been more drastic" in amending Senate legislation would likely be viewed as irrelevant to observers today.[19] Such is the modern view of the Senate as a vestigial organ rather than an independent, active body of Parliament.

Finally, identifying whether the Senate has generally hit the sweet spot between being a vigilant, independent house exercising its powers to prevent or correct undue legislative initiatives and one that is obstructing the will of the people is hardly a science. Simple descriptive statistics about amendment rates or the exercise of the legislative veto tell only a part of the story. For one thing, many of the Senate's amendments to bills are "technical" rather than substantive. They involve drafting corrections, changes at the request of government, or administrative improvements consistent with the purpose or objectives of the bill. One study analyzing the period from 1925 to 1963 found that 70 percent of the Senate's amendments to legislation were technical in nature, rather than fundamental changes to bills or their purpose.[20] This may go some way to explaining why a strong majority of Senate amendments are normally accepted by the House of Commons.[21] The Senate can also employ an "indirect veto" by delaying legislation or returning it with amendments shortly before an expected dissolution, as it did with a 1996 bill regulating negative option billing by cable companies.[22] Finally, an on-again, off-again exercise of "pre-study" of bills before they arrive from the House has sometimes seen the Senate propose amendments before the bills have received a final vote in the House, and the proposed Senate changes are incorporated into the Commons' version of the legislation.

As for the rarely used veto power, a general consensus has emerged that this should be reserved for particularly egregious legislative initiatives and with a high level of justification, limited to only a few situations. One possible list of contexts under which the Senate might defeat a bill outright includes: when it is of grave detriment to one or more regions; when it violates constitutional rights; when it is of grave detriment to linguistic or other minorities; when it is of such importance that the government should seek a new mandate; or when it is so repugnant that it represents a quasi-abuse of the legislative power of Parliament.[23]

Given evolving democratic norms, even this list might be overly liberal. For example, the idea that the Senate should ever determine when a sitting government should seek a new mandate is arguably an affront to the principle of responsible government, wherein the government must maintain the confidence of a majority of members of the elected House of Commons. The Senate is not the confidence chamber in Parliament, and arguably oversteps its proper role when it attempts to assert the power to do so (as it did during the 1980s, discussed below). In a broader sense, those who question the Senate's democratic legitimacy on the basis of its unelected nature might consider *any* use of the veto normatively unacceptable.

The upper house's exercise of amendment or veto powers is only part of the story. The Senate's sober second thought role has been important in another respect, specifically its committee investigations and special studies. C.E.S. (Ned) Franks, for example, points to influential committee investigations on land use in 1957 that had an important impact on agricultural legislation, and on science policy in 1967. He contends that the Senate's investigations are generally at a higher standard than similar work in the House of Commons:

> Reasons for the differences included: first, many extremely able and experienced Canadians sit in the Senate and contribute to this investigative work; second, investigations by the Senate are usually non-partisan; third, Senate investigations do not suffer from excessive exposure in the media; fourth, senators have the time and leisure to conduct diligent research and exhaustive analysis; and fifth, investigators can work on for many years, immune from the vagaries and demands of the electoral process.[24]

The long-term perspective of the Senate is an important element of its unique contribution and sober second thought role. The work of the Standing Committee on Social Affairs, Science and Technology to conduct a two-year study of health care in 2000–02 is an important example: if "undertaken by the House of Commons, it would take up nearly half of the members' entire term and, in this particular case, would have risked being disrupted by the fall 2000 election. Moreover, there would be considerable pressure to generate short-term results that would bolster the members' immediate electoral chances."[25]

Many of the Senate's defenders point to its committee work as the prime example of the institution's effectiveness. Even here, however, there is evidence that this may be overstated. Andrea Lawlor and Erin Crandall report that while a committee like the Legal and Constitutional Affairs Committee acts as "a workhorse for legislative review," even it only occasionally produces legislative change.[26] In their study of the work of Senate committees, Lawlor and Crandall thus report that "the Senate may not be as systematic a check on the power of the House of Commons as sometimes thought."[27]

Partisanship and Independence

There is a lack of clarity on the extent to which partisanship negatively affects the Senate's capacity to act with independence or as a vigilant check on executive power or poorly conceived legislation. Writing in 1926, Robert Mackay notes that the "most serious objection to the system of appointments is that it has failed to give to the members of the Senate the character of independence of party ties."[28] In the revised edition of his study nearly four decades later, Mackay still agrees with this sentiment but notes that a broader tradition of non-partisanship "seems to be more firmly established," basing this on a period from 1940 to 1960 when the Senate majority was held by a different party than the government and it not once rejected a government bill.[29] A more recent study by Jean-François Godbout presents the most comprehensive account of partisanship in the upper house. Godbout's analysis confirms a decline in party unity, at least among Liberals, in the 1940s. However, partisan voting in the Senate has generally increased in a linear fashion over time, to the point where since the 1980s voting unity levels for the two main parties exceeded 90 percent.[30]

Beyond voting patterns, there is qualitative evidence that the intensity of partisan behaviour in the upper chamber has ebbed and flowed over time. Indeed, Godbout notes that the Senate's activism usually increases in periods of divided government.[31] Personalities and leadership within the Senate are sometimes considered causal factors in these shifting tendencies. Raoul Dandurand was a long-time organizer for the Liberal Party in Quebec and a high-level adviser to Prime Ministers Wilfrid Laurier and Mackenzie King. He was appointed to the Senate in 1898, serving as Speaker of the Senate from 1905 to 1909 and as either Government Leader or Opposition Leader in the Senate from 1921 until his death in 1949. Dandurand adopted a fiercely non-partisan attitude towards the work of the Senate, something perhaps informed by the fact that he "had never been a member of the House of Commons, and, therefore, he was not imbued with the mentality of an almost mechanical self-subordination to a parliamentary party machine."[32] It is perhaps no coincidence that his death correlates somewhat with the end of less partisan voting behaviour by Liberal senators at the time. According to F.A. Kunz, in Dandurand's "image of the Upper house as a body of independent-minded elder statesmen coolly exercising judicial impartiality there was no room for a formal party machinery, which would only accentuate a spirit that ought to be extirpated by all means."[33]

In fact, in Dandurand's view an ideal Senate would not even have a Government Leader, and each minister would select individual senators to pilot legislation independently through the upper chamber. Further, he believed the Senate should not sit along party lines, nor should senators attend party caucus meetings (which he personally avoided) so as to "remain away from the political atmosphere of the Commons."[34] These ideas presage events following *Reference re Senate Reform,* which saw the elimination of the government caucus in the upper chamber. Dandurand's virtually *anti*-partisan view did not take complete hold in the Senate but was clearly influential during his leadership role there, as Mackay's and Godbout's analyses suggest. Even former prime minister Arthur Meighen, upon his own appointment to the Senate, became a convert to Dandurand's perspective, and subsequently argued that the "Senate is worthless if it becomes merely another Commons divided upon party lines and indulging in party debates."[35]

Dandurand's position on partisanship in the Senate is noteworthy as an indicator that the nature and extent of partisanship in the Senate is not a fixed or entrenched variable. In the broad context of Canadian history, his attitude is no doubt in the minority, but critics of the 2016 reform who decry the non-partisan appointments process as a departure from the Senate's proper design overstate their case. Undoubtedly most of the framers would have assumed patronage and partisanship as a feature of appointments, but the degree of partisanship, and the lack of balance prime ministers generally exhibited in making almost all of their appointments from individuals of their own party are not part of some ordained design. As Smith writes, "the long periods of one-party rule that followed Confederation and the expansion of the national party system into the provinces of Canada" were unforeseen events that may help explain why the Senate has not performed as the framers expected.[36] Without those intervening events, appointments to the upper house may have been more balanced and less afflicted with patronage. Regardless, there is no good reason that the appointing culture has clung to partisanship – let alone patronage – for as long as it has.

To the extent that the core role of the Senate was as an independent body capable of sober second thought, the evolution of partisan control is something that has worked against the institution's performance on this score. This is examined further in Chapter 5. Yet it is also worth noting in the present analysis that rule changes and procedural innovations within the upper house have, according to Godbout, been "introduced with the explicit goal of transforming the Senate into a more partisan chamber."[37] For example, the Liberals in 1984 abandoned the use of pre-study, and in 1991 changes by the Conservative majority increased the government's control of the legislative agenda. In Godbout's view, "these changes contributed to altering the dynamic of debates in the upper chamber by promoting divisions between Conservative and Liberal senators."[38]

Even when the Senate has evinced independence from the lower house, partisanship has arguably encouraged it to cross a line into pure obstructionism rather than sober second thought. The most prominent contemporary example of this is the Liberal-dominated Senate that greeted Prime Minister Brian Mulroney's government in 1984. Senate Opposition Leader Allan MacEachen's "ardent partisanship"[39] was at least partly responsible for a level of Senate obstructionism unprecedented in the modern era. That period saw the Senate refusing to approve a borrowing bill in 1985, playing "ping-pong" with the House over amendments to the *Drug Patent Act* for a full year from 1986 to 1987, and forcing an election after refusing to pass legislation for the free trade agreement with the United States in 1988.[40] The Senate's activism during Mulroney's second Parliament was no less obstructionist, as it defeated a compromise bill on abortion in a tie vote, delayed an unemployment insurance bill, and attempted to block the Goods and Services Tax (GST). Only after Mulroney took the unprecedented action of employing section 26 of the *Constitution Act, 1867,* enlarging the Senate by eight members, was the deadlock broken and the GST bill passed.[41]

The Mulroney period and a similar (although more mild) period of tension between a Liberal-dominated Senate and John Diefenbaker's

Progressive Conservative government[42] imply that the problem of partisanship can create unwanted deadlock between the two houses when the government does not control the upper house.[43] With the benefit of hindsight, some argue that "[c]lashes between the two houses were so inevitable from the start that it is difficult to believe that a politician as astute as Macdonald did not anticipate them."[44] The problem of appointments as an exercise of partisan patronage is one of the major sources of condemnation the institution faces, particularly when flare-ups between the two houses occur (or whenever a scandal involving the Senate surfaces).

To what extent might partisanship explain a generally deferential, less-than-fully-independent Senate? As it pertains specifically to amendments, Andrew Heard's statistical analysis suggests that the size of the government majority in the Commons has "a far greater correlation to Senate amending activity" than the partisan mix.[45] Some important qualifiers should be placed on this analysis, however. First, the statistical data are limited to the period from 1957 to 1988. Second, Heard's analysis does not appear to account for the difference noted above between technical amendments and substantive amendments to legislation. Nor does it attempt to assess the relative salience of the bills at stake under different configurations – if Senate activity during the Mulroney period was not quantitatively distinct, it was surely qualitatively so. Finally, the introduction of the non-partisan appointments process by Prime Minister Justin Trudeau in 2016 appears to have led directly to a considerable spike in amendment activity. By the end of the 42nd Parliament in 2019, 33 percent of the eighty-eight government bills that received royal assent were subject to amendments by the upper house. The non-partisan nature of the appointments seems to be a prime reason for this. This is one of the primary issues discussed in more detail in Chapter 5.

THE SENATE AS REPRESENTING REGIONAL INTERESTS

The Senate is composed of 105 senators, 24 for each of the regions (Ontario, Quebec, the Maritime provinces, and the four western provinces), 6 for Newfoundland and Labrador, and 1 for each territory. From the perspective of Canada's modern population distribution, this regional breakdown may seem archaic or esoteric, but like many aspects of Canadian constitutional development, much of it is simply derived from historical contingency, messy compromise, and path dependency. The upper house was initially established following a compact featuring the Province of Canada (Ontario and Quebec), Nova Scotia, and New Brunswick (Prince Edward Island declining to enter Confederation until 1873). In 1867, the seventy-two-seat chamber thus saw Ontario and Quebec each with twenty-four seats, with twelve each for Nova Scotia and New Brunswick, over some objections from the smaller Maritime colonies.[46] As relayed in *Dawson's The Government of Canada* text:

> Representation in the Senate was not seen in the 1860s as one of the democratic elements in the constitution. One indication of this was shown in 1873 when Prince Edward Island entered Confederation: the complement of senators was not enlarged to accommodate the new province, but four senators were taken away from the other two maritime provinces to keep the regional total at twenty-four.[47]

As western provinces joined or were created, they were "somewhat arbitrarily"[48] assigned two, three, or four seats until a 1915 constitutional amendment created a new region of twenty-four seats, six for each province. As a result, Peter Russell argues that the "need for Senate reform was built into the very foundations of Confederation."[49] In the modern period, the West in particular has a legitimate claim about its relative underrepresentation in the upper house.

From early on, the Senate's regional composition led observers to declare that the upper house was "the guardian of Provincial rights."[50] While the Senate's regional composition was, in terms of the compact arrived at by the framers in the Confederation debates, in part intended to defend the interests of the smaller provinces against domination by the larger ones (representation by population was the inevitable design intended for the House), the Senate's role in protecting regional interests is often incorrectly conflated with the notion that it is a voice for the provinces. As several scholars point out, the Fathers of Confederation expected senators to be independent of provincial governments. The intention was that the Senate would represent regional interests at the national level, not that it would act as a "house of the provinces."[51]

Prince Edward Island demanded equal representation of the provinces, but its Maritime counterparts did not push as hard.[52] The argument for equality of representation across the provinces (as in the US model) faced an uphill battle in the Canadian context, especially given the unique concerns of francophone Quebec, which was concerned about its numerical position in Parliament overall (this remains relevant to modern attempts at reform, as discussed below).

The federal appointing power was also an issue for some of the participants in the Confederation debates. As Mackay notes, "sectional representation and nomination by the central government seem irreconcilable in principle. It is probable that Macdonald and other leaders who favoured a strong union were convinced of this also, and saw in appointment by the federal government the means of weaning the sections from their particularism."[53] The agreement on regional representation has been described as "the key to federation, 'the very essence of the compact,' said George Brown. 'Our Lower Canadian friends have agreed to give us representation by population in the Lower House, on the express condition that they could have equality in the Upper House. *On no other condition could we have advanced a step.*'"[54]

If regional representation was obviously fundamental for the provinces, does that mean that the Senate's role as protector of regional interests is paramount? This question is fundamental to the Supreme Court's determination in *Reference re Senate Reform* that changes to the Senate's essential features require provincial consent. Some interpretations of what the framers intended suggest that their expectations of the Senate's role were not as lofty as Brown's rhetoric might imply. In defending against criticism of the federal role in appointments, George-Étienne Cartier pointed to Cabinet and even the lower house as providing for additional protections. This leads Mackay to conclude that "it is clear that the Fathers of the federation did not expect that the Senate would be the chief line of defence for the protection of provincial or sectional rights. The first great check on the central government would be in the federal nature of Cabinet; the upper house would be only a last means of defence."[55]

Kunz is even more cynical about what some of the framers intended, arguing that the agreement on regional representation was "a well-calculated political device used as a constitutional tranquilizer to palliate the sectional fears of the weaker partners to federalism from the numerical majorities of the House of Commons. In order that such fears might not endanger the ultimate outcome of the bargain, the value of the Senate as a reliable safeguard of provincial rights had to be stressed."[56] Kunz points out that even with the regional composition, the smaller provinces remain numerically weak in the Senate, and thus "the Senate as a bulwark of provincial rights was essentially a rhetorical device, a psychological rather than a political remedy ... an opiate of the provinces."[57] Other commentators argue that, rather than "a ploy to lure other partners to Confederation," the agreement on the upper house's composition more likely reflected "the Fathers' ambivalence about the machinery required for effective regional representation," something that in turn helps to "explain the tenuity of the Senate's ultimate institutional position."[58]

Many observers view the Senate's performance in fulfilling its role as a voice for regional concerns as ultimately weak.[59] It was not long before the Senate's role in protecting the interests of regions was overshadowed. The provincial rights movement, the first Interprovincial Conference in 1887, regional representation in Cabinet quickly becoming a powerful convention, and the role of the courts – particularly the Judicial Committee of the Privy Council – as arbiters of federalism all became much more influential in protecting provincial powers.[60] In practice, early commentators note that the upper house "has rarely been appealed to as the champion of provincial or section rights and, even when appealed to, it has not consistently supported claims to such rights."[61] One key example is the 1949 constitutional amendment granting Parliament authority over future amendments except in relation to a subset of matters, without provincial consent. Mackay notes that opposition to the amendment was far more vocal in the House than the Senate.[62] Nor were the provinces consulted regarding the 1915 constitutional amendment redefining regional divisions in the Senate and creating one region for the four western provinces.[63]

Moreover, modern executive federalism and the substantial growth in the importance of the provincial governments generally were simply not envisioned by the framers. In that sense, as Ron Watts argues, we risk assessing a representational role for the Senate that it was simply not originally designed to fulfill.[64]

Another account attributes the long-term challenge the Senate has faced in protecting regional interests to other changes in the political system, including the centralization of power in the hands of the government within a system of responsible government, and the increasingly democratic nature of Canadian society. Anti-Confederates in the Maritimes were deeply concerned that the number of seats granted to the region would not be sufficient to prevent their smaller provinces from being overwhelmed by those from Ontario and Quebec, but in Phillip Buckner's view, the seat count would become irrelevant once those other factors took hold.[65] The Senate would end up with insufficient power or legitimacy to act as a meaningful voice for the Maritimes. Similarly, Donald Savoie argues that the extent to which Macdonald's sober second thought role for the Senate has dominated the collective imagination of what the institution's primary role should be "has taken away from the Senate's most crucial role according to the constitution" – its role as regional voice.[66]

Other scholars argue that the Senate has occasionally served a useful function in looking out for regional interests. Despite his harsh rhetoric about the emptiness of the framers' promises regarding the upper house's regional role, Kunz argues the Senate from 1925 to 1963 was a "distinguished spokesman of the component parts of Canadian federalism" through its "revisory" and committee work.[67] He acknowledges that this was an auxiliary rather than leading role, however.[68]

Writing in a more contemporary context, Paul G. Thomas readily identifies a number of important instances when the Senate did act on behalf of regional concerns, including initiating amendments to a 1977 maritime bill that threatened to abolish all ports of registry and replace them with the single port of Ottawa; attempting amendments to the *Unemployment Insurance Act* under the Mulroney government that reduced benefits to seasonal workers (particularly affecting the Atlantic provinces); introducing tax credits for low-income individuals to a 1997 bill to harmonize the GST with provincial sales taxes in three Atlantic provinces; and introducing amendments based on Senate testimony of nearly two hundred individuals and organizations from the Prairies to a bill on the *Wheat Board Act* in 1998.[69]

The contemporary Senate offers its own examples. In 2019, a majority of senators on the Standing Committee on Transport and Communications voted to recommend against Bill C-48, the *Oil Tanker Moratorium Act,* and did so on the justification of regional concerns.[70] (The bill would ultimately pass.) This is a particularly interesting case because within a nominally "regional" context it offers competing provincial perspectives. On the one hand, the Government of Alberta vociferously opposed the legislation, with Premier Jason Kenney calling the law "a prejudicial attack on Alberta, banning from Canada's northwest coast only one product – bitumen – produced in only one province, Alberta."[71] On the other hand, British Columbia also had a direct interest in the legislation as providing environmental protection for its northern coast, on which basis that government articulated its support for the law.[72]

As this most recent example makes clear, the interests of the provinces should not be conflated with the representation of regions within a national Parliament. As noted above, the regional composition of the upper house is embedded in historical contingency and the relevance of several intersecting factors, including the presence of Quebec and Canada's linguistic and cultural duality (setting aside for the moment the presence of Indigenous peoples and the colonizers' complete antipathy towards any involvement in Confederation for them), the federal reality of the Constitution, and regionalism in a large and diverse new country. The regional basis for the Senate's composition begins to look less esoteric when the relevance of regionalism is taken into consideration, as it has been in other institutional contexts, including appointments to the Supreme Court and to the federal Cabinet, and, as Smith notes, even the federal regional veto act of 1996, legislation that further complicates Parliament's role and approach to the constitutional amending formula.[73] This reality further complicates Senate reform proposals and their consequences, as discussed in the next chapter.

THE SENATE AS DEFENDER OF PROPERTY

Another key role of the Senate as envisioned by the framers was the protection of property. This should be distinguished from a particular interest in defending the interests of the upper crust; indeed, the framers felt that the Senate would avoid one of the defects of the House of Lords by not containing a hereditary class, and that "the property qualifications would not be so high as to distinguish [senators] sharply from their fellow citizens."[74] The constitutional eligibility requirement of at least $4,000 in personal property (a sizable sum in 1867, but not as high a cut-off as some wanted) was as much designed to ensure the individual independence of senators as it was a reflection of the importance of class itself. It was important for Macdonald, for example, that senators would be "of the people."[75] The intention of the framers was thus that senators "do not sit for class, estate, or corporate interests that leaves them free to speak on all the issues that come before Parliament, and enables them to support or check Cabinet and Commons."[76]

While some critics argue that the Senate operates "on behalf of Canada's business community" and that its composition "gives an undemocratic advantage to business interests in their efforts to compete with other groups for influence in the policy arena,"[77] most systematic accounts of the Senate's performance over the years suggest otherwise. Kunz's 1965 analysis suggests that the Senate did not play much of a role in constraining the growth of the welfare state, although prior to the Great Depression there was some pushback in a few areas.[78] In his view, "the policy of the Senate during this period [1925–63] has been to check the political extremism of the 'positive state,' without obstructing its economic/social implications."[79] Franks's analysis of Parliament similarly pushes back against the idea of the Senate as a lobby for business interests, noting that "it would be more accurate to describe it as a defender of the rights of property, a function which it was intended to perform by the fathers of confederation."[80] And former senator and constitutional scholar Eugene Forsey writes that there was a lot of evidence that the Senate often acted *against* corporate interests, citing amendments to the drug patent bill in 1987, the refugee bills in 1988, and unemployment insurance legislation in 1989–90.[81]

As for the Senate's success as a defender of property, history – or, at least, historical analysis – has not been kind. As put bluntly by one observer:

> [T]he status of property as the basis of Canada's institutions quickly eroded. Institutional protections of property against federal encroachment withered, and universal enfranchisement ensued. The phenomenon of party dominance discouraged divergences by the Senate from the House of Commons. Time rendered the property requirements for appointment virtually meaningless. The Senate never fulfilled the functions meant for it, becoming instead a rubber stamp for Commons legislation and a burial ground for political patrons.[82]

The Senate's lack of interest in protecting, or its ability to protect, property rights has been so minimal that the institution's role in this regard has been all but ignored by the Supreme Court. In the 1979 *Upper House Reference,* the court declined to answer a question on the authority of Parliament to make changes to the qualifications of senators due to lack of specificity, noting only that the property qualifications entrenched in the *Constitution Act, 1867* "may not today have the importance which they did when the Act was enacted."[83] The 2014 *Reference re Senate Reform* does not even mention this aspect of the Senate's role, despite the fact that one of the reference questions explicitly pertained to the removal of property qualifications for senators. This is discussed in more detail in Chapter 4.

THE SENATE AS PROTECTOR OF MINORITY RIGHTS

The Senate is also cited as a protector of minority rights. Beyond its regional composition, prime ministerial appointments to the Senate have been preoccupied by representational concerns. Historically, prime ministers have been attentive to the need to ensure representation among Acadians in the Maritime provinces, francophones in Ontario and the West, English-speaking Catholics in anglophone provinces, and English-speaking Protestants in Quebec.[84] In the contemporary period, a more pluralistic set of diversity concerns have emerged, extending considerations beyond the historical linguistic and (narrowly) religious cleavages. The representation of women, people of different ethnic and racialized backgrounds, and Indigenous peoples has taken on a pronounced importance in Senate appointments, particularly as the House of Commons remains a relative laggard on several of these aspects of representation.[85]

The Senate has historically fulfilled its role of protecting minority rights "infrequently"[86] and "its record has not been impressive."[87] Writing somewhat weakly in the upper house's defence on this score, Kunz notes in 1965 that "it should be stressed, however, that there has been nothing dramatic about its role as a moderating influence on the executive, for the simple reason that there has been nothing dramatic about the attempts of the Executive to tread upon Parliament or the individual."[88] Notably, this analysis came before the *Charter of Rights and Freedoms* was established, with the courts, not Parliament, now widely regarded as the primary institution for the protection of minority rights. Smith states, however, that the framers "looked to Parliament's upper chamber as a shield. As sensitivity in the area of rights grows, so the Senate's role in the scrutiny of legislation in advance of judicial review may be expected to grow too."[89]

Contemporary accounts of the Senate's role in protecting minority rights are somewhat more positive.[90] Smith cites the prolonged Senate debate over the ending of denominational schools in Newfoundland in the 1990s as an example of the vigilance the Senate occasionally displays with regard to such rights issues.[91] And it is no doubt true that the Senate's committee work, particularly that of the Legal and Constitutional Affairs Committee, has provided some important oversight on rights issues in the modern era and tends to be more comprehensive than any parallel work in the Commons. Examples of this in relation to the renewed Senate are explored in Chapter 5.

Still, it is uncontroversial to say that the Senate's role in protecting minority interests remains largely overshadowed by other institutions in the Charter period. An example of the lack of attention to this particular role of the Senate is the fact that the upper chamber was not included as an authority to review a referendum question on the question of secession (for purposes of clarity) under the *Clarity Act*. The determination of whether a referendum question on secession was sufficiently clear, and whether there is a clear will to secede following the referendum vote, is left solely to the House of Commons. Smith argues that the *Clarity Act* removes "from the upper chamber one of its historic functions – to protect minorities – of whom among the most historic and central to the preservation of national unity are residents of Quebec."[92]

CONCLUSION:
IN SEARCH OF A MODERN ROLE FOR THE SENATE

Dawson's classic text on the Government of Canada concludes about Parliament's upper chamber that "[i]t would be idle to deny that the Senate has not fulfilled the hopes of its founders; and it is well also to remember that the hopes of its founders were not excessively high."[93] It is, of course, open to debate whether the original roles *as envisioned* by the framers remain relevant today. Yet a number of things bear on that discussion. First, the lack of formal constitutional change relating to the Senate – explored in the next chapter – means that both a plain reading of the Constitution and a consideration of the Senate's place within Parliament and the broader system of government cannot ignore the foundational reasons the upper house exists. Second, as considered in Chapter 4, the Supreme Court places significant weight in *Reference re Senate Reform* on the views of the framers in its own articulation of the Senate's role.[94] Third, as the preceding analysis suggests, these various roles may have evolved in different ways (for example, the disparate categories of people whose rights as minorities are legitimated are considerably more varied and numerous now than they were in 1867), but their core normative purposes have not changed.

Thus, while the modern Senate has a spotty record at best in fulfilling some of its roles, the normative justification for seeking to maintain them has not evaporated along with the Senate's general reputation. A primary question seems to be whether the Senate is best suited to fulfilling those roles, and whether it can do so with its current composition, powers, organization, and norms of behaviour. As the analysis in Chapter 4 will show, the Supreme Court emphasizes certain roles and not others, and engages in scant analysis of how these have evolved over time or even the degree to which the Senate has fulfilled them.

The discussion cannot end there, however. Each of the various roles of the Senate remains balanced against other interests, or even against each other. The Senate's independence and its role as a chamber of sober second thought is explicitly balanced against the democratic legitimacy of the House of Commons and the government of the day. The Senate's role as a defender of property might in some contexts come into conflict with its role as a protector of minority rights. And it is clear that the Senate's place as a national institution in a federal Parliament – particularly one dominated by the executive in the context of highly partisan organization – has, in the aggregate, diminished its potential role as a forum for regional representation.

The next chapter explores historical and modern reform efforts that seek to change the very nature of the Senate. Many reform proposals do not explicitly consider the Senate's role, or if they do, they appear to desire a strengthening of one role over, or even to the exclusion of, the others. This is a problem that will continue to plague Senate modernization efforts, and it is why this book begins with a focus on the Senate's myriad roles. Coherent and meaningful reform can begin only with explicit attention to what the reforms are desired to achieve. The next chapter concludes with a brief examination of more modest proposals for informal reform that would enhance the Senate's existing roles or simply improve the institution's performance in fulfilling them. The combined purpose of this chapter and the next is to provide context for the events leading up to and following the 2014 *Reference re Senate Reform*. The constraints imposed by the court in its reasoning, and arguably the inspiration for the 2016 reform to the Senate appointments process, are ultimately based on a particular conception of the Senate's roles. To what extent that conception meshes with the historical ones examined in the preceding analysis is the subject of Chapters 4 and 5.

2

A Brief History of Senate Reform

T HE SENATE OF CANADA sometimes seems like everyone's favourite target, the pariah of the country's constitutional structure. As Donald Savoie writes, "[m]ost who have looked at the Senate have labelled it 'a much-maligned institution' and 'a tarnished' appointed body."[1] It is, in David Docherty's words, often regarded as the "loony cousin" of the Constitution, "best not talked about."[2] Yet criticisms of the Senate, and the reform proposals accompanying them, often appear an inchoate cacophony of contradiction. The Senate is at once a useless, institutional rubber stamp and an activist, undemocratic meddler. An unnecessary organ, it should be abolished. Or it should be elected, so that its membership is empowered and legitimated to act. But it should also have fewer powers, to ensure it does not act as much as it might.

Among proposals for reform, we see scant attention to the broader political system and to unintended consequences of major reform to Parliament for power relations, democracy, and accountability. How many of those who favour abolition of the Senate also believe, in the context of other discussions about Canadian politics, that power is too concentrated in the hands of the executive, and especially the prime minister, and that the Opposition in the House of Commons is too weak? How many who seek to enhance the Senate's ability to exercise its famed role as a voice for the provinces (more accurately, regions) also recognize that Canada is already one of the most decentralized federations in the world? How many who favour an elected Senate also complain that the current Senate has complicated and slowed the legislative process?

The broad sense of dissatisfaction with the Senate's performance contributes to the more fundamental motivations behind calls for reform or abolition. These are especially rooted in the nature of the upper house as an appointed body. This chapter examines the various efforts at, and proposals for, reform. If the Senate has not worked as well as the constitutional framers had hoped, perhaps reform can strengthen one or more of these roles. Yet each reform proposal raises its own set of questions and concerns. Ultimately, reform of the Senate has failed over the course of a century and a half in part due to wildly disparate ideas about what the Senate should be (and whether it should exist at all), and in part due to the difficulties of institutional change under the Canadian Constitution. The Supreme Court considered some, but not all, of the potential unintended consequences of reform in *Reference re Senate Reform*. The analysis that follows thus provides important historical context to the court's 2014 decision.

REFORM AND ITS DISCONTENTS

Reform proposals for the upper house emerged not long after Confederation. As early as 1874, one member of Parliament, David Mills, moved that "our Constitution ought to be so amended as to confer upon each Province the power of selecting its own Senators, and to defining the mode of their election."[3] Another parliamentary motion in 1906 sought to abolish life tenure, limit the term of appointment to three Parliaments, and provide a mandatory retirement age of eighty years. That motion was withdrawn after debate, with an expanded version introduced again in 1908.[4] A senator moved for election of two-thirds of the Senate and the imposition of term limits of seven years in 1909.[5] Other motions for abolition emerged in 1909, 1910, and 1911.[6]

These early proposals, when Canada was barely out of infancy, might lead some to suggest that Senate reform has been a continuous preoccupation for almost the country's entire existence. Yet these were one-off proposals, often by individual parliamentarians, that stood little chance of success. It is more accurate to say that serious reform proposals were not entertained until the great constitutional debates began in the late 1960s and 1970s. Even in formal settings of early executive federalism, the Senate was rarely on the public agenda. A 1927 federal-provincial conference, for example, discussed Senate reform only vaguely "as a gesture to Parliament which wanted the provinces' opinions on the issue."[7]

Senate reform was not raised again by partners to Confederation until 1969 at another conference, in the context of Pierre Elliott Trudeau's proposals on broader constitutional reform. The ideas included more equitable representation for the provinces (to the benefit of the West); provincial appointment of one-half of the Senate; special powers for the Senate to review federal appointments, official language policies, and human rights legislation; and having the Senate's powers reduced to a suspensive veto.[8] After those talks broke down, and after Trudeau won the 1974 election, he publicly stated that the Senate would have to reform itself from within.[9] At that point in time, the only prime minister to get a meaningful reform bill through Parliament was Lester B. Pearson, during whose watch a mandatory retirement age of seventy-five was implemented for senators in 1965.[10] The only alteration to the Senate's powers came in 1982, when the amending formula entrenched in the new *Constitution Act, 1982* limited the Senate to a suspensive veto on major constitutional amendments.

As Ned Franks writes, reform proposals have not changed for several generations: "like the weather, everybody talks about Senate reform but nobody does anything about it."[11] From elections to changing the method of appointment to alterations to the Senate's powers, reform proposals are all variations on a handful of themes. The Senate's defenders argue that reform proposals generally suffer from vagueness or are simply not well considered,[12] and that there is little effort to consider the potential impact or unintended consequences of changes to the upper house on Parliament or the broader system of government.[13] This is in part because some proposals are designed to meet particular political ends rather than improve Parliament's functioning, or even that of the Senate itself. Certain proposals, like the famed "Triple-E" Senate scheme, are more designed to improve representation of the West in Canadian governance, or even as a response to regional alienation stemming from the National Energy Program (NEP).[14] As discussed below, this contributes to a reform idea that neglects or even works against other aspects of the Senate's role.

At the same time, the rallying cries for reform or abolition of the upper house emerge most vociferously during times of controversy or conflict. These historical trends are useful when thinking about the proposals the Supreme Court confronted in *Reference re Senate Reform*. When the Senate is functioning as normal, few in the political class initiate or raise Senate reform as a matter of public importance. As Robert Mackay notes, reform proposals are most often generated when the government faces obstruction, especially when the Senate majority opposes a new governing majority's legislation. "It is on such occasions," writes Mackay, "the demand for Senate reform has arisen, a demand likely to be forgotten when the grim reaper has provided enough vacancies to enable a new Government to be assured of a majority of its friends in the upper House."[15]

Criticisms of the Senate as undemocratic, illegitimate, or unrepresentative are so commonplace when speaking of the institution that it is difficult to know, as David E. Smith ponders, "how much of this criticism is echo."[16] According to Franks, "the work done by the 'Actual Senate' is vital to the effective functioning of Parliament. Unfortunately, the 'Imaginary Senate' is the model usually held up by its critics and the media – in MacGregor Dawson's words, a nearly vestigial body that is 'so sluggish and inert that it seemed capable of performing only the most nominal functions.'"[17] Along similar lines, Helen Forsey writes:

> The problem is not the Senate's existence as an unelected body, its fictional redundancy or its real or imagined powers; the problem is the

way its place in our democracy has been misrepresented and its proper functioning undermined. When a government uses its power of appointment to fill Senate vacancies with party hacks and nodders, it undercuts that body's legislative and investigative functions by replacing fairness with bias and expertise with incompetence.[18]

There is a chance that some of the Senate's defenders risk being too dismissive of what motivates reform proposals. As Ronald Watts notes, the Canadian Senate has the least perceived public legitimacy among major federations.[19] Modern democratic norms make an appointed upper house look positively archaic, especially when countries that share our system of government, like Australia, have demonstrated that elected upper chambers can work. The western provinces have a legitimate complaint that the regional composition allots them under 23 percent of the Senate's seats when they comprise nearly 32 percent of the population. These distinct concerns need to be taken seriously. However, many reform proposals, as discussed in the remainder of this section, either are premised on a questionable understanding of the role of the Senate or suffer from faults, including consequences for Parliament or the broader system, that their proponents do not sufficiently address.

Two broad categories of Senate reform options have occupied modern constitutional debate. The first category seeks to create a Senate that is a representative of the provinces, and the second attempts to democratize the upper house through the introduction of elections.

The Senate as a House of Provinces

The idea of a "House of the Federation" or a "house of provinces" type of Senate has at times received at least some consideration from the federal government as a means of placating provincial partners in the context of broader constitutional reform efforts. The 1978 constitutional amendment bill, for example, proposed a House of the Federation, selected by indirect election by provincial legislative assemblies and the House of Commons. As Smith notes, at "the end of the 1970s, the problem the second chamber needed to repair had nothing to do with the question of accountability and everything to do with improving federal-provincial relations."[20]

The German Bundesrat has been a favourite model for this category of Senate reformers in Canada. The 1979 report of the Task Force on Canadian Unity (co-chaired by Jean-Luc Pépin and John Robarts) recommended a Senate composed of appointees of the provinces in its style. Critics argue that such a reform would not be consistent with the realities of Canadian political practice, as "the Bundesrat structure, personnel, and operation are as divorced from Canadian Senate traditions and practices as is German administrative federalism from the jurisdictional concerns that dominate Canadian federalism."[21] Moreover, the preoccupation of reformers dedicated to this model "focuses on neither sectional nor regional but rather provincial interests defined by territory and articulated by provincially appointed or periodically elected senators."[22]

Keith Banting notes that the two proposals would actually result in considerably different functions for the Senate. With its mix of appointments from both the federal and provincial levels, the House of the Federation proposed in 1978 presumed an independence on the part of the senators from either federal or provincial governments, with freedom to defend the interests of regions as they saw them. By contrast, the House of the Provinces proposal more explicitly operated on the basis of the representation of *provincial governments*.[23]

According to Smith, the "vocabulary of reformers who want to make the Senate more sensitive to provincial issues suggests that they are willing to limit the independence of senators."[24] This indicates a shift in perspective about the purpose of the Senate, with senators implicitly envisaged as provincial delegates rather than independent parliamentarians. This threatens to skew the original role of the Senate as a forum for the consideration of *regional* interests. As Franks writes, provincial governments "present a very biased view of regional concerns," adding that they are even more executive-dominated than the federal level and are incentivized to blame the federal government for all of their ills.[25]

He adds:

> There are fashions in parliamentary reform as much as in clothes, pop
> music and architecture, and the idea of a "House of the Provinces" has
> now lost favour. Many of the proposals were highly asymmetrical, giving
> the provincial governments ways of influencing the federal government's
> use of its powers, but giving Ottawa virtually no power to influence the
> provinces when they challenged important federal interests.[26]

An effort to alter the Senate's composition or role such that its focus
becomes one of narrowly representing provincial views – as opposed to
broadly considering regional interests – and incorporating them into
the centre of power at the federal level risks exacerbating the already
tremendous centrifugal forces in Canadian federalism. Why this would
be desirable in one of the most decentralized federations in the world
is unclear.

Regardless, it is questionable whether such proposals would achieve
the desired results. So long as partisanship played a central role in the
appointments process, even if shifted to the provincial level, senators
would be motivated to act in a manner consistent with partisan interests. As Jack Stillborn notes, "unless political parties are content to
remain purely regional protest parties, they are under ceaseless pressure
to develop policies that can result in their election in Ontario and
Quebec."[27] This criticism extends even to more modest proposals, such
as the idea that the Senate ought to sit in provincial delegations rather
than partisan ones:

> The belief that the pervasive influence of party and party discipline
> within a Westminster-model political system such as Canada (which is
> a necessary feature of that sort of system of responsible parliament
> government) can be overcome by moving furniture is an obvious mis-
> conception. The further insinuation that a homogenous provincial
> policy somehow can emerge from the suppression of party identification
> (though some scholars have noted the potential and actual decline of
> parties in this respect) is another obvious oversimplification.[28]

There is scant evidence that senators appointed on the basis of partisan identification, or elected in largely partisan campaigns, would be willing or able to shed the obvious constraints of their party identification in favour of loyalty to the views of their provinces (or even more specifically, the stated position of whoever currently holds power in their home province).

An Elected Senate

By the late 1970s, competing visions for a new upper house were part of the political discourse on Senate reform. British Columbia and the Quebec Liberals favoured a house of provinces, to emphasize the voice of regions. Elected proposals, by contrast, "would strengthen ties between national legislators and citizens in all regions of the country."[29] As Peter Russell writes, "[t]hese competing approaches to Senate reform were built on very different understandings of the Canadian political community."[30] One early proposal on elections – advanced by a 1984 Report of the Special Joint Committee of the Senate and the House of Commons on Senate Reform – endorsed the idea that only elections could advance the cause of regional representation.[31] Later proposals included the 1985 Royal Commission on the Economic Union and Development Prospects for Canada (Macdonald Commission), the 1985 report of the Alberta Special Select Committee on Upper House Reform, the 1992 proposal of the Special Joint Committee on a Renewed Canada (chaired by Gérard Beaudoin and Dorothy Dobbie), and the 1992 Charlottetown Accord.[32]

The leading model for an elected Senate quickly became the Triple-E (equal, elected, effective) proposal emanating from Alberta. A Canada West Foundation task force report outlined a number of serious perceived defects of the status quo, including that the Senate's appointed nature is deleterious in the modern age given contemporary democratic norms, contributing to the lack of status (effectiveness) of senators within Parliament.[33] A second issue is the lack of provincial input or consultation in the process of federal appointment. In the report's words, "[i]f the *fact* of appointment denies Senators the legitimacy of an electoral base, the *mode* of that appointment denies Senators the legitimacy of a provincial base."[34] Thus, senators lack accountability and are be-holden only to the prime minister who appointed them. Finally, the regional, rather than provincial, basis for representation is, in the report's view, arbitrary and manipulative, as it "perpetuates the political dom-inance of the larger provinces in both chambers of the bicameral legis-lature."[35] Moreover, the regions as established are hardly homogeneous political units with consistently shared goals. Building off the Canada West Foundation report, the report of the Special Select Committee out of Alberta became the basis for the Triple-E Senate proposal.[36]

The Triple-E scheme contains normative strengths, not only because it satisfies widely held democratic expectations but also because it gen-erally seems more fair. Triple-E's supporters can point to the upper houses in other federations to support the idea that the constituent units should receive equal representation.

Yet commentators raise a number of critical objections. Watts notes that while advocates of Triple-E cite the United States and Switzerland as comparator states, the nonparliamentary form of executive-legislature relationship in those countries makes their relevance for Canada ques-tionable.[37] Nonetheless, Watts argues, Australia, which shares Canada's system of government and has a Triple-E–style upper chamber, is often ignored by critics. To some extent, this latter point is true, especially in relation to critics who claim that an elected upper house in a parlia-mentary system would be unworkable. Yet commentators have con-sidered the Australian example and they raise legitimate concerns about the impact of an elected upper house on responsible government.[38] In 1975, Australia suffered a constitutional crisis after the Senate rejected a money bill and the governor general decided to dismiss the prime minister. For concerned Canadian observers of Senate reform, the events emphasize the considerable uncertainty about the respective roles of the two houses in a dual elected context.[39] Moreover, the political stakes and the questionable interpretation and application of the governor general's reserve powers were never properly resolved in Australia,[40] raising concerns about the 1975 events as a precedent for the future.

Such concerns over how responsible government might operate – or indeed, become abused – under an elected upper house were explicitly raised in previous government reports. A 1978 Government of Canada paper argues that whereas an elected upper house is viable in a congressional system like that of the United States, "the dependence of the Executive on the confidence of the elected Lower House in a parliamentary system makes the election of the Upper House inappropriate."[41] The 1979 report of the Pépin-Robarts Task Force on Canadian Unity points to the Australian experience and notes that it "illustrates the problems that can arise in a parliamentary system when there is a conflict between two popularly elected Houses. It also argues that an electoral process would tend to enhance the role of political parties, so that party concerns, rather than regional concerns, would tend to dominate the activity of an elected Upper House."[42]

The Triple-E proposal also suffers for its particularistic conception of the Canadian political community. As Smith notes, the idea focuses on territorial federalism rather than its cultural underpinnings, which makes it unlikely to receive support from Quebec or the broader francophone population.[43] Russell, writing in the context of the Charlottetown Accord negotiations, states that for Quebecers, "the triple E Senate proposal threatened more than their power – for many, it threatened their very identity. Treating Quebec as simply a province like all the others appeared to deny Quebec's special place in Confederation as the homeland of a founding people."[44] To some extent, the Triple-E Senate idea seeks to correct perceived defects in federalism that are better addressed in other institutional forums.[45] In Franks's view, a Senate reformed along these lines would not alleviate federal-provincial conflict but would instead be more likely to enhance and entrench it.[46]

As for the democratic argument, commentators as early as F.A. Kunz argue that "there is much demagogy in repeating nineteenth century liberal slogans about the virtues of elected offices. What is important is that Canada's political system is democratic; the Senate is part of that system."[47] Along similar lines, Smith argues:

> The assumption that election confers legitimacy and the absences of election its opposite is treated as a self-evident rather than a demonstrated truth. Since, for better or worse, the Senate is an appointed body, to

chastise its members for not being elected and to dismiss their work for that reason seems a profitless exercise. More than that, it is self-defeating, since it undermines the lower house as well. Abundant evidence exists to demonstrate significant public dissatisfaction with the way the popularly elected chamber works.[48]

The Canadian governance system is replete with unelected actors who exercise considerable policy influence, including judges,[49] officers of Parliament such as the auditor general and the conflict of interest and ethics commissioner,[50] political staffers,[51] and the bureaucracy writ large.[52] Although a considerable academic literature exists debating the role of courts especially,[53] few would argue that the courts are *illegitimate* by virtue of their unelected status. Instead, the debate has focused on the extent and use of their policy-making powers, and the degree of deference they ought to show to legislative decision makers.

The Senate's staunchest defenders see the role of the upper house in similar terms: it may be powerful, but so long as it exercises its influence in an institutionally appropriate manner, its appointed nature helps provide it with a useful advisory function, a usefulness that would evaporate if it became an elected replica of its lower house cousin. Moreover, there is also the risk that elections would narrow the diversity of personalities and backgrounds of people who are willing to become senators. Smith worries that an entire class of professionals (doctors, teachers, social workers, farmers, journalists, and so on) "whose contributions to the work of the Senate are among the institution's greatest assets would not choose to run for election."[54]

By the time of the Charlottetown Accord, Senate reform was of deep symbolic importance, particularly for the West and somewhat for the Atlantic provinces, given perceived political dominance by Central Canada. Deadlock arose over the Senate's powers regarding ordinary legislation and over seat distribution among the provinces.[55] When Ontario agreed to provincial equality, it was on the condition that the Senate lose its legislative veto (except in cases of taxation affecting natural resources – a legacy of Western resentment of the NEP).[56] Senate elections would take place at the same time as those for the

Commons, and senators would be banned from serving in Cabinet. Russell notes that these two changes arguably run counter to each other in institutional logic:

> Electing senators in a general election would tie in Senate campaigns to the contest among political parties for seats in the House of Commons. This would tend to undermine the objective of having senators give priority to regional interests over loyalty to the platform of any national political party. At the same time, barring senators from the cabinet would prevent any of the senators, no matter how prominent they might be in a national party, from serving in the cabinet, the crucible of national policy-making. Further, it would create an elected second chamber, quite unlike Australia's triple E Senate, in which the government had no ministers to explain or defend its policies ... Perhaps the kindest thing one can say about this Senate plan is that it does not appear to have been carefully thought through.[57]

To get Quebec on board, the negotiations then agreed to ensure that Quebec would never fall below 25 percent of seats in the House of Commons ("[t]he first ministers might have benefitted by spending a little more time with their pocket calculators," Russell notes). Quebec premier Robert Bourassa also obtained the important concession that provinces could decide, instead of direct elections, to have senators selected by the provincial legislature "so that its senators could be viewed as delegates from Quebec's National Assembly."[58]

The ultimate failure of the Charlottetown Accord is difficult to pin on any one factor. The accord covered such a litany of issues, including establishing Aboriginal self-government and entrenching Aboriginal government as an order of government in Canada, recognizing Quebec as a distinct society, making changes to the constitutional amending formula, the inclusion of a social charter, and changes to the *Charter of Rights and Freedoms,* among other fundamental alterations. Different elements of the accord were unpopular in different parts of the country, and the national referendum rejecting the deal led to serious consequences, including the near–break-up of the country in the 1995

Quebec referendum on secession. After decades of "mega-constitutional" politics and deal making, any appetite for formal constitutional change evaporated after the accord's demise, to the point that, nearly three decades later, few have seen their hunger for constitutional reform return.

The Triple-E Senate proposal itself, however, would live on for some time through advocacy by the Reform Party, which won a significant breakthrough in the 1993 general election. Reform's support for Senate reform, which continued through its evolution into the Canadian Alliance and eventual merger with the Progressive Conservatives to become the Conservative Party, are explored in more detail in Chapter 3.

The only other move to implement elections began in 1989, when, in an informal effort to effect change, the province of Alberta held Senate nominee elections in order to try to persuade the federal government to appoint the winners of those elections. Pressure from the Reform Party and the province compelled Prime Minister Brian Mulroney, "somewhat reluctantly," to make one appointment from the first such elections.[59] Jean Chrétien refused to acknowledge the elections during his time as prime minster, but Stephen Harper would ultimately appoint four more senators who had won Albertan votes in the 2004 and 2012 elections.[60] The implications of the *Reference re Senate Reform* for provincial elections of this kind is discussed in more detail in Chapters 4 and 6.

Senate Abolition

The final major change promoted in some corners is the abolition of the Senate altogether. Serious discussion of abolition was not a major feature of academic analyses of the upper house until Colin Campbell's 1978 book, as most other scholars until that time accepted the status quo.[61] Other types of reform would not resolve Campbell's primary criticism of the institution (that the Senate is a "lobby from within" for business interests), and Senate elections, in Campbell's view, would cause serious problems for the general functioning of Parliament.[62] For Campbell, then, abolition is preferable to reform because the Senate's role is counter to modern liberal democratic norms, and reform efforts have failed.[63]

The main political force in Canada favouring abolition has been the Co-operative Commonwealth Federation (CCF) and its successor, the New Democratic Party (NDP). As Smith notes, abolition of the upper house is a plank in most socialist platforms in Australia and the United Kingdom, "[b]ut there is another explanation for the antipathy of the [CCF] and the New Democratic party: historically, labour and social democratic parties (including the Australian Labor party) look upon federalism as an impediment to their policy objectives. Thus, for some at least, an upper house in a federal system has two strikes against it."[64]

As with the issue of electoral reform for the Senate, most scholars of Parliament are deeply critical of proposals for abolition. Watts argues that the comparative evidence makes clear that abolition would be a "serious mistake," as "all other major federations of any significant size have found it necessary to establish and maintain bicameral federal legislatures."[65] Janet Ajzenstat writes that abolition would only further concentrate power in the hands of the prime minister, and that the framers recognized this.[66] And Smith writes:

> Abolition of the Senate would not only be inconsistent with Canadian federalism, it would destroy it. In a unicameral Parliament, presumably based at least as closely upon the principle of rep-by-pop as now, Ontario would dominate the chamber ... the Senate and its final weapon, the absolute veto (or even a suspensive veto), would have disappeared. The regional, sectional, provincial, and associational rights the Senate was established to protect would lack an institutional forum in which to be heard.[67]

An obvious corollary to these arguments is the presumption that the Senate fulfills an important function. The preceding discussion of the Senate's various roles suggests that the upper house does not fulfill all of them in a robust manner; however, those practices most consistent with the sober second thought role, of deliberation, of delay and long-term perspective, are the qualities most prized by the Senate's defenders. Abolition would mean the elimination of that counterweight to the exigencies of efficiency and executive dominance imposed by and on the lower chamber.

A further issue has been the ham-fisted and completely unprincipled proposals for, and attempts at, abolishing the Senate. Over the course of generations, from the first CCF leader, J.S. Woodsworth, to the NDP under Thomas Mulcair in 2011, motions have been advanced (and defeated) in Parliament to starve the upper house of its funding.[68] Even if these gambits had been successful, the effect would not have been abolition but a paralyzed, dysfunctional Parliament, left unable to pass legislation.

Along similar lines, Mulcair, Harper, and former premier of Saskatchewan Brad Wall each endorsed the idea of letting the Senate die by "atrophy" – that is, the idea that the prime minister could simply stop making Senate appointments altogether. This particular proposal flies in the face of the Constitution itself, wherein the governor general (in practice, the prime minister), is arguably *obligated* to make appointments by virtue of the language of section 32 of the *Constitution Act, 1867.*[69] Regardless of constitutionality, as with stripping the Senate of its funding, a long-term policy of refusing to make appointments would simply leave Parliament unable to function or pass legislation. The question of how to formally go about abolition was also put to the Supreme Court in *Reference re Senate Reform,* and is discussed in Chapters 4 and 6.

The Teflon Senate? Briefly Considering the Failure of Reform

Canada's historical inability to reform the upper house is not explained by a lack of appetite for change. When the Senate is not openly reviled, it is barely tolerated. Yet its critics differ too much on what to do about it: those who wish to strengthen the provinces "in the centre" of Canada's federal institutions would like to see a provincial role in appointments. Those who emphasize the democratic legitimacy issue would like to see the upper house elected. Within both of these categories there are a litany of perspectives on whether or not to reduce the Senate's powers (a key issue is whether the Senate should retain its current powers or have them reduced to a suspensive veto), whether changes ought to be made to the Senate's composition, or what electoral system should be used. Another group of critics would like to see the Senate abolished altogether.

The lack of consensus also reflects legitimate substantive concerns that many of the proposals augment or alter the Senate's various roles. Stillborn is correct when he argues that many proposals ignore "the practical reality that each additional role is likely to dilute the effectiveness of the Senate in performing central roles":

> This concern would seem to be raised by proposals for an elected Senate that, for example, take for granted its retention of traditional roles as a chamber of sober second thought but do not address the fact that the basis for the suitability of the Senate as a place of second thought is that, since they are free from the pressures of constituency and electoral duties, senators have the time to consider issues in a manner different from that of the House of Commons.[70]

Similarly, schemes to transform the Senate into an institution that narrowly represents the interests of *provincial governments* belie the Senate's place as a national body for the consideration of national policy. Even proposals that would prioritize or supercharge the Senate's role of regional representation pose challenges, in that they may have unintended consequences or even obliterate the purpose of regional representation. The concerns of Victoria are different from those of Prince George, as are those of Toronto and Thunder Bay. An elected Senate that made senators answerable to a geographic constituency along the lines of MPs may not enhance regional representation as much as make the upper house more partisan than ever. (Quebec has Senate constituencies, but these were originally designed in part to ensure minority English and Protestant representation.)

More fundamentally, as noted above, the different reform proposals seem to conceive of the Canadian political system in varied and even contradictory ways. The most prominent of these is the tension between

Canadian federalism as a purely geographic institution on the one hand, and, more fundamentally, as a cultural or "founding nations" institution on the other, as reflected in the West's support for equality of seat distribution across the provinces and the desire of Quebec (and others) for special status. The different frames and understandings of the Canadian Constitution have only grown more complex in the modern era. Reform languishes because no proposal can capture them all. As Smith writes, the "constitution is about fiscal federalism and linguistic federalism; it is about two nations (perhaps) and First Nations; it is about executive federalism and representational federalism; it is about the common law, the civil code and an entrenched charter of rights."[71] Smith argues, correctly in my view, that this is why specific reform efforts are so episodic and relatively ephemeral. The Triple-E scheme, for example, has nothing to say to Quebec or Indigenous peoples.[72]

Put simply, there is little agreement about what the Senate should do. That fact does not mean that the Senate is a vestigial organ of Parliament. In fact, it remains vital for particular conceptions of the Canadian constitutional being, which is precisely why abolition remains so unlikely. What would abolition do for the concerns of Quebec and the Atlantic provinces, particularly as the population of those provinces continues to drop as an overall proportion of the country's? What compensation would be sufficient in the context of constitutional guarantees to the smaller provinces that their allotment of House of Commons seats would not fall below the seats they are guaranteed in the Senate? That the Senate could be abolished or reformed in isolation from the rest of the system, and specifically without changes to the House of Commons, is a far-fetched proposition.

Absent consensus, and factoring in the historical difficulties of amending the Canadian Constitution (before and after the entrenchment of the amending formula in 1982),[73] it is little wonder the Senate looked very much the same in 2014 as it did in 1867. These difficulties, and the implications of the Supreme Court's reference opinion for broad constitutional change, are examined in Chapter 6.

MODEST AND INFORMAL REFORM PROPOSALS

If major reform of the Senate is effectively off the table, there is no shortage of more modest or informal proposals to improve the institution. Rather than transforming the upper house by fundamentally altering its role, a number of observers have argued in favour of changes that would strengthen its existing roles. The long-standing failure of formal reform proposals has led leading scholars like Russell and David Docherty to conclude that the path forward is informal change along these lines.[74]

Perhaps the most efficient way to reform the Senate in this manner is for the Senate itself to take the initiative and make changes to its own rules. As Andrew Heard writes, the "appointed Senate may still have a valuable role to play in the legislative process, even in the modern democratic context, if its goal is to refine legislative proposals while ensuring that elected MPs have the final say."[75] Heard envisions two key changes that could be integrated into the Rules of the Senate. The first would regulate the behaviour of its members in order to mitigate scandal and the appearance of impropriety. Such rules might address past problems of truancy, the need to shore up conflict of interest standards, senators' expenses, and residency requirements.

The second change Heard proposes would see the Senate establishing rules "to self-limit its legislative powers and define a clearer relationship with the House of Commons."[76] One such change would see the Senate effectively eliminate its ability to indirectly veto legislation via delay. Heard suggests that the Senate Rules "could state that a bill emanating from the House of Commons shall be deemed to have received third reading in its original form 6 (or 12) months after its introduction."[77] He also suggests that the Senate's formal veto power could be constrained by requiring supermajority or even unanimous support for votes defeating government bills.[78] Further, rule changes could also eliminate the Senate's capacity to play repeated ping-pong with the House over legislative amendments.[79] Critics might argue that these self-imposed reductions in the Senate's formal powers would prevent it from fulfilling its sober second thought role and enable the House and the government to more easily ignore proposed amendments. To counter this argument, Heard points to the success of the British House of Lords despite its having retained only a suspensive veto, noting that from 1999 to 2007 roughly half of its amendments to bills were subsequently accepted by the House of Commons.[80]

It is not quite clear whether Heard's proposals would meet constitutional muster. Do self-imposed changes to the Senate's powers require provincial consent under the amending formula? Heard argues, in a nutshell, that parliamentary privilege over the internal operation of the independent Senate ought to shield such changes from constitutional scrutiny; in other words, the Rules of the Senate enjoy special constitutional status.[81] This argument is explored in more detail in Chapter 6 in the aftermath of the logic advanced by the Supreme Court in *Reference re Senate Reform*.

Along similar lines, Smith lists a set of actions that the Senate could undertake on its own volition to improve its work and reputation, including: establishing a regional affairs committee; spending more time travelling to all regions of the country; increasing the use and number of senators participating on standing and special committees for policy investigations; enhancing its role in scrutiny of regulations and delegated legislation; investigating the effects of international treaties prior to their adoption by government; better explaining the rationale for amendments; and increasing the number of sitting days.[82]

Other informal proposals focus on the Senate appointments process. Long before the 2016 changes (discussed in detail in Chapter 5), several scholars advocated reforms that would remove a degree of discretion from the prime minister in selecting senators. Smith proposes an independent vetting commission, with non-partisan membership, that would report to Parliament rather than the prime minister (a similar proposal by James McHugh would have the appointments process established in the Senate itself).[83] In Smith's view, the "most glaring weakness of the Senate appointment process is the fact that it is perceived as an exercise in patronage. Successive prime ministers have been perceived as abusing their powers and making appointment on the basis of partisanship."[84] He and others point to the United Kingdom's House of Lords Appointments Commission, established in 2000, as an exemplar.[85] The purpose would be to establish a convention that the prime minister appoint from a shortlist of four or five candidates identified by the commission.

Gil Rémillard similarly advocates a system that reinforces the political independence of senators, but would go further than merely making the selection process somewhat independent from the prime minister. Rémillard would prohibit senators from taking part in party caucuses and avoid appointing senators to Cabinet with the exception of the Government Leader.[86] A number of scholars also advocate a set of non-partisan appointments, such as the "crossbenchers" in the United Kingdom (the Australian Senate also has a crossbench section, but it is normally reserved for elected members of minor parties, like the Greens).[87] Finally, there are also proposals that prime ministers be required to fill vacancies within a set period of time.[88] This would directly address the recent claim by some politicians that the Senate could be left to die on the vine through a policy of not making appointments, as criticized above, as well as a historical problem of prime ministers leaving specific Senate seats vacant to their own political advantage.[89]

A reformed appointments process that emphasizes the existing role of the Senate is hardly a new idea. For example, Kunz, writing in 1965, discusses a non-partisan, merit-based process along the lines of what the Liberal Party would end up promising in its 2015 campaign platform:

> To give the Senate an even more non-partisan character, it has been suggested that either the power of appointment should be taken out of the hands of the prime minister and placed in those of various professional bodies, or that appointments should be made, not on the basis of political allegiance, but on "merit," as "a positive recognition and acknowledgment of community responsibility."[90]

The problem of the role that patronage plays in appointments has been a central feature of criticism of the Senate going back decades. In their long-standing text, J.A. Corry and J.E. Hodgetts complain that "the exigencies of party leave little room for recognizing distinguished public service which is not of a specifically political nature."[91] Yet it is interesting to consider that the political class became preoccupied by large-scale or formal constitutional changes to remake the Senate while practical, more modest proposals to improve its functioning (and indeed, its legitimacy) went largely ignored. It arguably took the Supreme Court's closing of the door to the prospects of grander constitutional reform in 2014 for a government to recognize informal change as the obvious path. This is explored in more detail in Chapter 5.

Some proposals are more ambitious and relate more directly to the way the Senate positions itself as a policy-maker. Helen Forsey's design for a "People's Senate" would see the upper house break down omnibus bills, initiate electoral reform, be more aggressive in conducting investigations, secure "[o]ur children's future" with environmental legislation, exhibit a willingness to object to passing legislation – including budgetary legislation – if it threatens public institutions like Library and Archives Canada or the CBC, "explore options for limiting the power of the Cabinet to ratify binding international agreements" like the Canada-China Foreign Investment Protection and Promotion Agreement or agreements on Trade-Related Aspects of Intellectual Property Rights, constrain executive power, and even attempt to change the rules regarding prorogation of Parliament.[92] If pursued, many of these initiatives would dramatically overstep the Senate's appropriate role in its relationship with the House of Commons. Moreover, such activism could backfire, hurling the Senate into another abyss of criticism and causing long-term damage to its legitimacy. Even informal changes to the institution can do damage if not tempered by a consideration of the Senate's appropriate role within Parliament.

CONCLUSION:
THE END AND THE BEGINNING OF SENATE REFORM

The preceding analysis suggests that efforts at major reform of the Senate have failed because reformers cannot agree on what the Senate should be. Even seemingly clear objectives, such as ensuring that the upper house is a venue for the protection of provincial interests, are caught in a tension regarding how Canadian federalism ought to be conceived. The regional composition originally entrenched in the Confederation bargain was designed to ensure protection for smaller provinces and for Quebec. Proposals that seek equality of representation among the provinces arguably ensure the former but do so at the expense of treating Quebec just like any other province. However legitimate such a view might be, it is politically unpalatable for many.

Similarly, proposals for an elected Senate threaten to abandon, in practice, a sober second thought role for the upper house entirely. So focused on the democratic legitimacy of the institution are proponents of the electoral option that they pay little heed to the risks and unintended consequences of creating a competitor to the House of Commons, with all of the dubious implications for responsible government such a change would entail.

Abolitionists, who seem to recognize many of the risks of reform described here, seem to understate or ignore the further concentration of power handed to the executive by removing yet another check, however relatively weak the Senate's role in that regard has been. Abolition is also the least likely of all options simply by virtue of the fact that smaller provinces and Quebec have no incentive to eliminate the added degree of representation in Parliament that the upper chamber affords them.

Reference re Senate Reform may make these fundamental reform proposals all the more moot. Efforts to bring about significant changes require provincial consent, an increasingly unlikely proposition after 2014. Moreover, none of the historical challenges and barriers to reform have been addressed. Among critics of the upper house, no clear consensus has emerged about what ought to be done.

None of the analysis here will necessarily convince opponents of the Senate that an unelected legislative body is appropriate in a twenty-first-century democracy. I have come to believe that the Senate is not the undemocratic monstrosity its fiercest critics decry, for much the same reason we give other unelected actors considerable policy influence, be they judges or the auditor general. But this is somewhat beside the main point: we have the Senate we have, and we have been unable to reform it, both for reasons of disagreement about its role and as a result of historical contingency. The Senate can be a functioning part of an obviously democratic system, and it can perform better than it has in executing its various roles. The preceding discussion has outlined proposals that have for some time been part of the policy discourse on how to do that. Such ideas would come to represent the full panoply of options for action on the Senate in a context of formal constitutional stasis imposed, in part, by the Supreme Court's 2014 reference decision.

As the next chapter explores, the Conservative government under Stephen Harper confronted the reality that formal reform, after decades of mostly unsuccessful mega-constitutional politics, was undesirable. Harper decided to advance significant reform proposals through ordinary legislation, eventually posing a series of reference questions to the Supreme Court for determination of their constitutional validity. Chapter 3 examines the full context in which the court would come to hear those questions.

3

If at First You Don't Succeed:
The Harper Government and the Senate

THE LEAD-UP TO *Reference re Senate Reform* has its roots in the reform efforts advanced by the federal Conservatives under Prime Minister Stephen Harper. Although these reforms originated with the Reform Party and its advocacy for a Triple-E Senate, the Harper government modulated its proposals in the hope that unilateral changes passed by ordinary statute would achieve its objectives. Unwilling to engage in major constitutional negotiations with the provinces through a formal amendment process, the Harper government instead sought to introduce legislation to implement senatorial term limits and consultative elections for Senate appointments.

A number of developments during the period from 2006 until the Supreme Court decision in 2014 seem significant. First, there is some evidence of foot-dragging on the part of the Harper government with respect to its own legislation. Some of this appeared as a strategic attempt to maximize electoral advantage, particularly when the government was in a minority context and a possible election campaign always seemed to be around the corner. The second development was the explosive Senate expenses scandal, which emerged in 2012 and plagued the Senate for the next three to four years. As described below, it would also implicate the Prime Minister's Office (PMO). Finally, a constitutional challenge by the province of Quebec, through a reference to its own Court of Appeal, would eventually prompt the federal government to pose its own set of questions to the Supreme Court.

The Supreme Court was thus confronted with a series of questions relating to consultative elections, term limits, property qualifications, and even abolition. Heading into the reference, there was some degree of uncertainty as to whether Parliament enjoyed unilateral authority to enact certain reforms. This chapter concludes with a brief discussion of the political and legal debate prompted by the reference.

THE HARPER GOVERNMENT'S LEGISLATIVE INITIATIVES

At the federal political level, it was the early Reform Party that carried the Triple-E torch. Jonathan Malloy notes that in that early period "the Triple-E Senate was perhaps the single greatest objective of the party."[1] While there is some evidence that the passion for a Triple-E Senate may have resided more among the party's grassroots than its leadership, including leader Preston Manning himself,[2] the pledge to pursue Triple-E reform continued as late as the party's 1997 federal platform.[3] During its transition to the Canadian Alliance brand under leader Stockwell Day, the party retained the Triple-E Senate as a long-term ambition, although its rhetoric and promises regarding the Senate were much more muted by the turn of the twenty-first century. The Canadian Alliance's 2000 federal platform's only mention of the Senate pledged that an Alliance prime minister would "appoint only Senators who have been directly elected in their home province/territory as a first step towards having an effective Senate elected on an equal basis."[4] By 2004, the Conservative Party stood united under a new banner following the merger of the Canadian Alliance and Progressive Conservatives. Harper, the party's leader, approached Senate reform with the understanding that formal constitutional change was off the table and the Triple-E idea no longer had a vocal and prominent advocate at the federal level.[5]

The period of mega-constitutional politics[6] from the late 1960s to the early 1990s saw only one success, in the *Constitution Act, 1982,* and produced extreme tensions over national unity. It was followed by a period of constitutional exhaustion. To this day, intergovernmental negotiations to attempt major constitutional change remain a non-starter. Observers literally speak of "opening the Constitution" as if it were Pandora's box.[7] So do Canada's political leaders. As recently as 2017, after the Quebec government released a 177-page document outlining a vision of Quebec's role in Canada and laying out constitutional arguments, Prime Minister Justin Trudeau immediately shut down the prospects for any discussion, publicly stating that "we are not opening the Constitution."[8] The lack of creativity among Canada's political actors, and the unwillingness to engage each other even on discrete matters of reform, is a major contributor to what I have described elsewhere as a constitutional straitjacket.[9]

In this sense, Canada's fraidy-cat political culture around constitutional change explicitly conditions how governments approach reform, arguably compelling them to look for shortcuts to achieve informally what they cannot achieve through the formal amending procedures. This sort of unilateralism is also arguably consistent with the Harper government's "open federalism" approach to intergovernmental relations, in which each order of government was given wide latitude to exercise discretion within its jurisdictional areas of authority, and which largely avoids engagement in major intergovernmental negotiations.[10] For some critics, the Harper government's eventual failure to reform the Senate, and the outcome of the 2014 *Reference re Senate Reform,* is the direct result of the illegitimate manner in which the reforms were attempted.[11]

The Conservatives' 2006 campaign platform promised to "[b]egin reform of the Senate by creating a national process for choosing elected Senators from each province and territory," and also promised "further reforms to make the Senate an effective, independent, and democratically elected body that equitably represents all regions."[12] Having secured a minority government, the Conservatives faced a relatively strong opposition in the House in addition to a Liberal-dominated Senate. Nonetheless, they immediately implemented plans to initiate reform, including establishing a Special Senate Committee on Senate Reform.

One of the matters referred to the Special Committee was Bill S-4, which would have amended the *Constitution Act, 1867* to limit senatorial terms to eight years (senators already appointed at the time the act came into force would continue to hold their seats until the mandatory retirement age of seventy-five). In an unprecedented appearance for a sitting prime minister before a Senate committee, and one designed in part to emphasize Senate reform as a top priority for his government, Harper noted that the "government proceeded with this proposed legislation first because it believes Parliament can act, without engaging other levels of government in a complex constitutional discussion or amendment process. Quite frankly, I would put it to you that terms of this duration, even if nothing else happened, would enhance the legitimacy of the Senate."[13] Harper acknowledged, however, that Bill S-4 alone "would not achieve the kind of accountability that the Senate and other legislative bodies require. Anything short of a democratic electoral process would fall short of what we ultimately need on accountability."[14] He thus noted that the government would soon introduce legislation to consult the electorate on appointments to the Senate.

Questions quickly emerged about the constitutionality of the term limits bill. The main issue was whether provincial consent was required under the constitutional amending formula. The amending formula contains no fewer than five separate procedures, including the general procedure (also called the "7/50 rule") requiring the agreement of at least seven provinces representing at least 50 percent of the population for major changes. Section 42(1)(b) of the *Constitution Act, 1982* specifically identifies changes to "the powers of the Senate and the method of selecting Senators" as requiring recourse to the general procedure. Section 44 permits Parliament alone to make changes affecting the House of Commons, the Senate, or the executive. Nowhere in the amending formula is senatorial tenure specifically mentioned. Department of Justice officials appearing before the Special Committee affirmed their belief that Bill S-4 fell "squarely within the ambit" of section 44 of the amending formula, which permits Parliament alone to make amendments affecting the Senate except for those specified as requiring the general procedure.[15] This was also the opinion of most of the expert witnesses before the Special Committee.[16]

Despite this analysis, the bill was silent on whether senatorial terms would be renewable. Harper noted to the Special Committee that the bill's silence on this question implied that it was possible for senators to receive subsequent reappointments.[17] Citing the *Upper House Reference* of 1979,[18] the Special Committee's report notes that any changes affecting the "fundamental features, or essential characteristics given to the Senate as a means of ensuring regional and provincial representation in the federal legislative process" could not be made by Parliament alone. Only a few witnesses raised this as a potential warning flag before the Special Committee; nonetheless, real misgivings were expressed by some witnesses about how eligibility for reappointment might change the attitude and demeanour of senators, and especially whether such a change would impair their independence from the government of the day. The Special Committee report also reflects witness testimony that, absent other changes, term limits would empower prime ministers to make many more appointments than they generally enjoy under the existing system.[19]

Although the Special Committee concluded that it was satisfied that Bill S-4 was constitutionally sound, the Standing Senate Committee on Legal and Constitutional Affairs was not. Its own report back to Senate amended the bill to set senatorial tenure at a non-renewable fifteen years, with the recommendation that the bill not proceed to third reading until the legislation was referred to the Supreme Court with respect to its constitutionality. The Liberal-dominated Senate adopted the committee report, effectively killing the bill.

Before the Senate completed its work on Bill S-4, the government introduced in the House of Commons Bill C-43, *An Act to provide for consultations with electors on their preferences for appointments to the Senate*. This was the first piece of legislation attempting to adopt consultative elections for prime ministerial appointments to the upper house. The consultative elections would coincide with the general election, in provinces with Senate vacancies. Conservative MP Scott

Reid stated during the debate over C-43 that it "attempts to deal in a non-constitutional way with the issue of making the Senate more democratic."[20]

Constitutional concerns were raised almost immediately, particularly since this bill more explicitly engaged the requirement that the general amending procedure be used for changes to "the powers of the Senate and the method of selecting Senators."[21] Reid argued that he was "not aware of any credible arguments that [the bill] is not constitutional," although he somewhat astonishingly pointed out that the legislation "successfully attempts to skirt the constitution by limiting itself and by not actually calling for the election of senators."[22] Reid continued:

> [I]t would violate the constitutionally enshrined principle that senators are appointed by the Governor General. However, they are appointed, and this is a convention that has sprung up in Canada since Confederation, on the advice of the prime minister. Therefore, if the prime minister's advice is guided by the choice of voters choosing to make a recommendation under the Senate Appointment Consultations Act, that would be constitutionally permitted.[23]

This is the logic that underpinned the Conservative argument that the introduction of consultative elections were not a change to "the method of selecting Senators." Everything hinged on the idea that the prime minister retained the final power of appointment, formally through advice to the governor general. The government would remain consistent on this point, including in its arguments before the Supreme Court seven years later. Moreover, the Conservatives could point to precedent at the time: Senate appointments made on the basis of Alberta's Senate elections process, first by Brian Mulroney in 1989 and the recently announced (at the time) selection by Harper of Bert Brown, who won an Alberta contest in 2004.

The debate would not progress much further than this, because Bill C-43 was never brought to a vote. It never progressed beyond second reading in the House of Commons, and the prime minister requested prorogation in September 2007. In the following session, the consultative election legislation was revived as Bill C-20. A separate bill to impose term limits on senators was introduced around the same time (Bill C-19). Neither bill made it to third reading either. It is difficult to say conclusively why this was so. The bills were introduced in November 2007 and the parliamentary session would not end until the following September (although, to be fair, in the case of Bill C-20 the Legislative Committee held hearings through the spring of 2008). Perhaps the Conservatives, recognizing their minority position, did not feel confident about the legislation's prospects. The possibility of another election (rumours began as early as the spring of 2007) may also have prompted them to reserve the Senate reform issue for another campaign. Indeed, the party's 2008 campaign platform promised the following:

> The Conservatives and Stephen Harper believe that the current Senate must be either reformed or abolished. An unelected Senate should not be able to block the will of the elected House in the 21st century. As a minimum, a re-elected Conservative Government will reintroduce legislation to allow for nominees to the Senate to be selected by voters, to provide for Senators to serve fixed terms of not longer than eight years, and for the Senate to be covered by the same ethics rules as the House of Commons.[24]

After securing another minority government in the 2008 election – and after two controversial prorogations in 2008 and 2009 – the government introduced Bill C-10, another piece of legislation designed to establish term limits. This time the law would set out non-renewable terms of eight years. However, the bill languished without even being referred to committee.

The 2011 election presented the Conservatives with their best opportunity to finally get reform through Parliament, as they secured a majority government. Their 2011 campaign platform explicitly argued that the government "has fought long and hard for Senate reform. Unfortunately, the Ignatieff-led Coalition has blocked us at every turn."[25] The government would no longer be able to use its minority position as an excuse for failing to make progress with Senate reform legislation.

When the new Parliament began sitting, the government promptly introduced Bill C-7, which packaged together the changes to senatorial tenure and the introduction of consultative elections. This time, the bill established term limits of nine years, and set out a system of consultative elections that could be administered by the provinces and territories themselves. Although the bill was brought forward for debate on seven occasions, the government never imposed a limit (something it had been willing to do often in the context of other legislation, by invoking time allocation),[26] and so it languished without ever being referred to committee. By late 2012 and into 2013, intervening events would soon derail even the majority government's ability to pursue its initiatives for the upper house. The first was the emergence of a scandal over Senate expenses. The second was a constitutional challenge to Bill C-7 in Quebec by way of a reference, which would eventually prompt the federal government to announce its own reference to the Supreme Court of Canada.

"ICE COLD CAMEMBERT AND BROKEN CRACKERS": THE SENATE EXPENSES SCANDAL

The first rumblings of trouble for the Senate emerged in a June 2012 report of the auditor general that found weaknesses in Senate administration of documents and verification practices for expense claims.[27] That initial report did not identify individual senators, but pointed to issues including the lack of documents to support proof of residence (senators are reimbursed a flat rate for each day they maintain a second residence if their primary residence is more than one hundred kilometres from Ottawa) as well as travel expenses with little or no evidence that the purpose of travel was parliamentary business.

Media reports began to inquire into housing allowances for Senators Patrick Brazeau and Mike Duffy, both Conservative appointees, and in December 2012 the Senate began an audit that included the question of Liberal Senator Mac Harb's primary residence. Travel expenses for Senator Pamela Wallin, another Conservative appointee, were later called into question as well. The Senate's internal process failed to find any questionable housing allowance claims beyond Brazeau, Harb, and Duffy, and in February 2013 the Senate hired external auditing firm Deloitte to review the three files.[28] In May, the Senate released its expense audits and the report by Deloitte. Harb was ordered to repay $51,000 and Brazeau $48,000, and the report noted that Duffy had already repaid $90,000. An examination of Wallin's expenses was still underway.[29] That month, the RCMP announced that it was examining the expense claims.

On the heels of all this news, the PMO was directly implicated in the expenses story when it was revealed that Harper's chief of staff, Nigel Wright, personally paid the $90,000 reimbursement for Duffy. Duffy stepped down from the Conservative caucus amid this new wrinkle in the controversy.[30] Wallin also resigned from the Conservative caucus amid the revelation that her travel expenses totalled over $321,000 under a three-year period.[31] In August, Harb resigned from the Senate entirely, and repaid $231,649 in expenses.[32] In September, it was revealed that Wallin had reimbursed the Senate for well over $138,000. In November, Brazeau, Duffy, and Wallin were all suspended from the Senate without pay for the remainder of the parliamentary session. In 2014, the RCMP laid charges of fraud and breach of trust against Harb and Brazeau, and charged Duffy with thirty-one counts of fraud, breach of trust, and bribery (Brazeau had other legal troubles that are not relevant to the current discussion). Although Wright was dismissed from the PMO, an RCMP investigation resulted in no charges of wrongdoing.

In June 2015, the auditor general released a major report based on an investigation requested by the Senate. The report examined the expense claims of 116 current and former senators, and found just under $1 million in questionable claims from April 2011 to March 2013.[33] Some of the senators implicated in the report provided reimbursements, but fourteen appealed and went to arbitration. The Canadian Press reported that the audit cost $23.6 million to produce (although nearly half of that amount consisted of expenses the auditor general's office would have incurred regardless), with the obvious implication that resources were being wasted.[34] However, this cynical view does not take into account the fact that changes prompted by the audit to shore up oversight on expenses could save money in the long run, and might also be instructive for other institutions or units in the government.

Retired Supreme Court justice Ian Binnie was appointed as a special arbitrator, and his report explored at length the issues involved in the Senate's administration of expenses, including the widely held view among many senators that the rules were ambiguous. In a stinging rebuke, Binnie notes that in his view, "however, the problem for many of the Senators singled out by the Auditor General was not so much the clarity of the rules as it was a casual attitude towards the limits of their entitlement."[35] Nonetheless, Binnie reduced the amounts to be reimbursed for ten of the fourteen senators who sought arbitration, noting that "I impute no bad motives to any of the senators ... They acted in accordance with what they believed to be their entitlement. Our disagreement, where it exists, is as to the content of that entitlement."[36]

The Senate expenses scandal had a marked impact on perceptions of the institution, at least for the years from 2012 to 2016, when it garnered intense media coverage. One public opinion poll in 2015 found that only 14 percent of Canadians believed the Senate should be left as it was, with 45 percent supporting reform and 41 percent in favour of abolition.[37] The apparent attitude of some senators in response to the auditing processes did not help matters. When asked if she was concerned about the auditor general's investigation, Senator Nancy Ruth complained about which expenses were being investigated, noting that in her own interview with auditor general staff there were questions about why she had ordered additional food on flights that came with breakfast included: "Well those breakfasts are pretty awful, if you want ice cold Camembert and broken crackers."[38] The statement made for great media coverage, reeked of oblivious entitlement, and seemed to epitomize everything Canadians disdained about the beneficiaries of appointment to the upper chamber.

Efforts to defend the Senate on the basis that the expenses scandal was largely about a few bad apples or that nothing about the problems with the financial claims was intrinsically tied to the Senate's appointed nature seem to ring hollow, even if those points are valid. When James McHugh writes that "[t]here is no evidence that elected Senators would have been less prone to this sort of scandal than appointed ones,"[39] he is correct, but try telling that to Canadian poll respondents in the midst of the media frenzy accompanying the story.

At the same time, books written about "our scandalous senate"[40] fall flat when the conclusions they draw about the entire institution are predicated on the scandal itself, in part because they were published prior to the conclusion of the expenses scandal, which seemed to end not with a bang but with a whimper – due in part to the fact that, however improper some of the expense claims might have been, they were ultimately found to have been not unlawful. Duffy was acquitted of all charges in 2016, and prosecutors subsequently dropped charges against Harb and Brazeau and ended their investigation of Wallin without laying charges. Couple that legal context with the changes to the appointments process brought in by the new Liberal government in 2016, and it appeared that the metaphorical page had been turned on the expenses story.

It is not clear why the Harper government did not use the expenses story to push harder to get its reform legislation through Parliament. One strategy would have been to push the narrative that reform was all the more needed. However, the government was undoubtedly feeling the pressure of its own connections to the scandal. Three of the senators most visibly implicated were Harper appointees, and the PMO's own involvement in the story, through the cheque written by Wright, compounded the government's political difficulty. It is most likely that the government simply did not want to engage with the Senate file at all, and so allowed Bill C-7 to collect dust throughout much of 2012 and 2013. However, a constitutional challenge by way of reference to the Quebec Court of Appeal would press the issue.

THE QUEBEC CHALLENGE AND THE LEAD-UP
TO THE SUPREME COURT REFERENCE

In April 2012, the Quebec government issued a reference to the Quebec Court of Appeal on the constitutionality of Bill C-7. The reference power allows governments to challenge the legality of bills introduced by another order of government, and many of the most significant references in Canadian history have involved intergovernmental disputes.[41] Specifically, the reference asked the Court of Appeal three questions. First, because the formal appointing power rests with the governor general, acting on the advice of the prime minister, the Court of Appeal was asked whether the office of the governor general was implicated by Bill C-7 in a way that would constitute a change under section 41(a) of the amending formula, thereby necessitating the unanimous consent of the provinces. The Court of Appeal answered in the negative, noting that section 42(1)(b) specifically enumerates "the powers of the Senate and the method of selecting Senators"; thus if Bill C-7 constituted such a change, it was properly conceived as falling under the general procedure's 7/50 rule.[42] Moreover, the Court of Appeal recognized that Bill C-7 explicitly sought to preserve the governor general's formal power in this regard.[43]

The second and third questions dealt specifically with whether the two major reforms – consultative elections and senatorial term limits of nine years – were in fact constitutional amendments under section 42(1)(b). The Court of Appeal ruled that they were. With regard to consultative elections, the Court of Appeal noted the clear purpose of the bill was that appointees to the Senate would be the winners of the elections, and indeed "to make the senatorial institution truly democratic."[44] Both the purpose and effect of the bill amounted to more than a mere consultation, and thus constituted a clear change in the method of selecting senators requiring the consent of the provinces under the 7/50 rule.

With regard to term limits, the approach of the Court of Appeal was to view the electoral proposals and the imposition of the nine-year term limit as fundamentally linked.[45] This is despite the fact that previous iterations of the legislation had seen the two reforms packaged separately, and the statement to the Senate Reform Committee by the prime minister that he viewed term limits as significant even in isolation from other reforms. The Court of Appeal also cited the Supreme Court's 1979 *Upper House Reference,* where it noted that at "a certain point, the reduction in the length of office could be detrimental to the proper functioning of the Senate."[46] The Court of Appeal, however, did not stipulate at what point such a reduction would have such an impact, and noted simply that it should be left to political actors to determine under the section 42(1)(b) process.[47] Nor did it analyze any of the evidence about the reality of senatorial terms, despite having evidence before it that, in practice, senators serve a median term length of just 9.8 years.[48]

By the time the Court of Appeal issued its decision, the Harper government had already issued its own reference to the Supreme Court of Canada. It had no doubt been hoping that this would render the Quebec challenge moot, but the Court of Appeal decided to issue its decision anyway (Bill C-7 had also died on the Order Paper after a September 2013 prorogation of Parliament). At any rate, the Quebec legal challenge left the federal government with little option but to defend its legislation in court.

HEADING INTO COURT: THE REFERENCE QUESTIONS AND POLITICAL CONTEXT

One of the advantages of issuing its own reference was that the federal government was able to frame the questions itself. As a result, the Harper government's questions to the Supreme Court were lengthier and more diverse than those posed in Quebec. First, the questions exhibited different variations on the term limits and consultative elections themes, reflecting (and directly citing) the various bills introduced in Parliament from 2006 through 2012. Second, the government added questions about eliminating property qualifications or abolishing the Senate entirely to reflect the panoply of major reform options. This coincided with past government statements that, absent its reform proposals, the upper house should be abolished.

The reference questions were as follows:

1. In relation to each of the following proposed limits to the tenure of Senators, is it within the legislative authority of the Parliament of Canada, acting pursuant to section 44 of the *Constitution Act, 1982,* to make amendments to section 29 of the *Constitution Act, 1867* providing for

   (a) a fixed term of nine years for Senators, as set out in clause 5 of Bill C-7, the *Senate Reform Act;*

   (b) a fixed term of ten years or more for Senators;

   (c) a fixed term of eight years or less for Senators;

   (d) a fixed term of the life of two or three Parliaments for Senators;

   (e) a renewable term for Senators, as set out in clause 2 of Bill S-4, *Constitution Act, 2006 (Senate tenure);*

   (f) limits to the terms for Senators appointed after October 14, 2008 as set out in subclause 4(1) of Bill C-7, the *Senate Reform Act;* and

   (g) retrospective limits to the terms for Senators appointed before October 14, 2008?

2. Is it within the legislative authority of the Parliament of Canada, acting pursuant to section 91 of the *Constitution Act, 1867,* or section 44 of the *Constitution Act, 1982,* to enact legislation that provides a means of consulting the population of each province and territory as to its preferences for potential nominees for appointment to the Senate pursuant to a national process as was set out in Bill C-20, the *Senate Appointment Consultations Act?*

3. Is it within the legislative authority of the Parliament of Canada, acting pursuant to section 91 of the *Constitution Act, 1867,* or section 44 of the *Constitution Act, 1982,* to establish a framework setting out a basis for provincial and territorial legislatures to enact legislation to consult their population as to their preferences for potential nominees for appointment to the Senate as set out in the schedule to Bill C-7, the *Senate Reform Act?*

4. Is it within the legislative authority of the Parliament of Canada, acting pursuant to section 44 of the *Constitution Act, 1982,* to repeal subsections 23(3) and (4) of the *Constitution Act, 1867* regarding property qualifications for Senators?

5. Can an amendment to the Constitution of Canada to abolish the Senate be accomplished by the general amending procedure set out in section 38 of the *Constitution Act, 1982,* by one of the following methods:

   (a) by inserting a separate provision stating that the Senate is to be abolished as of a certain date, as an amendment to the *Constitution Act, 1867* or as a separate provision that is outside of the *Constitution Acts, 1867 to 1982* but that is still part of the Constitution of Canada;

   (b) by amending or repealing some or all of the references to the Senate in the Constitution of Canada; or

   (c) by abolishing the powers of the Senate and eliminating the representation of provinces pursuant to paragraphs 42(1)(b) and (c) of the *Constitution Act, 1982?*

6. If the general amending procedure set out in section 38 of the *Constitution Act, 1982* is not sufficient to abolish the Senate, does the unanimous consent procedure set out in section 41 of the *Constitution Act, 1982* apply?

By framing the questions this way, the government was asking the Supreme Court to provide it with a blueprint for reform. There may also have been strategy involved: in the event the government did not like the answers it received from the court, it would have a clear and obvious target to blame for not fulfilling its campaign promises regarding the Senate.

It is worth recalling at this point that, despite the perceived precedent of the 1979 *Upper House Reference,* the constitutional questions remained far from straightforward. There are two principal reasons for this. First, the constitutional amending formula was entrenched in

1982, and thus the court was dealing with a very different constitutional context in tackling the reform questions in 2014. Indeed, many, if not all, of the answers the court provided in 1979 ought to be viewed as superseded by the 1982 amending formula. For example, the 1979 court's assessment of whether Parliament could effect the abolition of the Senate centred on a 1949 amendment enacting section 91(1) of the *Constitution Act, 1867,* which empowered constitutional amendments through a joint resolution of the two houses of Parliament. That provision was restricted to amendments affecting only matters of federal jurisdiction, or what the court deemed "housekeeping" matters.[49] The court's *Upper House Reference* opinion states that the proposed repeal of constitutional provisions establishing the Senate would substantially affect federal-provincial relations because it would "alter the structure of the federal Parliament."[50]

The Supreme Court similarly rejected the idea that Parliament could unilaterally limit the legislative powers of the Senate, alter the numbers and proportions of members as representing the provinces and territories (thus identifying regional representation as an essential feature of the Senate), or institute direct elections for some or all senators (which would again affect a fundamental feature of the Senate, its independence). Each of these issues was settled on the notion of Parliament's authority under section 91(1), which was repealed in 1982 when the amending formula was entrenched.

Second, the *Upper House Reference* left many questions unanswered. The 1979 court determined that it did not have a sufficient factual context to answer questions relating to changing the name of the Senate, changes to the qualifications of senators, changes to senatorial tenure, or other changes to the appointments process, including having some members selected by provincial legislatures, some by the House of Commons, or some by the lieutenant-governor of a province or some other body or bodies.

In light of this context, the 2014 court was confronted with a set of entirely unsettled questions (consultative elections, term limits, property qualifications) and one question where a completely new constitutional set of rules was at stake in the form of the amending formula (abolition). This new context had the effect of making at least one of the reference questions easier to handle. A prospective answer from the court on the issue of abolition was bound to be much more straightforward than the court's 1979 analysis because the Senate was mentioned in the amending formula itself, changes to which require unanimous approval of the provinces.

On the other questions, however, the answers were not necessarily self-evident from a reading of the constitutional text. The amending formula dictates that change to "the powers of the Senate and the method of selecting Senators" be conducted under the general amending procedure requiring approval of at least seven provinces representing 50 percent of the population. A change to *direct* elections as proposed in the 1979 reference would clearly be out of bounds for Parliament to effect unilaterally, but how would the court deal with consultative elections in which the prime minister, through advice to the governor general, retained the final authority to appoint? Moreover, the amending formula makes no mention of senatorial tenure or term limits whatsoever, so the court would confront the question of whether section 44, providing for Parliament alone to make changes affecting the Senate, would permit such a change.

It is worth noting that the weight of academic opinion, especially in relation to the legitimacy of Parliament enacting consultative elections without the consent of the provinces, stood heavily against the government (although prominent scholars, including Peter Hogg, argued in appearances before legislative committees that Parliament was free to pursue the reforms). Several of these writers were cited by the court in its unanimous 2014 opinion. Some argued primarily that the consultative elections proposal clearly violated the spirit, if not the letter, of the amending formula requirements, or amounted to a back-door attempt at constitutional amendment.[51] Others felt that the Supreme Court's decision in the *Upper House Reference* remained determinative and that the details surrounding the consultative elections proposal were similar enough to the direct elections at stake in that reference to require provincial consent.[52] Opinion about the validity of enacting term limits through ordinary statute was considerably more divided.[53]

One final event relevant to the Supreme Court's decision making in *Reference re Senate Reform* emerged shortly before the opinion was released, and it arguably sent a signal about how the justices might approach the questions at stake. On 21 March 2014, just over a month before the release of the *Senate Reform* decision, the court issued its opinion in a reference case involving the eligibility requirements for appointees to the Supreme Court, and the constitutional status of the court itself. A majority of justices determined that the eligibility requirements for justices of the Supreme Court, as outlined in sections 5 and 6 of the *Supreme Court Act,* are entrenched in the Constitution.[54] The reference involved the attempted appointment of Marc Nadon, a Federal Court of Appeal judge from Quebec. The statutory requirements of section 6 of the act requires that judges appointed to one of the three seats reserved for Quebec must be from the Quebec Court of Appeal or the Quebec Superior Court, or be a current advocate from the province. A central issue was whether section 6 ought to be read in conjunction with the general eligibility requirements of section 5 (requiring at least ten years' standing at the bar), in which case Nadon would arguably be eligible, or whether truly distinct rules for the Quebec seats and a narrow textualist reading meant that Nadon, despite his past experience, was ineligible. The majority rested on the latter.

A more fundamental issue at stake was whether Parliament alone could alter the eligibility requirements. The majority determined that it could not; any changes to the eligibility requirements require unanimous approval of the provinces because they fall under section 41(d) of the amending formula as part of the "composition of the Supreme Court of Canada."[55] The effects of this part of the decision – incorporating at least some of what was formerly regarded as an ordinary statute into the Constitution, and arguably limiting Parliament's authority to unilaterally alter aspects of the top court despite its original creation under that statute – signalled a commitment on the part of the Supreme Court to respect the federalist nature of the 1982 amending formula. While by no means determinative for the questions posed to the court about the Senate, a similar approach to those questions would make some of the Harper government's arguments about Senate reform all the more an uphill battle.[56]

CONCLUSION: THE STAGE WAS SET

The Harper government had an explicit objective of finding ways to incrementally and informally achieve substantive Senate reform without engaging in the protracted intergovernmental negotiations that had preoccupied the country from the 1960s to the 1990s. In the early years of two minority governments, the Opposition and even the Senate itself slowed and blocked legislative efforts at reform. There is also cause for speculation that the Harper government did not pursue reform as vigorously as it might have. Not long after securing a majority government in 2011, the Senate expenses scandal transformed discussion of the upper house into a minefield, especially after the PMO itself became associated with the story. Ultimately the government had little choice but to refer its reform proposals to the Supreme Court. The Quebec government's own reference ensured that the constitutionality of the reforms would be assessed by the top court at any rate.

The Supreme Court itself was presented with questions about the reform of a deeply unpopular institution in the context of a complicated amending formula upon which it had not ever significantly elaborated. This latter point is worth underscoring: not even in the Quebec secession reference of 1998 did the court expend any energy elaborating on the boundaries of the Constitution's various amending procedures. The court's oral hearings on the Senate questions took place prior to the reference dealing with the *Supreme Court Act*'s eligibility requirements. How the court might disentangle the various procedures, particularly as they related to the questions about consultative elections and term limits, was far from clear. The court's ultimate decision is analyzed in the next chapter.

4

The Decision

THE QUESTIONS CONFRONTING the Supreme Court of Canada in *Reference re Senate Reform* required it to elaborate on the various procedures of the amending formula for the first time since its entrenchment in the *Constitution Act, 1982*. The general amending procedure under section 38 requires that most major reforms be approved through resolutions passed by the House of Commons and the Senate and at least two-thirds of the provincial legislatures representing at least 50 percent of the population (the "7/50 rule"). Section 41 identifies a number of matters requiring unanimous approval of the provinces, including amendments to the amending formula itself. Section 44 allows Parliament alone to make changes to the federal executive, the Senate, or the House of Commons. However, section 42 outlines specific matters requiring recourse to the general amending procedure, which includes section 42(1)(b): "the powers of the Senate and the method of selecting Senators."

The full text of the reference questions to the court (set out in full in the previous chapter) asks the justices whether Parliament could employ changes under section 44's unilateral procedure to institute senatorial term limits and consultative elections, and to remove property qualifications for senators. The court was also asked under what procedures the Senate could be abolished.

The court found that provincial consent under the 7/50 rule would be required to establish consultative elections and term limits. Parliament would be free to eliminate property qualifications except in the case of Quebec, whose consent would be required given that the *Constitution Act, 1867* attaches the property qualification to senatorial electoral districts in that province. Finally, abolition of the Senate, which would necessarily require amendments to the amending formula itself, would require the use of the unanimity procedure.

In defending its reasoning, the Supreme Court relies heavily on the idea that changes to the "constitutional architecture" or basic structure of the Constitution require provincial consent. I argue that the court relies too heavily on the concept of constitutional architecture in its reasons when a slightly more narrow, more textually rooted approach would have been sufficient to arrive at a coherent dividing line between the various amending procedures and to establish a clear standard for future assessments of which procedures are required for changes relating to the Senate. Further, whereas the justices step too far in exploring aspects of the constitutional architecture, they do not go far enough in examining the amending formula's specific provisions, such as section 44 of Part V of the *Constitution Act, 1982,* where they fail to provide a logical justification for the minimal role they outline for Parliament in effecting changes to the Senate.

Given that the court's emphasis is on defining the basic structure of the institutions implicated by constitutional change, the court provides a surprisingly simplistic description of the Senate and its roles. After briefly describing the court's approach in this regard, this chapter examines each of the court's conclusions in turn.

HOW THE SUPREME COURT VIEWS THE SENATE'S ROLES

The Supreme Court provides only a brief description of the Senate and its roles. This is surprising because much of the reasoning the court later applies in answering the questions before it is, by its own logic, dependent on fundamentally understanding the essential features of the Senate and its place within the broader constitutional structure or architecture. While the court does not evince an obvious *misunderstanding* of the Senate's roles, its description of them is ultimately superficial. This may contribute to some of the questionable reasoning employed in certain elements of its decision. The court's description also omits important context and any real discussion of how the Senate operates in practice or how it has evolved over time.

The court begins by noting that the upper house was explicitly adapted from the British form of government – citing the constitutional preamble that Canada would have a "Constitution similar in Principle to that of the United Kingdom," and that Parliament would include "an upper legislative chamber made up of elites appointed by the Crown."[1] The court notes the "sober second thought" role intended for the Senate – without providing much elaboration on what that means, how it has been exercised, or how it *ought* to be exercised – and adds that the Senate "played the additional role of providing a distinct form of representation for the regions that had joined Confederation and ceded a significant portion of their legislative powers to the new federal Parliament."[2] The court acknowledges that criticism of the Senate reflects its failure in completely fulfilling either of these roles, including that it does not "provide meaningful representation of the interests of the provinces as originally intended."[3]

The Supreme Court's brief description of this point risks conflating the representation of regional interests at the national level with the specific interests of provincial governments. The idea that the provinces were intended to be represented in this latter sense is somewhat belied by the fact of federal appointment to the upper chamber. The court's emphasis on the Confederation debates for evidence about the role of the Senate is also interesting to the extent that it underscores an original-intent understanding that in other constitutional contexts the court is notoriously loath to explicitly contemplate.[4]

The other role briefly acknowledged by the court is that the Senate evolved to "represent various groups that were under-represented in the House of Commons" along ethnic, gender, religious, and linguistic lines, in addition to "Aboriginal groups."[5] There is no elaboration on whether or how the Senate actually performs this role.

Finally, it is noteworthy that the court makes no mention of the Senate's role in the protection of property, something explicitly contemplated by the property requirements for senatorial eligibility and directly implicated by one of the reference questions the justices were expected to answer.

STARTING PRINCIPLES: CONSTITUTIONAL ARCHITECTURE AND HISTORY

The court's approach to assessing the constitutional amending procedures begins with a starting point, articulated in the Quebec secession reference,[6] that constitutional interpretation involves examining "the constitutional text itself, the historical context, and previous judicial interpretations of constitutional meaning."[7] The justices also note that "constitutional interpretation must be informed by the foundational principles of the Constitution, which include principles such as federalism, democracy, the protection of minorities, as well as constitutionalism and the rule of law."[8] Notably, these are unwritten principles that the court itself articulated in controversial fashion in the Quebec secession reference. The court has been criticized for using unwritten principles in a manner that enlarges the conception of the judicial role and empowers justices to create constitutional obligations whenever it identifies a "gap" in the constitutional text.[9]

It is through these principles that the court concludes, as it has invoked in earlier cases,[10] that the Constitution ought to be regarded as having an "internal architecture"[11] or "basic constitutional structure,"[12] meaning that the Constitution "must be interpreted with a view to discerning the structure of government that it seeks to implement. The assumptions that underlie the text and the manner in which the constitutional provisions are intended to interact with one another must inform our interpretation, understanding, and application of the text."[13]

"By extension," the court writes, "amendments to the Constitution are not confined to textual changes. They include changes to the Constitution's architecture."[14]

Describing the Constitution's architecture is in line with a purposive approach to interpretation that seeks to capture the meaning of specific constitutional provisions and to prevent interpretations that conflict with or contradict the application of other components of the Constitution. It also underscores, as the justices point out, that amendments to the Constitution are not limited to textual changes but also apply to changes to the way the Constitution operates.

Therefore, on the one hand, an appreciation of the constitutional architecture ensures that specific provisions are interpreted to operate as parts of a coherent whole. On the other hand, however, too much dependence on the fundamentally vague notion of the basic structure of the Constitution may divorce specific provisions from their textual underpinnings and their basic meaning. A reliance on the concept of the Constitution's architecture also gives the justices considerable discretion in choosing how to locate and define specific issues depending on how they view the broader governing structure. Interpreting specific constitutional provisions with too much of a focus on the indeterminate constitutional structure rather than rooting analysis more directly in the text thus risks placing a great degree of dependence on the justices' ability to accurately describe the various institutions, conventions, and processes that animate the Constitution.

The Supreme Court also briefly explores the history of amendment in Canada. In speaking to a period prior to the enactment of the amending formula in 1982, the court notes that "in practice, throughout the 20th century, the federal government consulted with the provinces on constitutional amendments that directly affected federal-provincial relations, and obtained their consent before putting a joint address to the British Parliament."[15] This is, at best, a misleading statement. As noted in Chapter 1, the provinces were not consulted prior to the 1915 amendment that redefined the divisions of the Senate to accommodate the western provinces.[16] Nor were they consulted with respect to the 1949 amendment setting out section 91(1), which permitted Parliament to make amendments to the Constitution except for those falling under classes of subjects under provincial jurisdiction or the use of the English or French language.[17] Indeed, the 1949 amendment occurred over the express objection of the provinces.[18] Even the decision to end final appeals to the Judicial Committee of the Privy Council, making the Supreme Court of Canada the final court of appeal, was effected unilaterally over provincial objection.[19] In each of these instances, the provinces could credibly claim concern over potential impacts on federal-provincial relations.

CONSULTATIVE ELECTIONS

With respect to consultative elections, the federal government posed the following questions to the Supreme Court:

2. Is it within the legislative authority of the Parliament of Canada, acting pursuant to section 91 of the *Constitution Act, 1867*, or section 44 of the *Constitution Act, 1982*, to enact legislation that provides a means of consulting the population of each province and territory as to its preferences for potential nominees for appointment to the Senate pursuant to a national process as was set out in Bill C-20, the *Senate Appointment Consultations Act?*
3. Is it within the legislative authority of the Parliament of Canada, acting pursuant to section 91 of the *Constitution Act, 1867*, or section 44 of the *Constitution Act, 1982*, to establish a framework setting out a basis for provincial and territorial legislatures to enact legislation to consult their population as to their preferences for potential nominees for appointment to the Senate as set out in the schedule to Bill C-7, the *Senate Reform Act?*[20]

As noted above, under section 42(1)(b) of the *Constitution Act, 1982*, changes to "the powers of the Senate and the method of selecting Senators" must be made according to the general amending procedure. The federal government argued that the prime minister would retain full discretion to make the final decision on senatorial appointments under a system of strictly advisory elections, and therefore their implementation would not constitute a change to the selection process. The justices did not give much credence to this argument, noting that while in theory the prime minister might refuse to make appointments based on electoral outcomes, the very purpose of the reforms the government sought was "to bring about a Senate with a popular mandate."[21] They elaborate: "We cannot assume that future prime ministers will defeat this purpose by ignoring the results of costly and hard-fought consultative elections."[22] The justices thus state that the federal government's argument incorrectly privileges "form over substance" in its interpretation of the meaning of 42(1)(b).[23] If advisory elections are advisory in name only, then their implementation effectively provides a loophole to escape the requirements of the general amending procedure.

It is worth noting that this finding privileges a particular conception of "method of selection." The narrow reading espoused by the federal government views the executive's final decision-making authority as the central element. From a certain perspective, there is a logical coherence to this view. Historically, the actual process that precedes the formal recommendation of the prime minister and appointment by the governor general has been at the virtually unfettered discretion of the prime minister, who has been free to canvass and consult anyone for names to consider. Candidates were routinely selected on the basis of patronage and often as a result of past work of a partisan nature, but in theory, the prime minister has been free to make the final determination as the result of a committee of staffers in the Prime Minister's Office, the recommendation of Cabinet colleagues, or even the flip of a coin. In a narrow respect, the court's decision arguably creates an absurdity: a prime minister is free to consult with whomever he or she wishes except for the voting public.

Yet the court's reasoning also makes clear that the prime minister is not free to bind his or her decision-making authority in all practical senses. It is difficult to argue with the justices on this point: elections, even if technically consultative, come with the baggage of democratic legitimacy that makes it very difficult to foresee the appointment of winners of senatorial election campaigns becoming anything other than normal practice. As a result, advisory elections would mark a significant change in the way the final, formal decision to appoint is made, even if by conventional practice and not as a matter of formal law. In the result, the court's reasoning here provides at least a legitimate legal grounding for interpreting section 42(1)(b) so that it applies to establishing advisory elections.

The justices, however, extend their rationale for this conclusion beyond the scope of a contextual analysis of how section 42(1)(b) applies with respect to establishing advisory elections. In line with its emphasis on the constitutional architecture concept, the court describes the impact consultative elections would have on the operation of the Senate as an institution. The justices point out that the "framers sought to endow the Senate with independence from the electoral process to which members of the House of Commons were subject, in order to remove Senators from a partisan political arena that required unremitting consideration of short-term political objectives."[24] They further argue that

> the choice of executive appointment for Senators was also intended to ensure that the Senate would be a *complementary* legislative body, rather than a perennial rival of the House of Commons ... This would ensure that they would confine themselves to their role as a body mainly conducting legislative review, rather than as a coequal of the House of Commons.[25]

This conception of the Senate "shapes the architecture"[26] of the *Constitution Act, 1867.*[27] Advisory elections would constitute a significant change to the function of the Senate and, as a federal institution, such a change requires provincial consent.

A number of problems flow from the court's foray into describing the Senate's function. First, the justices' description of the Senate as a body of sober second thought and one that engages primarily in "legislative review" is somewhat simplistic. Studies of the upper house show that the classic sober second thought depiction is overstated, in part because the Senate has at times enjoyed more legislative influence than is normally recognized, as discussed in Chapter 1.[28] None of this is to suggest the Senate should be a competitive rather than a complementary body – although there were periods when it clearly acted in a more competitive sense (see the discussion of the Mulroney era in Chapter 1) – but there are important nuances to the Senate's function that the Supreme Court's depiction does not fully address.

Second, the court's emphasis on the proposed reform's impact – specifically, giving the upper house a "democratic mandate" – belies other potential changes that might affect the Senate's role vis-à-vis the House of Commons. It is not surprising that the court left unaddressed what other reforms to the appointments process might be permissible without requiring the general amending procedure. The justices were addressing the questions before them, and wading too deeply into hypothetical scenarios would be fraught with difficulty (and is also generally avoided in the context of references).[29] Nonetheless, by not resting their reasons on the determination that the particular electoral reform proposal falls under the ambit of section 42(1)(b), the justices clouded the issue of whether other, more modest reforms to the process are possible when they invoked the Senate's general attitude as a deferential body of sober second thought. Nor does the court's opinion rest solely on the fact that the proposed process would, in practice, be binding on the prime minister's discretion; it also emphasized that the specific nature of elections – and the democratic mandate they give the Senate itself – was particularly likely to alter the Senate's function.[30]

The court's opinion not only fails to provide guidelines about what changes Parliament might make to rules governing senatorial selection or even a consultative process that might draw up a list of potential candidates for appointment, but it also arguably clouds the issue more than if it had simply rested its reasons on its discussion of section 42(1)(b). This problem is more than hypothetical because, by the time the court rendered its opinion, other proposals had already been put forward in political debate.[31] Then-Liberal leader Justin Trudeau had already proposed abolishing partisanship and patronage as factors in the senatorial selection process. The non-partisan appointments process established in 2016 marks a departure from past practice, and could, over time, remove partisanship as a feature from the Senate entirely. The details of that process are discussed in the next chapter.

With regard to the establishment of an arm's-length advisory committee to develop a short list of candidates for the prime minister to approve, a number of interesting questions are raised in light of the court's opinion. The court's reasoning does not make it especially clear whether an amendment under the general procedure is required for a change of that nature, and it may depend on how much emphasis is given to the electoral nature of the impugned reforms of 2014. The court writes:

> The words "the method of selecting Senators" include more than the formal appointment of Senators by the Governor General ... The proposed consultative elections would produce lists of candidates, from which prime ministers would be expected to choose when making appointments to the Senate. The compilation of these lists through national or provincial and territorial elections and the Prime Minister's consideration of them prior to making recommendations to the Governor General would form part of the "method of selecting Senators." Consequently, the implementation of consultative elections falls within the scope of s. 42(1)(b) and is subject to the general amending procedure.[32]

It is not clear whether this applies to *any* list produced by *any* process from which the prime minister would be "expected" to choose names when making appointments, or if there is something particular to a list drawn from an electoral process. If the former, then the court's opinion may place much greater restrictions on the front end of the selection process than many observers previously contemplated.

As I wrote in 2015:

> From the perspective of the Senate's function, a merit-based process that removes partisanship and patronage from the appointments process would also confer added legitimacy to the Senate as a body. While not necessarily of the same magnitude or character as the democratic mandate

afforded by an electoral process, a non-partisan Senate composed of eminent Canadians appointed from a quasi-independent process would arguably mark a fundamental shift in the nature of the Senate's composition. It is conceivable that senators appointed via a non-partisan process, and whom the public came to view with more respect as a result of not being beneficiaries of patronage, would recognize, and be emboldened by, the added perceived legitimacy such a context afforded. Although unlikely to transform the Senate into a body that would act in constant competition with the House of Commons, such a change could nonetheless lead to more frequent legislative activity in the form of amendments and even vetoes to bills coming up from the lower house. The Court's reference opinion leaves much doubt about what degree of change in the Senate's function is sufficient to require a constitutional amendment under the general formula.[33]

As discussed in Chapter 5, increased legislative activity on the part of the Senate – particularly in the form of a pronounced increase in proposed amendments – was precisely what resulted from the 2016 reforms. The constitutionality of those reforms are examined in more depth in Chapter 6.

This question relates to another issue that is left unclear by the court's opinion: whether provinces are still free to run their own Senate elections. The reference asked whether Parliament could pass legislation to run its own elections or "establish a framework" for provinces to consult their electors.[34] Yet Alberta has long held Senate elections on its own initiative; indeed, a number of senators who have won these contests were subsequently appointed to the upper chamber. The court did not comment on this more informal (from the federal government's perspective) process, or on the legitimacy of these particular senators' standing in the Senate. From a constitutional perspective, it would be surprising if a province were somehow prohibited from canvassing its voters via plebiscite on any matter it wished. It is not clear whether the prime minister is now prohibited from exercising the discretion to appoint someone who had won one of these provincially administered contests.[35] This will also be addressed in more detail in Chapter 6.

TERM LIMITS

On term limits, the Supreme Court was asked the following:

1. In relation to each of the following proposed limits to the tenure of Senators, is it within the legislative authority of the Parliament of Canada, acting pursuant to section 44 of the *Constitution Act, 1982,* to make amendments to section 29 of the *Constitution Act, 1867* providing for

    (a) a fixed term of nine years for Senators, as set out in clause 5 of Bill C-7, the *Senate Reform Act;*
    (b) a fixed term of ten years or more for Senators;
    (c) a fixed term of eight years or less for Senators;
    (d) a fixed term of the life of two or three Parliaments for Senators;
    (e) a renewable term for Senators, as set out in clause 2 of Bill S-4, *Constitution Act, 2006 (Senate tenure);*
    (f) limits to the terms for Senators appointed after October 14, 2008 as set out in subclause 4(1) of Bill C-7, the *Senate Reform Act;* and
    (g) retrospective limits to the terms for Senators appointed before October 14, 2008?[36]

On the question of term limits, the court confronted arguably the most difficult issue of the reference. Unlike "the method of selecting senators," the specific issue of senatorial terms is not explicitly mentioned in the amending formula.[37] At issue with respect to term limits was whether Parliament could implement them unilaterally under section 44 or whether provincial consent was required under the general amending procedure. The justices concluded that, as with consultative elections, term limits could be implemented only under the general amending formula.

While noting that senatorial terms were not an issue encompassed by changes referred to in section 42(1)(b), the court states that provinces have an interest in any changes affecting the "fundamental nature or role" of the Senate.[38] Specifically, the justices write, "it does not follow that all changes to the Senate that fall outside of s. 42 come within the scope of the unilateral federal amending procedure in s. 44."[39]

The court's approach to interpreting section 44 is guided by its understanding of the historical context surrounding that provision. In 1949, the *British North America Act (No. 2), 1949*[40] inserted section 91(1) into the *Constitution Act, 1867* and gave the Canadian Parliament broad new authority over constitutional amendments:

> The amendment from time to time of the Constitution of Canada, except as regards matters coming within the classes of subjects by this Act assigned exclusively to the Legislatures of the provinces, or as regards rights or privileges by this or any other Constitutional Act granted or secured to the Legislature or the Government of a province, or to any class of persons with respect to schools or as regards the use of the English or the French language or as regards the requirements that there shall be a session of the Parliament of Canada at least once each year, and that no House of Commons shall continue for more than five years from the day of the return of the Writs for choosing the House; provided, however, that a House of Commons may in time of real or apprehended war, invasion or insurrection be continued by the Parliament of Canada if such continuation is not opposed by the votes of more than one-third of the members of such House.

Prior to this, only a minimal set of changes to the original *Constitution Act, 1867* could be made domestically, as permitted through a handful of specific provisions. In the 1979 *Upper House Reference,* the Supreme Court of Canada described section 91(1) as providing only for "housekeeping" changes to the Senate or House of Commons. These included increasing the number of members of Parliament (under section 52), establishing and changing electoral districts (section 40), changing quorum in the Senate (section 35) and amending the privileges and immunities of members of Parliament (section 18), and allowing provinces to make changes to provincial constitutions, so long as these did not affect the lieutenant-governor (section 92(1)).[41] The 1949 changes broadening the scope of federal amending authority were made without provincial consent:

> The federal position was that provincial consent was unnecessary because the new amending power was of concern to the federal government alone and could not be used to affect provincial powers. The provinces rejected this justification and claimed that section 91(1) could nonetheless operate to permit the federal government to enact amendments that would indirectly affect provincial interests in the federation.[42]

In *Reference re Senate Reform*, the court interprets section 44 as effectively a replacement for this old provision, and determines that, despite the broad textual language of section 44, Parliament can effect only housekeeping changes to the Senate. Section 44 is thus regarded as a circumscribed exception to the general amending procedure.[43]

There are historical and legislative reasons to think that the court's 1979 reference to section 91(1) as permitting mere housekeeping changes was wrong and far too narrow an interpretation. One contemporaneous account of the 1949 amendment, while acknowledging that section 91(1) was not a sweeping power to amend *any* federal part of the Constitution, argues that a correct description of the power would be as follows:

> a power mainly to alter the structure of the central government machinery and the rules governing its functions. For instance, the Senate could be remodelled or abolished; the basis of representation in the House of Commons could be changed; the rule providing that money bills should originate in the House of Commons could be repealed.[44]

These matters clearly go beyond the narrow housekeeping interpretation as generated by the Supreme Court in 1979, and which the 2014 court would simplistically apply to section 44 of the amending formula. Yet there are good reasons for favouring the broader understanding. Section 91(1) was widely perceived as a federal analog to the existing provision in section 92 giving provinces authority to amend their own constitutions. For that reason, the view that section 91(1) provided the federal government the amending authority formerly held by the British Parliament – specifically for matters on which the two houses of Canada's Parliament did not need to consult provinces before making the amendment request – was a sensible one.[45] Moreover, parliamentarians in the United Kingdom who passed the 1949 amendment believed that the exceptions explicitly stated in section 91(1) were sufficient to protect provincial interests, and thus the federal government would now have amending authority for all but "very important sections" of the Constitution.[46]

Nonetheless, consistent with its architecture approach, the Supreme Court of Canada determined in 2014 that any changes that might alter the Senate's function or role, or have any implications for the provinces, require provincial consent. In the context of term limits, the justices state that

> the Senate's fundamental nature and role is that of a complementary legislative body of sober second thought. The current duration of senatorial terms is directly linked to this conception of the Senate. Senators are appointed roughly for the duration of their active professional lives. This security of tenure is intended to allow Senators to function with independence in conducting legislative review. This Court stated in the *Upper House Reference* that, "[a]t some point, a reduction of the term of office might impair the functioning of the Senate in providing what Sir John A. Macdonald described as 'the sober second thought in legislation'": p. 76. A significant change to senatorial tenure would thus affect the Senate's fundamental nature and role.[47]

It is notable that the court acknowledges its statement in the 1979 *Upper House Reference* that held that the imposition of mandatory retirement age "did not change the essential character of the Senate"[48] and could therefore be regarded as a legitimate exercise of unilateral action by Parliament. Constitutional scholars who have noted that the amending procedures as they relate to the Senate were an attempt to "codify" the court's opinion in the 1979 reference have also argued that it would be acceptable for Parliament to enact term limits of a certain length under section 44: "The items specified in section 42 should be regarded as an exhaustive list of matters deemed fundamental or essential, as those terms were utilized in the *Senate Reference*. To hold that the unilateral federal power in section 44 is subject to a further limitation along the lines suggested would lead to needless uncertainty and ambiguity."[49]

Importantly, the court explicitly refused to address the seemingly pertinent question of why a retirement age might fall under the category of "housekeeping" but the imposition of terms limits of *any* length or design do not. The justices write that "[i]t may be possible, as the Attorney General of Canada suggests, to devise a fixed term so lengthy that it provides a security of tenure which is functionally equivalent to that provided by life tenure. However, it is difficult to objectively identify the precise term duration that guarantees an equivalent degree of security of tenure."[50]

The court's refusal to engage in a line-drawing exercise here is problematic to the extent that line drawing is precisely what was being asked of it. The structure of the federal government's reference questions on term limits was clearly designed to encapsulate a range of alternatives. The questions posed to the court provide a clear indication that guidance was sought as to whether certain types of term limits might be enacted under section 44 even if other types could not. By not addressing the question of whether a non-renewable term limit long enough to avoid altering the basic function of the Senate or the role of senators is feasible, the court sidestepped a contradiction and logical flaw in its approach to interpreting section 44.

Presuming the validity of the court's own interpretation of section 44's development, there is no reason to believe that Parliament would not be theoretically free to unilaterally lower the mandatory retirement age of senators to seventy or sixty-five. However, it is not free, according to the court, to unilaterally enact a non-renewable term limit of fifteen years. The idea that one of these changes would alter the fundamental features of the institution and the other would not is difficult to comprehend. By refusing to engage with this question, not only has the court failed to deliver a good standard by which some matters may fall under different procedures in Part V but it has also arguably gutted section 44 to an unreasonable degree.

The justices' refusal to distinguish between different types of term limits is also contrary to existing evidence that not all term limits would alter how the Senate functions. Fixed terms would undoubtedly run the risk of impairing the Senate's independence if they were renewable. Similarly, excessively short term limits might make a Senate appointment a brief mid-career stint, something that might alter senators' approach to their role and skew their decision-making incentives. But there is little evidence that lengthy, non-renewable terms would pose similar dangers. As Christopher Manfredi writes in his expert submission for the reference, the "average age at which individuals have been appointed is 57, which means that, had the nine-year fixed term applied since 1867, the average senator would have left the Senate at age 66 and would not have expected a lengthy post-Senate career."[51] Moreover, the mean and median lengths of senatorial service since 1965 have been 11.3 and 9.8 years, respectively.[52] The imposition of lengthy non-renewable terms – be they nine, twelve, or fifteen years – would not constitute a departure from the Senate's existing reality, nor could it realistically be thought to alter the Senate's fundamental features or operation.[53]

PROPERTY QUALIFICATIONS

Sections 23(3) to 23(6) of the *Constitution Act, 1867* require that senators own property (and personal net worth) of at least $4,000. The court was asked whether it is "within the legislative authority of the Parliament of Canada, acting pursuant to section 44 of the *Constitution Act, 1982*, to repeal subsections 23(3) and (4) of the *Constitution Act, 1867* regarding property qualifications for Senators?"

The court determined that Parliament could remove the general net worth requirement but that a full repeal of the property requirement required the consent of the Quebec legislative assembly, given that section 23(6) specifically requires senators from Quebec to have real property in the electoral division for which they are appointed, or to be resident in that division.

This was perhaps the most straightforward of the reference questions posed to the court. Indeed, the court rendered its decision on the net worth requirement in four short paragraphs.[54] Yet given the court's emphasis on the intentions of the framers and its sensitivity to modifications to the role of the Senate in the context of other reforms, it is somewhat surprising that the court did not engage at all in the question of whether the property requirements were connected to the role of the Senate in protecting property rights. In fact, the justices apparently do not think protecting property rights *is* one of the Senate's roles. There is no mention of it, despite its wide recognition in the academic literature, as discussed in Chapter 1. The justices merely note that "there is nothing in the material before us to suggest that removing the net worth requirement would affect the independence of Senators or otherwise affect the Senate's role as a complementary legislative chamber of sober second thought."[55] This narrow focus on the Senate's sober second thought role leads the court to conclude that the removal of the property requirements would have no impact on "the interests of the provinces," as supported by the fact that none of the intervening provinces opposed the repeal in their submissions to the court.

Two possible conclusions flow from the court's omission of the Senate's role as a defender of property. One is the implication that the Senate has not fulfilled this role, or that it has somehow fallen into obsolescence. It is unlikely the court is implicitly relying on this logic. If the Senate's performance or failure as active defender of property authorizes a reform that relates to that role without provincial consent, this is arguably just as true with regard to the Senate's other roles, such as its role as a defender of minority interests. Perhaps the amount at stake, however considerable in 1867, is in the modern period so insignificant that this bears on the court's reasoning. But if that were the case, why not say so?

The second possible explanation for the court's reasoning is that it simply does not believe the property-related aspect of the Senate's role is as important as its role in defending regional interests or in conducting sober second thought. Yet this belies the court's focus on the intentions of the framers when it otherwise discusses the Senate's role in other parts of the opinion.

In its own way, the property requirements part of the court's decision highlights the problems with a focus on constitutional purpose and structure. The justices adopt an approach to balancing the different amending procedures in a way that maximizes their own discretion to emphasize, downplay, or ignore altogether certain features and functions of the institution. The court's focus is on whether reforms affect the essential features of the Senate, but it does not explain how or why certain features are essential.

ABOLITION

On the issue of abolishing the Senate, the Court was asked the following questions:

5. Can an amendment to the Constitution of Canada to abolish the Senate be accomplished by the general amending procedure set out in section 38 of the *Constitution Act, 1982,* by one of the following methods:

   (a) by inserting a separate provision stating that the Senate is to be abolished as of a certain date, as an amendment to the *Constitution Act, 1867* or as a separate provision that is outside of the *Constitution Acts, 1867 to 1982* but that is still part of the Constitution of Canada;

   (b) by amending or repealing some or all of the references to the Senate in the Constitution of Canada; or

(c) by abolishing the powers of the Senate and eliminating the representation of provinces pursuant to paragraphs 42(1)(b) and (c) of the *Constitution Act, 1982?*

6. If the general amending procedure set out in section 38 of the *Constitution Act, 1982* is not sufficient to abolish the Senate, does the unanimous consent procedure set out in section 41 of the *Constitution Act, 1982* apply?[56]

Although the question on abolition was perhaps just as straightforward as the property qualifications question, a number of odd or erroneous arguments arose during political debate over the issue. For example, Robert Ghiz, then-premier of Prince Edward Island, spoke out against Senate abolition because it would mean his province "would be down to one member of Parliament" as a result of the constitutional guarantee giving Prince Edward Island the same number of members of Parliament as it has senators.[57] The premier's fears were unfounded, however, because section 41(b) of the amending formula preserves the number of members in the House of Commons for each province such that they do not fall below their number of senators "at the time this Part comes into force."[58] In other words, the abolition of the Senate would not reduce the number of members of Parliament to which Prince Edward Island is entitled (four) barring a unanimous amendment that alters section 41(b). Prince Edward Island's veto would protect it from such a result.

With respect to Senate abolition, any change to the amending formula itself requires unanimity under section 41(e), and the Senate is referenced throughout Part V. The federal government attempted to argue that the Senate could be abolished under the general amending formula without amendment of the text of Part V, as references to the Senate in Part V would be viewed as spent provisions following any general amendment to do so. Notably, section 47 of Part V provides the Senate with a suspensive veto that requires the House of Commons to adopt a second resolution after 180 days if the Senate refuses to adopt an initial resolution to amend the Constitution under any of the procedures other than sections 44 or 45.[59] The federal government argued that, because the Senate could be overridden after 180 days under section 47, references to it in the amending formula were incidental to its abolition. It is worth noting that such logic could be flipped on its head: the fact that the Senate itself was granted the power to delay amendments for 180 days only underscores its relevance and the significance of its presence in Part V. The ratification of resolutions to amend the Constitution when provincial consent is required is a difficult process, and a 180-day delay could result in an intervening election in some provinces. During the ratification process for the Meech Lake Accord,[60] the election of the Clyde Wells government resulted in Newfoundland and Labrador's revocation of its assent to the accord and contributed to the failure of the constitutional package.[61] For this reason, the Senate's suspensive veto should be regarded as having substantive, in addition to symbolic, significance.

For its part, the court concluded correctly that:

> Part V was drafted on the assumption that the federal Parliament would remain bicameral in nature, i.e. that there would continue to be both a lower legislative chamber and a complementary upper chamber. Removal of the upper chamber from our Constitution would alter the structure and functioning of Part V. Consequently, it requires the unanimous consent of Parliament and of all the provinces (s. 41(e)).[62]

CONCLUSION: A DEEPLY IMPERFECT LOGIC

The rationale employed by the Supreme Court of Canada in *Reference re Senate Reform* raises a number of issues with respect to Senate reform specifically and future constitutional amendment generally. In the context of their reasoning regarding changes to the method of selecting senators, the justices' reliance on the amorphous notion of the constitutional architecture clouds the definable limits of method of selection under section 42(1)(b). While it would be unreasonable to expect the reference opinion to account for every hypothetical reform option, the court should be counted on to provide clear guidelines about the scope of the relevant provisions in Part V. Instead, the reasoning adopted by the justices adds to, rather than alleviates, the uncertainty over what other changes to the appointments process might be feasible without formal constitutional amendment and provincial consent. This is not to argue that the court reached an incorrect decision on whether consultative elections fall under the ambit of section 42(1)(b), nor is it to suggest that only a narrow, textual reading of the Constitution is the appropriate jurisprudential approach. However, the appeal to the Constitution's broader architecture introduces ambiguity where a focus on a contextual reading of 42(1)(b) would have sufficed.

Not only does the court's appeal to constitutional architecture lead it to introduce problematic uncertainty into its discussion of the imposition of term limits, it also leads the justices to an incorrect conclusion regarding Parliament's ability to enact changes unilaterally under section 44. The court's explicit refusal to distinguish between the federal government's ability to enact a retirement age under section 44 and its logic that term limits, regardless of length, require the consent of the provinces under the general amending procedure lacks logical consistency and arguably erodes section 44 to a problematic degree. The justices' rationale also flies in the face of available evidence about the conceivable impact that lengthy, non-renewable term limits would have on the Senate's function and essential features. The structure of the questions on term limits posed to the court makes it clear that the justices were being asked to examine whether some types of term limits might avoid implicating the general amending procedure even if others do. By sidestepping this question and explicitly refusing to engage the matter of whether lengthy term limits might not alter the Senate's function, the court effectively avoided dealing with the central issue at stake. The effect of this is to minimize section 44 in a manner not necessarily compatible with its historical context or even with the court's stated rationale.

While the court arrived at the correct conclusion with regard to changes to the property qualifications of senators, the fact that it did so without any discussion or acknowledgement of the Senate's role as a defender of property belies its own fundamental approach as grounded in constitutional architecture or the "essential features" of the Senate. The inability or refusal to address this aspect of the Senate underscores a degree of incoherence. The justices effectively privilege certain roles for the upper house over others, and the lack of acknowledgment or discussion in doing so makes those choices appear arbitrary.

5

Informal Reform and a New Appointments Process: A Renewed Senate?

FOLLOWING ON THE HEELS OF the 2014 *Reference re Senate Reform* and the 2015 federal election came a major, informal reform of the appointments process to the upper house. How has the Senate's functioning evolved since that change? After providing an insider's perspective on the reform itself, I will investigate how the elimination of patronage and partisanship as a basis for appointments has affected the Senate's performance. Contrary to the concerns expressed by some critics, the Senate has successfully navigated the changes to its composition, often by proposing amendments to improve legislation. Although there are clear signs that a more independent Senate has made the legislative process more challenging and complex from the government's perspective, it has not translated into the obstructionism feared by some critics. The Senate has not attempted to block legislation outright or engaged the House of Commons in repeated "ping-pong" of bills. While there has been a notable increase in amendment activity, the Senate has routinely bowed to the wishes of the House in either accepting or rejecting amendments.

One of the most significant challenges relating to getting the government's legislative agenda through the upper house has been organizational: with the majority of senators no longer in a formal party caucus, the institutional benefits derived from getting large groups of senators "on the same page" has been lost. Government ministers quickly learned that they needed to work harder in relation to certain bills in order to ascertain, keep track of, and gain senatorial support for bills. Public servants have also had to work harder in some instances, providing a greater number of technical briefings to smaller groups of senators, reflecting the disparate range of opinions and lack of information flows that existed in the partisan era. Finally, the role of the Government Representative Office in the Senate has been important for shepherding legislation through the Senate and negotiating timelines and votes in an efficient manner.

The Trudeau government's initiative to establish a "non-partisan, merit-based" appointments process was met with considerable criticism, largely revolving around concerns about a renewed Senate's potential for activism and dysfunction. An assessment of the Senate's general performance, with an examination of its record thus far, is warranted. Included here is an exploration of the progression of two controversial bills from the perspective of key players involved in order to provide a snapshot of some of the legislative challenges faced in the renewed upper chamber.

The analysis that follows draws on interviews conducted from August 2018 to March 2019 with Senator Peter Harder, Government Representative in the Senate; Senator Yuen Pau Woo, facilitator of the Independent Senators Group (ISG); Senator Joseph A. Day, Senate Liberal Leader; Senator Yonah Martin, Deputy Leader of the Opposition in the Senate; a senior staff member of the office of the Leader of the Opposition in the Senate; in addition, there were five not-for-attribution interviews with senior public servants in federal government departments and central agencies. The analysis incorporates their perspectives on the Senate's functioning and the evolution of its relationship with the government.

AN INSIDE LOOK AT REFORM
OF THE SENATE APPOINTMENTS PROCESS

During the 2015 federal election campaign, the Liberal Party under Justin Trudeau promised to enact a new non-partisan, merit-based appointments process for the Senate of Canada. Once the Liberals formed government, an independent advisory board was established to submit names to the prime minister for consideration. I provided non-partisan, unpaid advice to the government on the role and design of the new appointments process. This included the drafting of a proposal that largely became the basis for the reform. In this section, I will briefly outline the reform process and incorporate some observations based on my own limited involvement. I will not divulge specifics on what was said in various telephone conversations and conference calls, as I consider that to be confidential. I should also note that my own involvement was limited to advice; I was not a party to the formal decision-making process in the Prime Minister's Office (PMO) and Privy Council Office (PCO) and was far from the only person providing input. My objective here is to provide a broad background to the development of the policy, with my own insights into that process.

Upon the invitation of Gerry Butts, who would go on to become Prime Minister Trudeau's principal secretary, I had initially provided non-partisan expert advice to Trudeau and his advisers soon after he became leader of the Liberal Party and in the run-up to the anticipated *Reference re Senate Reform.* For the most part, my interactions at that point were aimed at giving Trudeau and his team a sense of the constitutional limits or impediments to reform, as well as some idea of how the Supreme Court of Canada might rule (I would also later provide advice to the PMO on reforms to the Supreme Court appointments process and the selection of a new chief justice). I provided similar advice to Trudeau and his advisers after the court released its decision in April 2014. At this point, the Liberals were developing their platform ahead of the 2015 election, and were aided by Matthew Mendelsohn, a former professor of political science from Queen's University who had gone on to work as deputy minister and head of the Democratic Renewal Secretariat in the Ontario government and then director of the Mowat Centre, a now-defunct Toronto-based think tank attached to the School of Public Policy and Governance at the University of Toronto. After the election, Mendelsohn would also assist the new government in transition, and would then become deputy secretary to Cabinet in charge of a new Results and Delivery Unit in the PCO.[1]

Well before the election, Trudeau publicly stated his intent to adapt the appointments process to ensure that it was "merit-based and non-partisan." In January 2014, the Liberal leader expelled all Liberal senators from caucus, declaring that they would no longer have formal affiliation with the parliamentary machinery. He justified the decision by noting that the "Senate is broken and needs to be fixed."[2] He argued that the

> Senate was once referred to as a place of sober, second thought. A place that allows for deliberation on legislation, in-depth studies into issues of import to the country, and, to a certain extent, provide[s] a check and balance on the politically driven House of Commons. It has become obvious that the party structure within the Senate interferes with these responsibilities.[3]

The announcement came as a shock to the senators and their staffers.

Although I have no first-hand insight into the specific decision to build a firewall between the elected Liberal caucus and the Senate, it is safe to say that it was influenced by the ongoing Senate expenses scandal. The decision was met with some confusion (and likely hurt feelings) among Senate Liberals, but even on the day it was announced some suggested they were "becoming increasingly comfortable with the decision, the longer they had to think about it."[4] Liberal Senate Leader James Cowan told the media that "what Mr. Trudeau has courageously done today is to set us free and allow us to do the job we're here to do – without any interference or direction from colleagues in the other place."[5] The announcement was met with scorn by the other political parties. Prime Minister Stephen Harper tauntingly remarked, "I gather the change announced by the leader today is that unelected Liberal senators will become unelected senators who happen to be Liberal."[6]

What many commentators perhaps did not know is that the decision to remove senators from the party's caucus was not unprecedented.

R.B. Bennett, angry at the "general rebelliousness of Conservative Senators" during his time as prime minister, permanently ejected them from his caucus.[7] They did not return until 1938, when his successor became leader. In fact, this has been a relatively common occurrence throughout Confederation, albeit "not in order to encourage or maintain [senatorial] independence of the party or of the Commons, but apparently because they were not wanted."[8]

The decision to separate senators from caucus activities would go hand in hand with the Liberal plan for the Senate appointments process, although it was not until after the election that the new government would think through the specifics. As noted above, I was asked to develop a draft outlining the objectives and design of an advisory body to recommend names to the prime minister. The goal was to establish an advisory body of prominent, esteemed Canadians who would follow a merit-based process to make recommendations on Senate nominations.

The advisory board was established in two phases. A transitional phase saw a board established to advise on appointments in light of the immediate need to fill vacancies that had built up during the latter part of the Harper government. Harper had refused to make appointments following the Supreme Court's ruling in *Reference re Senate Reform*. At the time the Liberals formed the government, there were twenty-two Senate vacancies, and the provinces of Ontario, Quebec, and Manitoba were among those with considerable vacancies (Manitoba was down to half of its normal representation). A permanent process would then deal with subsequent vacancies. Nonetheless, a single board was developed for both phases, with the provincial members rotating as needed.

The advisory board is modelled on existing judicial appointment advisory committees and the short-lived Advisory Committee on Vice-Regal Appointments, and is composed of five members: three permanent federal members and two members from each of the provinces or territories where a vacancy is to be filled.[9] The board itself is intended to be independent and non-partisan, and the thought was that eminent Canadians with various records and types of public service would be appointed to make recommendations to the prime minister. The Independent Advisory Board for Senate Appointments was established by an Order-in-Council on 19 January 2016 and included among its members Huguette Labelle, a former governor of the University of Ottawa and a Companion of the Order of Canada; Dawn Lavell Harvard, president of the Native Women's Association of Canada; Daniel Jutras, a dean of law at McGill University; and Yves Lamontagne, a psychiatrist and leading figure in the field of medicine.[10]

The transitional phase saw the advisory board consulting with over four hundred organizations in the relevant provinces to seek potential senatorial candidates, with the organizations asked to nominate individuals who met the constitutional and merit-based criteria. The board would recommend a list of five names to the prime minister for each vacancy. After the initial appointment of seven senators in the transitional phase, the first cycle of the permanent process was launched. At that time, Canadians were invited to apply directly for Senate positions through an online application process. The self-application aspect was the most significant departure from the draft proposal I had written for the PMO and PCO, and I discuss its implications further in the conclusion.

A primary challenge in developing the advisory process was outlining merit-based criteria under which the members of the advisory board would do its work. The ultimate criteria published by the government emphasize non-partisanship, a knowledge requirement, personal qualities, and qualifications relating to the Senate's role.[11] The non-partisanship criterion is not intended to *prohibit* potential candidates who have a history of partisan service; instead, it requires individuals to demonstrate to the advisory board that they have the capacity to act in an independent and non-partisan fashion, and to disclose past political involvement. Unfortunately, according to at least one member of the board, "[w]ord circulated that former politicians need not apply, and, if they did, they stood little chance."[12] It is also worth noting that a key feature of an independent Senate is that its members can organize as they wish. Thus, the government could not require Senate candidates to pledge that they would not sit in a partisan caucus or engage in partisan activities.

Senatorial candidates must also demonstrate an understanding of the legislative process, the Constitution of Canada, and the role of the Senate itself. Notably, the written criteria describe the Senate "as an independent and complementary body of sober second thought, regional representation and minority representation."[13] In terms of personal qualities, candidates are expected to evince adherence to principles of public life, ethics, and integrity. Finally, in terms of qualifications, the advisory board seeks out individuals with high levels of relevant experience, which may include one or more of the following: legislative or policy experience at the federal or provincial/territorial level; service to the community, which could include one's Indigenous, ethnic, or linguistic community; or recognized leadership or achievement in one's profession or field of expertise. My personal hope regarding the latter experience category is that it would lead to greater diversity in the types of persons who sit in the upper house, especially in terms of professional background. As discussed further below, that has not necessarily materialized, and the lack of ideological diversity among the recent Senate appointees is a fundamental point of contention. In addition to the traditional merit-based criteria, representational concerns are also important to the government, and so gender balance, Indigenous representation, and the representation of Canada's linguistic and ethnic communities are emphasized as additional considerations in the process.

Donald Savoie, who served on the board as a member for New Brunswick, reports a positive experience: "The process worked as intended. I did not see or feel any interference from the political level. All Canadians were free to apply, and our deliberations were held in a non-partisan and professional way."[14]

The overall objectives of the new appointments process are multifaceted. Although Trudeau emphasized partisanship as one of the Senate's ills, the renewed Senate remains at least quasi-partisan, even as the Independent Senators Group comprised a majority of the Senate's membership at the end of 42nd Parliament in June 2019 (59 of 105 seats). Even assuming that some form of a non-partisan appointments process remains in place over the long term, if certain senators stay until their mandatory retirement age of seventy-five, there could be Conservative partisans in the upper house beyond the year 2040. Thus, to the extent that a fully non-partisan Senate was an objective of the reform, it was an aspirational, long-term one, rather than an immediate proposition.

By contrast, patronage as a consideration in appointments was immediately eliminated. No one can credibly claim that senators appointed under the new process have been so on the basis of reward for partisan service, and few appointees have demonstrable party ties. In this respect alone, the reform arguably constitutes the most significant change to the Senate in Canadian history, albeit a potentially ephemeral one if a future prime minister opts to return to the old approach.

Another goal of the process is to produce *better* appointments. Whether this is the outcome is debatable, and a more subjective argument. Although the Senate has long been criticized as a house for party bagmen, its defenders have long argued that the work of the Senate has often been of a higher standard than that of its elected counterpart. Further, a cynical but not illegitimate argument might suggest that eliminating patronage and inserting merit-based criteria has more of an impact on optics than on producing a substantively better group of senators. On this score, the work of the renewed Senate requires some long-term evaluation.

A NEW APPOINTMENTS PROCESS, A NEW SENATE ACTIVISM?

Critics of the Liberal government's reforms to the Senate appointments process have argued that eliminating partisanship as a key criterion for selection would render the upper house even more undemocratic, activist, or simply unworkable.[15] Legal scholar Adam Dodek warned that a lack of partisanship may make organization of the Senate difficult, noting how it is a "critical and constitutional part of the day-to-day process of legislating in Canada. It is needed to pass the government's legislation":

Politics is a team sport. There are only so many mavericks who have the personality to be lone wolves. Most of us want and like to be part of a group – especially those who are attracted to public service. Eradicating partisanship may also be undesirable. What the Trudeau government will have to come to grips with is that the Senate is not an expert panel of independent, diverse voices – although it may serve this function at times, and serve it well.[16]

Not long after the first round of appointments under the new system, national columnist Andrew Coyne complained that the Senate's willingness to propose amendments to a number of bills constituted an "anti-democratic outrage."[17] Writer Gordon Gibson warned that the situation was a "constitutional crisis waiting to happen."[18] The concern was that emphasizing an independent Senate would embolden senators with a newfound perceived legitimacy that would encourage activism.

In terms of its aggregate behaviour in the 42nd Parliament, one early study suggests that the Senate's amendment "activism" is not significantly greater than in other modern Parliaments.[19] As examined in Chapter 1, there are different ways to analyze amendment activity, including as a percentage of bills introduced or as a percentage of bills that receive royal assent. It is therefore difficult to make meaningful comparisons across Parliaments, particularly when examining a relatively short period. As Paul Thomas notes, any statistics need to be interpreted cautiously, and numbers alone do not indicate whether proposed amendments are substantive or technical, nor do they provide "the wider political context in which the Senate was attempting to modify a given bill – for example, whether the same party controlled both houses."[20] Nonetheless, by the end of the 42nd Parliament, the Senate had amended twenty-nine government bills (sixteen in the final year alone – a legislative rush towards the end of the Parliament was particularly tumultuous), representing 33 percent of the total.[21] This is a significant increase in modern practice, harking back to the early decades of Confederation, when the Senate played a more active role.

Despite this jump in amendment activity, the Senate has not engaged in obstructionism by rejecting legislation outright (something that has occurred five times since 1988) or playing multiple rounds of ping-pong by repeatedly returning bills with amendments to the House. In fact, with respect to every bill but one (a transportation bill[22]) that passed with amendments by the Senate in the most recent Parliament, the Senate's amendments have either been accepted by the House or, where its amendments have been rejected, the Senate has dutifully passed the legislation as originally passed by the House.

If it is clear that the new Senate has not been particularly obstructionist, it is less clear from these simple statistics to what extent its increasing independence has made the legislative process more difficult.[23] In what follows, I explore the extent to which the executive – ministers and public servants – has had to adjust to the new realities of a larger and diverse group of non-partisan senators, and how the senators themselves have adjusted to their newfound independence.

TWO SNAPSHOTS OF LEGISLATIVE WRANGLING: BILLS C-45 AND S-3

As the number of independent senators has increased over time, the executive, particularly public servants tasked with helping usher legislation through the upper chamber, has faced a host of challenges. With most senators no longer part of partisan caucuses, the highly individualized and disaggregated environment of the new Senate means that technical briefings by public servants on complex or highly salient bills are often given to small groups, or even one senator at a time. Tracking support on contentious legislation is increasingly difficult. And procedural surprises, whether the result of the disparate views of individual senators, the relatively high number of inexperienced senators (a partial result of the high number of vacancies in the Senate at the time the Liberal government came to power), or an emboldened Conservative opposition, have, in the view of some observers, caused additional complexity and delays.

These difficulties presented themselves during the course of the 42nd Parliament in relation to a number of bills, two of which I explore here. The processes around these particular bills were identified, in interviews with relevant players as well as by a relatively high level of media scrutiny, as generally representative of the challenges faced by the renewed Senate.

Bill C-45

Bill C-45 legislated the legalization and regulation of marijuana sales. It was introduced in April 2017 and did not receive royal assent until June 2018. From the perspective of some interviewees who were closely following the marijuana file, the process in the House of Commons was carefully choreographed. The Standing Committee on Health met for "intense, marathon sessions" that began prior to the House's return from summer break, ultimately proposing amendments supported by the government and the New Democratic Party. The Senate process stood in stark contrast, with the bill eventually referred to five different committees for in-depth study, a move one public servant describes as "kind of unprecedented." The mandates of the various committees cut across "umpteen" ministers' portfolios, with many ministers appearing more than once before committees.[24] There was also a constant threat that the Senate would reconvene the committee of the whole to invite additional ministers.

Bill C-45 was viewed by some observers as a test case at a time when the Senate was trying to figure out its future. Some interviewees, though not all, describe the C-45 process in the Senate as "not pleasant" and "harrowing." Public servants, tasked with the provision of all materials to support the Senate's review of the bill and supporting their minister, were involved in unusually intensive outreach to senators. The highly individualized nature of dealing with the ISG members in particular appears to have generated a sense among those involved in the process that it was a marked departure from what was usually necessary under the old partisan Senate. According to one public servant, the new process "frankly felt almost American." Officials at Health Canada worked closely with Department of Justice counterparts to help steer the bill through the upper chamber, with one public servant noting that "I think they [Justice] had enough experience to forewarn us that the Senate was an independent beast."

The government delayed its initial timelines for pot legalization as a result of the extensive Senate scrutiny, pushing back the original target of 1 July 2018 to 17 October. The Senate ultimately proposed forty-six amendments to Bill C-45, many of which the government accepted. Thirteen of the Senate's substantive amendments were rejected, including a proposal to affirm the right of provincial governments to ban home cultivation, a provision to create a public registry of investors in cannabis companies, and a ban on the distribution of logo-branded pot merchandise. Notably, a late motion in the Senate to return the amendment on banning home cultivation to the House a second time was defeated in a 45–35 vote. That same day, the Senate voted 52–29 to pass the bill.

Some of the senators apparently required an explanation of why "reasons" were not attached by the House of Commons when some of the amendments were rejected.[25] Certain senators also seemed to behave as if ministers of the Crown were "somehow accountable to them, instead of to Canadians."[26] There is a widespread view among different actors familiar with the process that Senator Harder, as Government Representative in the Senate, worked to educate senators that their role was to scrutinize but not to somehow try to hold ministers to account (i.e., the difference between proposing amendments and demanding that ministers or the House provide "reasons").

It is unclear just how concerned the government was during the C-45 process about obstructionism or the threat of a ping-pong match with the House via multiple rounds of amendments. Some interviewees noted that a long game of ping-pong was unlikely, while others were concerned about "mischief" and aggressive tactics by the Conservative opposition. The Conservative senators operated as a bloc, and engaged in activities like bringing props to committee or less than respectful questioning at committee. Three Conservative senators even travelled to Washington, DC, to speak with US attorney general Jeff Sessions about Canada's pot legalization.[27]

Bill C-45's sponsor in the Senate was Tony Dean, who publicly noted that he thought the Senate functioned well throughout the process.[28] Dean is credited by observers with taking a read of the situation and what was required to navigate the new political reality in the upper chamber, ensuring that people were briefed and attempting to have a constructive, non-partisan discussion. Yet it is Harder who is cited as instrumental in getting agreement on a timeline and holding the final vote.[29] This is something even the opposition Conservatives acknowledge. A senior staffer in the office of the Leader of the Opposition in the Senate, who cited Bill C-45 as an example of negotiation and how the Senate has been functioning generally well, points out that "until [Harder] stepped up for proper negotiation, the bill wasn't going anywhere ... There were some trust issues." While public servants and members on different sides of the issue generally thought the C-45 process proved effective, not everyone was satisfied. Independent Senator André Pratte was angry that the bill passed without the more substantive amendments posed by the Senate, and questioned whether the government took "amendments into consideration seriously."[30]

Bill S-3

Bill S-3 dealt with registration of Indian status under the *Indian Act*. It was introduced in the Senate because of a backlog in the House.[31] The legislation was in response to a Quebec Superior Court decision that existing registration rules violated the equality rights provision (section 15) of the *Canadian Charter of Rights and Freedoms*. The old rules meant that Indigenous women who married non-Indigenous men lost their status, while Indigenous men who married non-Indigenous women did not. Bill S-3 was intended to resolve the remaining issue of treating the female hereditary line the same as the male line.

The technical complexity of the legislation presented many of the same challenges for the government and public servants as Bill C-45. In their view, it was difficult to explain to senators and to stakeholders why the rules were drafted the way they were. There were many more technical briefings than usual, with more independent senators, who had more fractured views. The minister's office was also more involved than it normally would be. The government adopted a two-stage approach to the broader inequities in the *Indian Act* registration process. The immediate issue was to be addressed under Bill S-3, with consultation on broader issues to proceed later (a consultation report was tabled in Parliament on 12 June 2019, but Parliament was dissolved shortly thereafter).

The government also needed the legislation to move quickly because the Quebec Superior Court initially gave it only eighteen months to resolve the constitutional issue, but as a result of Senate opposition to the bill, the government was forced to request extensions on two separate occasions. Witnesses appearing before the Standing Senate Committee on Aboriginal Peoples were generally very critical of the legislation, wanting more inclusive language that went beyond the court's requirements, something that was picked up on by many senators. The bill initially sought to reverse discrimination for individuals who had lost their status since 1951. An intensive period of negotiation followed, and the government agreed to a set of amendments, while rejecting others, in order to get the bill passed.

Among the Senate's amendments to the bill was a provision implementing the new rules in all cases dating back to 1869. The government agreed to implement the change, though only after a consultation period. This consultation was completed in June 2019, but no action to initiate further amendments occurred due to the dissolution of Parliament in anticipation of the federal election.[32] According to estimates by the Parliamentary Budget Officer, up to 35,000 Canadians were immediately eligible to register as Status Indians at a cost of roughly $55 million in annual benefits, but once the new rules permit registration for family lines going back to 1869, as many as 670,000 individuals will be eligible.[33]

As with Bill C-45, the process under Bill S-3 left those involved with the clear impression that the new Senate presented distinct challenges. One public servant notes never having been involved in a bill with so many amendments put forward by the upper house. This was interpreted by some within government to mean that the current Senate may have less deference towards the views of the government or the

House; senators seem more willing to play an active role and attempt to represent voices that have not always been heard.

Interviewees note that the Bill S-3 process was illustrative of a spike in lobbyist activity and the apparent openness of some senators to lobbyists and stakeholders. There is a clear perception among public servants that there is a different or more significant impact in this area than in the past.[34] This perception is borne out by data beyond merely the Bill S-3 process: records from the Office of the Commissioner of Lobbying show that lobbyists made contact with senators in 2017 twice as often as in 2016, and six times as often as in 2015.[35] Most of these contacts involved independent senators. At a 2018 Institute for Research on Public Policy (IRPP) roundtable on the Senate, Elizabeth Roscoe noted that lobbying communications with senators numbered roughly 450 per year from 2011 to 2014, rising to 700 in 2016 and 1,450 in 2017.[36] At the same roundtable, Yaroslav Baran noted that where lobbyists previously focused their activity on ministers and opposition leaders, independent senators have become more of a focal point because they "are more concerned with substance and can respond to stakeholders' views by amending legislation or influencing other politicians."[37] A recent study by Aengus Bridgman examining lobbying activity through the end of the 42nd Parliament provides further confirmation that independent senators have received disproportionate attention from lobbyists.[38]

As is apparent from this brief account of the progression of high-profile bills through the upper house, the increasing complexity of the new Senate environment has presented challenges for the executive. It is important not to overstate the dynamics at play. The majority of government bills presented to the Senate have progressed with little of the drama associated with these more controversial or prominent pieces of legislation. Nonetheless, the Senate's record so far and the views of the relevant actors on how the less partisan, more independent culture is proceeding raises a number of questions: How is the Senate organizing itself to adjust to its new composition? How is the government – from ministers to public servants – reacting to and cultivating the new relationship? And finally, what do the current challenges mean for the future of the Senate and its relationship with the government?

THE SENATE IN TRANSITION

One of the most direct consequences of the reform to the Senate appointments process is that a majority of senators no longer have partisan affiliation. As of the summer of 2020, the ISG comprised the largest group of senators, with two other non-partisan senator groups, the Canadian Senators Group and the Progressive Senate Group, also eventually forming. The Conservative Party caucus, the only explicitly partisan senators remaining, stood at twenty-one members. The purpose of the ISG is not to act as a caucus or even as an ideologically coherent faction; instead, it exists to protect the independence of senators and to provide a structure for the representation of non-partisan members in the broader coordination of the upper chamber's work, including the composition of committees. The ISG has a facilitator (loosely analogous to the leader of old government or opposition caucuses) whose role is to represent and help coordinate the group's interests.

This organizational mandate means that the ISG should not be regarded as a traditional caucus. There are no whipped votes. In fact, the individual independence of ISG members is prized. One result of this is that in the initial year or two following the reforms, information flows and organization in the context of the legislative process were challenging. Under the traditional partisan Senate, senators generally sat as members of the governing or opposition caucus, where they received political briefings on various pieces of legislation and coordinated on partisan messaging surrounding the government's legislative agenda. Senators appointed under the new system of appointments do not coordinate on the substance of individual bills in this manner. This reality accounts for many of the apparent logistical difficulties in relation to Bills C-45 and S-3.

The ISG has taken steps to address some of the organization and information-sharing difficulties. It is developing practices to emphasize information sharing as well as coordination on sharing knowledge and expertise for scrutinizing bills through the use of secretariat resources and voluntary measures. Information and outreach data are compiled on shared drives for ISG members to access. Senators with shared special interests on particular files will take the lead (sometimes as the sponsor of a bill, but not always) to help keep colleagues up-to-date. Part of this latter innovation stems from recognition that individual senators do not have the time or resources to devote to comprehensive scrutiny of every piece of legislation. They are thus beginning to learn to rely on colleagues to share the burden and to prevent unnecessary duplication of efforts.

According to ISG facilitator Senator Woo, there is an expectation that over time, as these forms of coordination are implemented, the problems faced by public servants will become less acute and will require less hands-on management and even fewer technical briefings to small groups or individual senators.

These coordination efforts are procedural. None of the organizational endeavours imply that ISG members will adopt similar substantive views on pieces of legislation or that the coordination encompasses how they will ultimately vote. Yet it is significant that the ISG recently adopted the Charter of the Independent Senators Group as a way of formalizing its organization, the role of the ISG, and the responsibilities of the facilitator and deputy. The charter explicitly limits the ISG membership to non-partisans, which precludes anyone who is a member of another recognized party or parliamentary group, a member of a caucus of the House of Commons, or someone who has direct involvement in the activities of a recognized political party registered under the *Canada Elections Act*, including public endorsements or fundraising for political parties or one of their candidates.[39] The charter outlines the purpose of the ISG as follows:

> Members of the ISG have joined together for the purpose of affirming and protecting each Senator's freedom to vote as he or she sees fit in respect of their parliamentary duties, and to enhance the ability of in-dividual Senators to conduct their functions as parliamentarians. By sharing expertise, pooling resources and providing mutual support, ISG Senators:

a) contribute to the planning and coordination of Chamber business and committee work;

b) share information and assist ISG Senators with their administrative needs;

c) coordinate collective action on issues related to Senate administrative processes and practices that the ISG has designated or may designate, as the case may be, as priorities or matters of common importance to all members of the ISG;

d) respect that each Senator can only fulfill the role of Senator if she or he maintains their right to express views that are aligned with the Senator's own judgment;

e) build on ongoing efforts to modernize the Senate in terms of its culture, rules and practices, in order to strengthen the work of the Senate as an effective, respected, and non-partisan Chamber of sober second thought that is complementary to the House of Commons.[40]

In view of these efforts, Senator Woo suggests that some of the problems faced by senators and public servants during the Bill C-45 or S-3 processes might be transitory.

From the perspective of Senator Joseph Day (at the time serving as leader of the Senate Liberal caucus, later becoming interim leader of the Progressive Senate Group until his retirement in January 2020), a lot of the adjustment stems from both the rapid nature of the reform and no clear outcome for what the Senate should look like after the changes to the appointments process. Day notes that "part of reacting to Mr. Trudeau's decisions was a lack of guidance on where we should go ... we're struggling with procedure often when it would be better to get into the substance of how things should be changed." The considerable number of new appointees has also made it difficult for the ISG to adjust, according to Day:

[T]he learning of the role of senator and being given the opportunity and time to develop an appreciation of how the individual can participate and contribute is not as smooth a transition as it could be or should be ... In Mr. Harper's time when he appointed a larger number at one time, filling a big number of vacancies, they came into the Senate and we noticed the same thing. The ability of these individuals to be nurtured along, to learn the process and to appreciate the unwritten but important aspects of the Senate were lost [as a result of the sheer number of new senators].[41]

Procedural adjustments are not the only factors influencing the evolution of the renewed Senate. Two other variables are significant: the composition of the Senate – the size of the ISG, especially relative to the size of the opposition Conservative caucus – and the relative inexperience of the recently appointed senators. Each factor has influenced the posture of different senators in relation to bills since 2016. Further, they are factors that the government, and particularly the Government Representative in the Senate, has had to account for when steering legislation through the upper chamber.

Upon Senator Harder's appointment as part of the first nomination group of seven independent senators under the new process, the Conservatives enjoyed a majority in the Senate and on every committee (as well as chairing most of them). As Government Representative, Harder was tasked with getting agreements among the various Senate leaders on managing major bills, in particular having conversations with then-Leader of the Opposition Claude Carignan, in order to work out an understanding to allow votes to take place and to prioritize certain bills for advancement. A prominent example of this early legislation was Bill C-14, which legislated eligibility requirements and laid out certain regulations for medical aid in dying. Harder notes that "we were able to get an agreement amongst the leaders on how we would manage the bill – I do think it worked quite well."[42]

Over time, as the independents grew in number and eventually outnumbered the Conservatives, adjustments were necessary. Harder and the ISG reached interim agreements with the Conservatives about the composition of committees in order to achieve greater proportionality of representation. There is a clear sense from Senator Harder that while in some ways the growing number of independents makes the job easier, it has also freed the Conservatives to oppose legislation in a more strident fashion. As Harder explains, the Conservatives could "exercise their opposition stance without fear of defeating legislation because of numerical superiority." Harder cites Bill C-45 as an example of this, where the opposition members voted against the bill at second reading, let alone third, which was fairly unusual. "In an odd way," Harder states, "both procedurally and substantively the Conservatives [have flexed their] muscles more" as their numbers have fallen. Despite this, negotiations between the various caucus and group leaders on C-45 ensured the bill's eventual passage. This reflects a broader context of consultation among the Senate's leadership. Senator Day notes, for example, that the various leaders meet every Tuesday morning (during sitting weeks) to discuss priorities and any challenges, a spirit of cooperation among four leaders (Harder, Day, Larry Smith, and Woo at the time of the interview) that he argues has been very helpful.

The Conservatives have a different perspective. In the view of Senator Martin, it is ISG members whose behaviour has changed as their numbers have grown, in part due to an expectation that simple majority rule would create an easier time for getting what they want done at the committee level and on the Senate floor. Some of the rules that give minority parties power, especially power to complicate procedural matters, have, in Martin's view, proven frustrating for the ISG. Examples of such rules include the fact that time allocation can be placed at only one stage of debate on an item if there is no agreement between parties, and the ability of every senator to introduce a variety of motions during debate (Martin notes that these same rules frustrated the Conservatives when they held the majority). According to Martin, there has been a resulting erosion of trust on committees as ISG members have sought to change rules, and this erosion of trust has affected the day-to-day sittings.[43]

Senator Woo notes that the Opposition has generally wanted to show that they are being a good opposition while also not wanting to create a dysfunctional Senate. However, in some ways the growing membership of the ISG made Harder's job more difficult. Where in the past he could reach an agreement with Conservative opposition leaders (previously Carignan, later Senator Larry Smith), the Government Representative and the ISG facilitator "can't have the same conversation as he has with the opposition leader," Woo points out, "because I don't whip my members."[44] It should be noted that there is not a lot of evidence of formal whipped votes in partisan caucuses either. Nonetheless, negotiations on timelines and on prioritizing certain bills will undoubtedly become more complicated in a context where the "leader" cannot reliably speak for the group, or even necessarily predict the behaviour of its members.

Senator Day largely concurs, but notes that a lack of support from the government made Harder's job more difficult than it otherwise needed to be:

> He's performing something we've never had before. That would be a difficult job for anyone to do. He had no experience in the Senate ... He's not in my view given the support of government for him to perform the role it would appear he's expected to perform. So he's sitting there learning his job every day, and he's a capable person and is adjusting nicely but it has not been an easy road for him.

Day argues that Harder could do the job a lot better if he were a member of Cabinet and had more clear and direct organizational support from the government. Senator Martin also emphasizes this point, noting that "Harder is Government Leader, but not [really]," because he is not at the Cabinet table, and this has made his task more difficult.

Woo notes that because the numbers game has changed so much in the Senate over the course of just a couple of years, there is a broader and different dynamic in the upper chamber. "The traditional duopoly of decision-making and direction between government and opposition has been disrupted," Woo states. Meanwhile, the formal Rules of the Senate were not changed during the 42nd Parliament to incorporate non-government, non-opposition input into various decisions around bells, time allocation, or committee selection. In practice, some of these processes have been adjusted on an ad hoc basis, but future changes cannot be made without buy-in from independents.[45]

Like Harder, Woo sees the opposition Conservatives becoming more strident in their approach over time, as the change in numbers has also "created a dynamic whereby the opposition has gone from playing the role as the responsible loyal opposition that is trying to make the Senate work to one now that is basically ... exercising its prerogative as the opposition and not much more." When they were a larger group, there was a sense that the Conservatives had a greater willingness to avoid being disruptive. Now that they are a more distinct minority, "they've left all the responsibility of ensuring the Senate is working to the government and to the ISG. They're doing that for a strategic reason: if the ISG functions to make things work smoothly, allow bills through, the Conservatives will accuse them of being Liberals. If the ISG is more disruptive, the Conservatives will still criticize."

One public servant suggests there is evidence that this dynamic has encouraged greater organization among the independents:

> [A]t a certain point it became clear the [opposition was] highly organized and tactically had all the advantage. And at a certain point you saw the Independents start to behave more as a group, with a common interest. They entered into this process kind of altruistic, acting in good faith, and that optimism was extinguished by some of the partisan attacks ... and then Independents start to organize a bit more.[46]

The overall dynamic came to a head in April 2019, when Harder proposed a "programming motion" to impose strict deadlines on eleven bills at various stages of the Senate's legislative agenda. The proposal was withdrawn after negotiations between the various Senate leaders apparently broke the impasse, leading to agreement to expedite much of the legislation but to drop deadlines on three controversial bills.[47]

From the perspective of the Conservative opposition, the task is not to stop the government's agenda – particularly on matters that were in its election platform – but to use the Senate as a voice for raising legitimate concerns. According to one senior staffer, "we can't fight on what's being done but on how it's being done." Therefore, on key pieces of legislation the Opposition has negotiated with Harder to get what they view as sufficient time for scrutiny of bills and a sufficient number of witnesses at committee to "create a legislative track record we can use when things go bad." Nonetheless, the Conservatives are open about the fact that they view it as being up to the government to ensure that the Senate functions smoothly. So while the process that led to the passage of Bill C-45 demonstrates, from the Opposition's perspective, that the Senate is working, the government "left a lot on the table" before the summer break in 2018.[48] Bills on environmental assessment, workplace harassment, and other issues "all got stranded because [Harder] said 'you have to sit,' to which the answer is 'who's responsible for quorum in the Senate? Not us. The government is.' So, the prime minister chose to go the independent route and can't guarantee quorum."

The Senate's current composition reminds us that the renewed upper house remains in a transition period. With a sizable partisan opposition still in place, it is not yet a fully non-partisan, independent body. That shifting dynamic makes it difficult to predict how much things will continue to change, although one factor may help stabilize things over the medium to long term: the growing experience of the independent senators.

It is apparent that some of the tensions over whether the Senate would act in an obstructionist manner during the Bill C-45 process emanated, to some degree, from the relative inexperience of some of the independent senators. If the perception among some of those involved with the C-45 process is accurate, some senators came with a view that ministers "answer to" the Senate as if the upper house were the confidence chamber. Similarly, simple procedural misunderstandings – such as whether messages from the Commons rejecting amendments should spell out reasons in a manner similar to the written reasons of appellate courts, for example – suggest that a learning curve might alleviate the temptation among some senators to assert the Senate's authority to interfere more directly with the government's agenda.

How some of the new senators conceive of the nature of their independence also may need adjustment over time. For example, some ISG members apparently adopted the view that it would be inappropriate for them to meet informally with, or be lobbied by, Cabinet ministers in relation to specific pieces of legislation. Senator Woo acknowledges this attitude among some of his colleagues, noting that there are some "doctrinal issues" independent senators are working through, and one is the relative distance they should keep from the "political class." Over time, he expects that there will be more nuanced and less dogmatic views on this. "It's not difficult to understand that one can obviously talk to a minister and still be independent, so I don't think that will be a big problem in the years ahead," Woo notes. The struggle for some senators has thus far been a desire to demonstrate that they are independent not only in name but also in practice, and to take pains to avoid even the appearance of conflicted behaviour or external influence. "Many will want to air [*sic*] on the side of caution, but [there is] no contradiction in speaking to a minister and still holding an independent view."

It is important not to overstate this particular issue. One senior public servant notes that Senate question period with ministers has been helpful and a means for ministers to build relationships within the upper chamber. Senator Harder also states that some ministers' relationships with senators have been helpful in the context of marshalling support for certain pieces of legislation.

Thus far, this analysis has examined the different facets of the renewed Senate's evolution as challenges or problems. Yet to the extent that the increased complexity, greater diversity of viewpoints, and forthright efforts to scrutinize legislation in line with a sober second thought role create challenges, they are perhaps properly characterized as a feature, rather than a bug, of the government's reform to the appointments process.

This is a sentiment echoed by various players in or involved with the current Senate. As one public servant notes, "the extent of the reform is completely under-appreciated outside of Ottawa. I don't think Canadians understand how significant a reform it has been, and how detrimental it has been to the government's interests – and the government doesn't get credit for it." Senator Woo concurs, stating that "it is precisely in the nature of a more independent Senate that you'll have more independent views! The views will be disparate and will require greater management on the part of public servants to address questions." Woo adds that this is precisely why the ISG created its charter.

THE FUTURE OF THE SENATE:
ASSESSING THE RENEWED SENATE'S PERFORMANCE

Delays and the Legislative Agenda: A Function of Increased Scrutiny

Controversy over the renewed Senate did not boil over until the end of the 42nd Parliament. As noted above, by April 2019 an abortive plan to invoke a quasi-omni-time allocation on a number of bills made headline news. There were also deep divisions over a handful of bills. Perhaps most illustrative was Bill C-69, which brought in a substantial overhaul of federal government environmental assessment legislation. Alberta premier Jason Kenney called Bill C-69 and a related piece of legislation, Bill C-48, the *Oil Tanker Moratorium Act,* "a prejudicial attack on Alberta" for their prospective impact on Alberta's oil industry.[49]

As the CBC reports, "[t]he Senate passed an unprecedented 188 amendments to Bill C-69 after months of study and a cross-country committee tour to regions most affected" by the legislation.[50] The government accepted 99 of those amendments (although it altered 37 of them), but rejected 90 percent of those proposed by Conservative senators. The amendments strengthened the role of provinces in the review process, gave the government of the day less control over the ability to alter project review timelines, and strengthened the independence of the new Impact Assessment Agency of Canada. As with other pieces of high-profile legislation, the Senate accepted the House of Commons adjustments to the bill and passed it without further changes.

Despite a flurry of legislative activity – not unusual at the end of the Parliament – only one noteworthy government bill died at first reading in the Senate, but that bill (C-98, enabling a public complaints and review commission of the Royal Canadian Mounted Police authority in relation to the Canada Border Services Agency) had been presented to the Senate just a day before the dissolution of Parliament. Criticism that the Senate obstructed the government's legislative agenda does not ring true under such a circumstance. Even if the complexity and challenges associated with the changes to the Senate's composition created delays, it is unclear to what extent the delays were the fault of the ISG or the Conservative opposition. The Conservatives were not shy about using procedural tactics to stall bills, even in the name of ensuring they were thoroughly vetted. The Conservative Senate whip, Don Plett, was accused of delaying important bills, including Bill C-69, on this basis.[51] How then to attribute such delays to the renewed appointments process?

Critics of that process have asserted that eliminating partisanship would either encourage senators to become obstructionist or effectively render the upper house unworkable or dysfunctional. Yet the general picture, according to my analysis, is of a robust and active chamber fulfilling its role while adjusting to its new composition. Although there is evidence of a strong willingness to propose amendments, this is distinct from obstructionism, for which there is little evidence. More significant for the present analysis is that despite delays with certain pieces of legislation, there is little evidence of dysfunction either.

From Senator Harder's perspective, the Senate has come through the most difficult part of its transition:

> I do think we are no longer in what I call the experimental stage, that the notion of a less partisan, more independent Senate that is complementary to the House of Commons is taking root ... I don't think it would be easy to turn the clock back to the *status quo ante*. I think that's significant. The conduct of the Senate has been such that the early concerns among some people that we would either be a rubber stamp or a committee that would oppose anything, hasn't happened. [There is] a good deal of confidence that you can have a less partisan and more independent Senate that doesn't impede government.[52]

It is significant, Harder points out, that he has so far never used time allocation, noting that it was used some twenty-five times in the previous (2011–15) Parliament. Recent events, including the aforementioned programming motion to expedite the legislative progress on a number of bills, put this boast in context, however. It should also be noted that the Senate's Government Representative can only propose time allocation, as under the Senate's rules it must be approved by a vote in the chamber. Further, the Senate has generally accepted messages from the House about its amendments. "I'm reasonably serene that the Senate exercises the independence that the prime minister says he wanted," Harder states.

Senator Woo generally concurs with this view, although he notes that the transition period is not quite over. "The Senate is partially independent [but] has a partisan caucus that can significantly hold back the full flowering of an independent upper house that is unelected and complementary to the House," Woo states. In his view, the new appointments process is working and is producing appointments "on par with the best we've seen under the [old] partisan process. That is not a statement of 'we're better than they are,' but the new batch do come to Senate without political connections and involvement of previous connections, and I think Canadians like to see that." A senior staffer with the Conservative opposition thinks the informal adjustments made to the legislative process and committee system have been fruitful: "I see no signs that it's not working."

Senator Day takes a historical view, noting that things have not changed so dramatically from the recent past:

> An outsider might not appreciate some of the things in the Senate ever since I arrived. Even in Harper's time we proposed amendments. I can remember [the Conservative government's] first piece of legislation, Bill C-2, and that went back and forth several times. There were over 80 amendments to that bill ... Ping pong is unusual, but does happen and is there as a tool for Parliament to use and for the Senate to use. And it usually happens when the House of Commons starts taking for granted the role of the Senate. And they're not doing that now – maybe there's more effort on behalf of the executive to inform senators about objectives and goals of the legislation.[53]

Day does not make any predictions about how the Senate's legislative process and relationship with the government will proceed, but his comments suggest that he is sanguine about the Senate's current attitude towards the legislative process.

Senator Martin notes that increased amendment activity is not necessarily reflective of a more robust sober second thought role in the newly reformed Senate, but instead is at least in part a result of the lack of an explicit government caucus and opposition caucus. "The ISG is sort of acting like the government caucus, but they're not. When you have a group that isn't congruent with how they're behaving – that incongruency, that misalignment ... makes everything more challenging for everyone." ISG senators do not sit in the governing caucus and so they cannot weigh in on legislative proposals, "so no wonder there are more amendments."[54] Further, many of the amendments are narrowly technical rather than substantive changes to bills. Martin adds that the inter-party/group discussions (at the leaders' level, the deputy level, and the caucus/group level) are starting to look more the way they did pre-reform; nevertheless, the incongruencies in the ISG role create gaps and challenges.

In an interview conducted in 2018, a senior public servant notes that while the overall legislative program in the Senate is different, it has not slowed things down. "One thing people assume is that things are taking longer," the public servant notes, but "we would say there's not a lot of evidence for that yet."[55] This was before delays with certain bills, such as Bill C-59, *An Act respecting national security matters,* became apparent. Bill C-59 took a full year to get through the Senate. By 2019, an apparent legislative backlog had developed, although this is not uncommon at the end of a Parliament. Moreover, serious delays remained the exception rather than the rule. Still, one analysis after the 42nd Parliament ended found that the length of time a government bill spent in the Senate more than doubled over the previous Parliament (from 2011 to 2015, bills spent an average of twelve sitting days in the upper chamber, compared with an average of thirty-one days for the 2015–19 period, excluding appropriation bills).[56] This is perhaps not too surprising given the sharp increase in Senate amendment activity. Further, a handful of bills, such as S-3 and C-59, no doubt disproportionately exacerbated the increase.

Since the Trudeau government seemed to get virtually its entire legislative agenda through Parliament in the end, it is difficult to draw normative conclusions that the Senate "delays" are in themselves a problem. In fact, at the end of the Parliament, critics of the Senate, such as columnist Andrew Coyne, seemed to be left with much more speculative concerns, such as the notion that the "mere threat" of the Senate's ability to "deflect the will of the people's elected representatives" might somehow be enough to "deter governments from introducing legislation, or ensure it is drafted in such a way as to avoid a confrontation." Examples of this are not forthcoming, however, although in Coyne's view "it would be hard to imagine there weren't some."[57] My own analysis suggests that the outcome of the 42nd Parliament is consistent with the goal of renewed independence: increased scrutiny on government legislation. This will never be acceptable to those who do not countenance an appointed upper house, but neither is it reflective of an attack on the democratic mandate of the elected lower chamber.

Future Organization: Will Challenges Worsen?

That the Senate has thus far functioned well in a complex new context is no guarantee that it will continue to do so. A number of questions and issues remain uncertain, particularly as the number of independent senators continues to increase. What will be the impact on the legislative process in the Senate once there is no longer an established, recognized, and partisan opposition caucus? Thus far, the Senate has organized the transition through informal agreements between the various groups. Eventually, changes to the formal Rules of the Senate may be necessary in order to recognize the new reality and satisfy independents that resources, committee spots, and procedures are allocated or organized fairly. What form should these changes take?

One of these issues was partially taken up by the Special Senate Committee on Senate Modernization, which issued its first report in October 2016. The report included a number of recommendations: update committee membership rules to ensure that senators who do not belong to a political party can more fully participate, introduce televised debates in the Senate, and establish rules to divide certain omnibus bills so that their substance can be properly reviewed by committees.[58] Changes were effected in 2017 to ensure that groups not affiliated with organized political parties received some funding for legislative duties.

One of the most important recommendations was to allow for the recognition of non-partisan caucuses in the Rules of the Senate. A proposal to organize the Senate around regional caucuses was advanced in a 2016 report by former senators Michael Kirby and Hugh Segal.[59] In their view, "over the years, an excessively partisan Senate became less fair-minded as it mirrored the House and the Prime Minister's Office. Rules advantaged partisanship while sober second thought became an infrequent experience."[60] Without regional representation as a central organizing principle for the Senate, Confederation would not have occurred, the authors argue. Senate caucuses organized by region would not mean "like-minded senators can't gather around voluntary groupings: a military affairs group; a minority languages group; a free enterprise group; an anti-poverty group; or even a politically like-minded group. But partisan affiliation should no longer provide the sole basis for authority or a route for any government to subvert independence."[61]

The formal Rules of the Senate need to be adjusted precisely because they currently serve to entrench partisanship. As Kirby and Segal note, "Independent Senators must secure proportional rights vis-à-vis partisan Senators in order to play a meaningful role in the management of the Senate agenda, rules on committee membership, the way the Senate budget is spent, and so on. As things stand now, the Independent Senators have no access to funding for research, which is granted to 'parties' only."[62]

As noted, some of these issues have thus far been dealt with informally. Other formal changes to the rules, particularly as the number of remaining partisan senators continues to dwindle, may be necessary, but Kirby and Segal's solution – structuring the Senate around regional caucuses – was not met with broad consensus. Independent senator André Pratte, for example, objected to the proposal because of the "risk that senators will come to see all the issues coming before the Senate only from the perspective of their region. Since the region will be the chamber's organizing principle, it will become senators' dominating preoccupation ... fixated on advancing its interests. Canada does not need yet another institution fostering regional tensions."[63]

In the short to medium term, there are also signs that it may be difficult to achieve changes to the Senate's formal rules. A senior staffer in the office of the Leader of the Opposition notes that the government's entire legislative agenda would be at risk if there appears to be a government-led effort to initiate changes (I interpret these comments to include anything pushed by the Government Representative's office). In this Conservative staffer's view, the consensus model the Senate has been operating on should continue to work. During the 42nd Parliament, Senator Harder was clear that the formal organization and question of caucuses "is for the Senate to decide, not for me."[64] His own hope for the final year of the 42nd Parliament was that the Senate would devote its time to the legislative agenda. "A lot of energy and time would be taken up with internal organizational issues, which could distract from our legislative role. I would be on the side of [continued] organic evolution." Senior public servants note that while there was initially plenty of public debate about the Senate's formal organization, particularly the regional caucus proposal, they have not heard much discussion behind the scenes in the last year or two.[65]

Another problem stems from the fact that certain changes to the *Parliament of Canada Act*,[66] such as those to move the Senate away from one strictly designed on a partisan government-opposition basis, need to be initiated by the House of Commons. Senator Woo recently called on the prime minister to initiate formal changes in law and fulfill his promise to finalize the Senate's transition to full independence. He was quoted in the media as saying, "I have been in the Senate now for two years and what I've learned is that the road map depends on him (Trudeau) to finish the job."[67]

It is an open question whether the Senate needs a fixed and designated opposition caucus. As independents come to dominate the upper chamber, it is more likely we will see an increasingly dynamic process instead: a shifting opposition, varying in membership and size, on an issue-by-issue or bill-by-bill basis. Independence by definition means that senators will not vote in lockstep on a wide-ranging set of issues. This is not to say that senators will not coalesce over broad areas of policy, be it fiscal conservatives, environmental activists, or members with particular views on criminal justice policy. There is no reason to think the Senate needs a dedicated group of senators as "the Opposition"; it is not the confidence chamber, and it does not exist to oppose the overarching legislative agenda of the government. The fact that it has traditionally had a formal opposition caucus is fundamentally the product of its historical partisanship. If the new appointments system is maintained and the partisan era comes to an end, it is not clear why the Senate's organizational vestiges should be maintained.

It is not clear that the Senate needs to be organized in formal caucuses either. Despite the concerns of critics that a Senate composed of un-tethered independents is unworkable, the record so far suggests the opposite. Like-minded senators will still coalesce over shared interests in particular issues or policy areas, and can do so in parliamentary groups rather than formal caucuses. Senate groups continued to evolve along these lines in the 43rd Parliament. In late 2019, eleven Con-servative senators, former Conservatives, and ISG members formed the Canadian Senators Group, designed to promote regional interests and regarded as a small-c conservative faction of the Senate.[68] Shortly after, the Independent Liberal Senate caucus rebranded itself as the Progressive Senate Group, abandoning its partisan identity with the stated intent of attracting other members on the basis of shared ideological outlook.[69] For the first time in Canadian history, there were no Liberal-affiliated senators in Parliament. By the fall of 2020, the two new groups had thirteen and eleven members, respectively. As different groups form along ideological or other grounds, it is possible the ISG itself will eventually disband (although at the time of writing it accounts for forty-four of ninety-five occupied Senate seats).

It is unclear to what degree the Senate's organizational needs require formalization at the level of substantive issues or coinciding with characteristics like ideology or regional representation. The core organ-izational requirements may be largely procedural, ensuring equitable staffing of committees and a relatively efficient process for getting bills scrutinized and voted on. The type of information-sharing and procedural innovations advanced within the ISG may constitute the minimal requirements needed to ensure that the Senate functions smoothly in a post-partisan era. The only substantive changes that may be needed are those relating to equitable distribution of resources.[70] Nonetheless, it is clear the current Senate, as of this writing, is beginning to sort this out for itself. This is not a prediction about how the Senate will ultimately organize. Independence also exists at the level of the institution, and the Senate will organize as it sees fit. Yet the fact that it has functioned with an increasingly large group of independent senators along precisely the parameters I have described is highly suggestive.

Are the Independents Independent? The Real Test of Reform

One of the outstanding questions about the upper house's future behaviour is whether independents will continue to operate with a reasonably deferential stance to the legislative agenda of the government. When speaking of Harder's role in getting the government's legislative agenda through the Senate, Senator Woo notes that an increasing number of independents might make his job easier, but notes there are no guarantees. One public servant expects that legislating will become increasingly difficult, and formal changes may be necessary or the pace will slow and legislating will "quickly become very uncertain" as senators assert themselves.[71] By contrast, another public servant believes that the government has adjusted and become more strategic in its dealings with the Senate.

There are reasons to be uncertain about how things will progress in the Senate. Senators appointed precisely on the basis of their independence, and in a process that came to involve an application process, might reasonably expect not to go to Ottawa merely to facilitate an institutional rubber stamp for government legislation. Critics of the reforms to the appointments process expressed concern on these grounds. Moreover, key aspects of Trudeau's approach to appointments seem to encourage a representative aspect to the role of senator. For example, he has made a concerted effort to increase the number of Indigenous members of the upper house, appointing nine Indigenous senators in under three years (at the end of the 42nd Parliament, there were twelve Indigenous senators, representing over 11 percent of seats). The renewed Senate may become an important site for the protection of Indigenous interests.[72] Others have similarly noted that the new conditions in the Senate enable feminist senators to come together in the name of women's representation.[73]

Another, more cynical element to this is the supposition by some critics, as noted above, that because the current ISG members frequently support government legislation, they are somehow Liberals in all but name. One analysis of recorded votes in the Senate from the beginning of the 42nd Parliament to July 2018 reveals that ISG members appointed by Trudeau vote with the government 84.2 percent of the time, compared with ISG members appointed by previous prime ministers (77.2 percent), Senate Liberals (76.8 percent), and Conservative senators (20.1 percent).[74] The implication of this assertion is that when a new government takes power, the renewed Senate may become an antagonistic and obstructionist institution (particularly if that new government is Conservative).

One unique, if not outright bizarre, criticism suggests that the Liberal government is able to "co-opt" independent senators by having them sponsor government bills or "launder" the government's own amendments to legislation through the Senate.[75] The implication is allegedly that without an organized (partisan) opposition, it is "far easier for the government to co-opt more senators and compromise them from doing their jobs of holding government to account."[76] There are two problems with this argument. First, freedom from partisan constraint makes it unlikely that a senator could be co-opted by serving as the sponsor of a bill. It seems far more likely that senators would sponsor a bill they agreed with, and simply refuse to do so in the context of a bill they objected to or had concerns with. Moreover, if co-optation is a concern, it is surely a bigger concern in the context of partisan Senate caucuses, where the co-optation is formally entrenched! The second problem with this argument is that it is not the role of the Senate to hold the government to account. The upper house may serve as a check, and is empowered to apply legislative brakes when needed, but it is not the confidence chamber. It is the House of Commons that holds the government to account. This is not to say the Senate cannot play a role in the broader accountability function of ensuring transparency, responsiveness, and effectiveness on the part of government through its legislative vetting and long-term research and advice capacities. Holding the government to account, however, is the function of the House.

It is certainly true that the real test of the non-partisan behaviour of the Trudeau-appointed independents is a long-term one. It is not clear whether their voting behaviour reflects ideological support of the current government or a non-partisan approach that generally respects the government's capacity to pass its legislative agenda. As noted above, senators appointed under the new process are expected to have a clear understanding of the role of the Senate as a chamber of sober second thought. In other words, there is a presumption that independent senators in particular will have a normative conception of their role, and that of the institution, that guides their behaviour. In political science, the study of role norms finds that they can be influential in shaping and constraining the behaviour of various actors, including independent and unelected ones, like justices of the Supreme Court of Canada.[77] Further, such actors are sensitive to the expectations and opinions held about them by other actors and the general public.[78]

Despite this, there is a legitimate concern that the type of senator appointed under the new system, in ideological terms, fits a broadly construed centre-left ideological portion of the political spectrum. In speaking with various senators about the Senate's activity (interviewed on the record for this analysis as well as in informal conversations), there is a real concern among some that certain members of the ISG would find Conservative attempts to roll back certain legislative initiatives unpalatable. If this is true, and the Senate were to adopt a more hostile posture to the legislative agenda of a government of a different political stripe, the upper house would be seriously undermining its own legitimacy and position. Independent senators should care about the reputation and legitimacy of the Senate; if they do, they will not risk it by inappropriately exceeding the limits of the Senate's proper function.

Whatever attitudinal trajectory senators adopt in the future, the record thus far suggests that the Senate has adjusted, albeit with challenges, to its burgeoning independent status. A sizable contingent of non-partisan senators will occupy the upper house for years to come, even if a new government were to take power and revert back to the old system of appointments. Thus far, the Senate is operating largely within the parameters a merit-based, non-partisan appointments process would ideally produce.

CONCLUSION

The recent change to the appointments process, done informally and at the discretion of the prime minister, arguably constitutes the most significant alteration to the Senate in its history. Although it is not clear whether future prime ministers will retain the independent, non-partisan advisory process, the reform might also end up being one of the most important legacies of the Trudeau government. The longer the new process remains in place, the harder it will be for future prime ministers to revert to the old system of patronage.

A major reason for this is that, as the preceding analysis has shown, the renewed Senate is working. Despite inevitable challenges and adjustments, the upper house is fulfilling its advisory role as a chamber of sober second thought. It has not engaged in obstructionism. Nor has it created serious disruptions to the government's legislative agenda. Moreover, in important instances it is improving legislation.

The difficulties the renewed Senate has faced derive largely from added complexity and constraints on information flows that result from senatorial independence and the partial (thus far) elimination of partisan caucuses. A growing number of divergent views among independents has made the work of ministers and public servants – tasked with getting legislation through the upper house – considerably more demanding in certain contexts. This may be a feature, not a bug, of the changes to the Senate. A more independent Senate, a Senate that is more responsive and active, will inevitably create more work for the government and add to the complexity of the legislative process. As the preceding analysis suggests, ministers and public servants are learning to become more proactive in this regard. Moreover, given that the manner in which some senators have conceived of their independence has contributed to the uncertainty, be it from an increased willingness to propose amendments or an unwillingness to meet informally with Cabinet ministers for fear of impinging on independence, it is likely that as they become acculturated to the Senate's norms this too will evolve.

Nonetheless, there are also reasons to be cautious about drawing firm conclusions about the success of the renewed Senate. There is clear evidence that the Senate remains in a period of transition. As noted in the preceding section, the Senate has not yet adopted formal changes to its rules to accommodate non-partisan groups or to establish an adequate and equitable distribution of resources for them. Thus far, the government has maintained the position that it is for the Senate to decide for itself, but it may need to initiate action if a bill to amend the *Parliament of Canada Act* implicates spending.

Moreover, it is not clear what further adjustments might be prompted as independents continue to be appointed. What does a Senate virtually full of independents look like? How will it organize itself? Will it need to create a new set of caucuses, whether on regional grounds or some other division? Or will it simply adapt procedures to accommodate the new fluidity and dynamism that comes with non-partisan, independent senators? And if it does adjust procedurally to this new reality, will independent senators be emboldened to act in an increasingly activist or even obstructionist manner, as critics of the reforms have argued? It is perhaps too soon to tell.

Thus far, the evidence suggests that the renewed Senate has the potential to become a significant success story. No longer negatively viewed as a patronage institution, let alone a partisan one, a recently disgraced institution may witness an unprecedented level of legitimacy. If it manages to conduct itself as the complementary, rather than competitive, body the Supreme Court of Canada describes in its 2014 *Reference re Senate Reform* opinion, it may fulfill the ideals envisioned by its defenders. This includes serving a useful function of providing legislative and policy advice and acting as a safety guard for Parliament's legislative agenda. It might also continue much of the valuable work the historical Senate often carried out: long-term study and commissions on policy issues of concerns to Canadians that members of Parliament rarely have the time to engage in. Time will tell.

6

A Constitution in Stasis? Prospects and Problems
for Future Constitutional Change

*R*EFERENCE *RE SENATE REFORM* was an unprecedented opportunity for the Supreme Court of Canada to elaborate on the
dividing lines between the amending formula's various procedures. The purpose of the reference was also to provide clarity on
possible options for reform of the Senate. On both scores, the court's
opinion is problematic for two reasons. First, the justices minimize
Parliament's unilateral capacity to introduce even modest changes like
senatorial term limits, characterizing section 44 of the amending formula as a very narrow exception to the general amending procedure.
As I have argued, the court does this without sufficiently addressing
the logical inconsistency of its approach, one that frames the introduction of a retirement age as "housekeeping" but presumes that even
lengthy non-renewable terms would amount to a change to the Senate's
essential features. The court's approach clouds what feasible reforms
might possibly be made to the Senate that *do not* affect its core roles.

Second, the court's appeal to the basic structure or architecture of
the Constitution ultimately obscures rather than clarifies the dividing
line between the various amending procedures. This may have the effect
of chilling future attempts at constitutional change or, at the very least,
increasing contestation and future legal challenges to reform efforts.
The effect of this is to further empower the Supreme Court itself to

dictate future constitutional change. Greater clarity through more co-herent guidelines about the scope of the various amending procedures would have reduced this uncertainty. In that respect, *Reference re Senate Reform* was a failure.

Despite this overall criticism, a major reform to the Senate appoint-ments process was implemented in 2016. In this chapter, I examine why the new "merit-based, non-partisan" process was validly realized – not even by Parliament alone, but through the exercise of prime ministerial discretion – and stands as a constitutional example of reform. I also examine why, despite this successful instance of informal consti-tutional change, *Reference re Senate Reform* increases the prospects of Canadian constitutional stasis, even to the point of rendering other existing laws potentially invalid and possibly wreaking havoc on unwrit-ten parts of the Constitution, including constitutional conventions.

INFORMAL REFORM: WHY THE NEW SENATE APPOINTMENTS PROCESS IS CONSTITUTIONAL

The 2016 reform to the Senate appointments process establishes an advisory board that prepares a shortlist based on a set of merit-based criteria (described in Chapter 5). The final appointing power is reserved to the prime minister (formally through advice to the governor general). Yet in 2014, the court's decision in *Reference re Senate Reform* rejected consultative elections as a method of reform even though the proposed reform preserved the prime minister's final appointing power. How then is the process established in 2016 constitutional?

The Supreme Court's approach to assessing the amending formula left unclear the extent to which the prime minister might introduce new elements – even informal ones – into the process leading up to the final selection of senators if they might constrain his own discretion. The court emphasized that the amending formula's reference to "method of selecting Senators" applies to

the entire process by which Senators are "selected." The proposed con-sultative elections would produce lists of candidates, from which the prime ministers would be expected to choose when making appointments to the Senate. The compilation of these lists through national or provincial or territorial elections and the Prime Minister's consideration of them prior to making recommendations to the Governor General would form part of the "method of selecting Senators."[1]

Yet even if the method of selection as enumerated in the amending formula applies to the "entire process," surely prime ministerial discretion is not eliminated entirely. Prime ministers have variously consulted their Cabinet, political staffers, and party officials when making senatorial appointments. The court's opinion could not reasonably be interpreted to contemplate a change in the method of selection stemming from whether a prime minister asks political staff to draw up a list or instead gets names from Cabinet members.

Two key considerations may help draw a line between legitimate unilateral changes and those that require formal amendment with provincial consent. The first is the distinction between an effort to formally establish a process in law (and thereby attempt to bind future prime ministers to a particular process) versus informally constituting a committee or some new process of consultation before making an appointment. The 2016 reform is a product of the prime minister's discretion to make appointments. It is established informally, on an effective ad hoc basis, in contrast to the Harper government's proposal to entrench an electoral process in law (either via federal law or in cooperation with the provinces). The result is that any continuation of the new process depends on an affirmation and conscious choice of future prime ministers to adopt the same method of selection. By contrast, under the Harper government's proposed reform future prime ministers would have been forced to dismantle a formally established process or avoid the pressure of the "democratic mandate" conferred upon Senate nominees by an electoral process, something the court emphasized it felt was unlikely. The formal versus informal nature of the reform is thus one important factor.

This raises a fundamental question of whether these sorts of distinctions amount to constitutional hairsplitting. The notion that a prime minister can implement certain reforms but only if he or she does so informally speaks to the flexibility of our constitutional architecture, perhaps, or it may simply expose a fundamental logical inconsistency within the court's interpretation of the amending formula. By implication, the court's opinion raises the question of in what context such informal processes might nonetheless produce binding force, and therefore perhaps tip a particular process into unconstitutional territory, but a straightforward reading of the opinion does not provide us with an answer.

Despite this lack of clarity, a second key factor might be found in the court's appeal to the Senate's essential features. Recall that in addition to the binding nature of consultative elections, the court found that the democratic mandate inherent in an electoral process, even a consultative one, would change the fundamental nature of the Senate itself, transforming it from a complementary body into a competitive one. The new merit-based, non-partisan appointments process does not alter the Senate's basic functioning in this way. Indeed, if the analysis in the preceding chapter is correct, the 2016 changes only *enhance* the traditional role of the Senate as a chamber of sober second thought. As I have written elsewhere, "[i]n a strict sense, it is impossible to know what the Court would say on this point if the Trudeau government's reform is ever subject to a constitutional challenge. This is because the Court's reliance on the amorphous constitutional architecture concept clouds more than it clarifies the scope of the various amending procedures."[2]

Nonetheless, the fact that the 2016 reform does not alter the Senate's fundamental roles seems to be a significant factor. Coupled with the informality – the fact that the process does not propose to bind future prime ministers through a change in law – it seems difficult to argue that the reform stands as a formal change to the method of selection requiring provincial consent.

What objection might someone make to the new process on the basis of the court's rationale in *Reference re Senate Reform?* One plausible argument is that the new process effectively eliminates the partisan nature of the Senate, something that has been a reality since

Confederation, and thus counts as a change to its fundamental features. There is an easy response to this: partisanship is simply not considered one of the roles of the Senate, whether by the court in *Reference re Senate Reform* or among the framers, relevant actors, or scholars of the Senate (as explored in Chapter 1). In fact, the court noted in 2014 that the "framers sought to endow the Senate with independence from the electoral process to which members of the House of Commons were subject, *in order to remove Senators from a partisan political arena* that required unremitting consideration of short-term political objectives."[3] It would be incorrect to interpret this as the court *prescribing* the elimination of partisanship. The court's comments are clearly embedded in the context of the electoral proposal. But this understanding of the Senate's independence goes to the point that the 2016 reform strengthens rather than deviates from the Senate's role and purpose.

Another objection might be premised on the notion that the 2016 reform constitutes an illegitimate "amendment by stealth"[4] by seeking to effectively create a new, binding convention surrounding appointments. Richard Albert argues persuasively that the Harper government's proposal for consultative elections was an attempted constitutional amendment by stealth by virtue of transforming the process into one guided by conventional rule where prime ministers faithfully appoint the winners of elections. The problem, in Albert's view, is that the "regularity of the practice would cause politics to override law."[5] Importantly, this convention would effectively be imposed rather than emerging organically and with the support or consensus of the relevant actors, something generally viewed as required for the evolution of constitutional conventions.[6]

The question, then, is whether the Trudeau government's reforms similarly act as a constitutional amendment by stealth by raising the spectre of grudging compliance by future prime ministers. Contrary to the court's suspicion that prime ministers would feel compelled to adhere to the results of consultative elections, there is evidence that other actors do not feel particularly bound to the 2016 process. In the lead-up to the 2019 election, for example, Conservative leader Andrew Scheer repeated that he would return to the old patronage appointments process if he became prime minister.[7] This emphasizes why the discretionary and informal nature of the reform helps to solidify its constitutionality. It is little different than if prime ministers historically have relied on Cabinet, political staff, or pulling names out of a hat when selecting senators. Few, if anyone, would have asserted that the exercise of such discretion amounted to a change of the "method of selecting" senators.

There remains an open question of whether the reform will eventually evolve into a convention. The longer the Senate has to adjust to its new reality, and the longer a merit-based, non-partisan selection process is in place, the more difficult it may be for future prime ministers to return to the old patronage system. But this just returns us to the distinctions noted above. Unlike a formal legal process incorporating a "democratic mandate" like consultative elections, the informal process established in 2016 does not alter the Senate's role. Any consideration of whether to continue it will be based on broader political factors – particularly the legitimating effect the elimination of patronage has on the institution, and a resultant preference in public opinion in favour of the new system. Indeed, one recent poll found that 77 percent of Canadians preferred the new system, with only 3 percent expressing a desire to return to patronage appointments.[8] Rather than grudging compliance with an imposed convention, a decision by future prime ministers to retain the new system will evolve in the more traditional or organic way, and before it can be said to solidify into a convention, it will require broad consensus among relevant actors.

FUTURE REFORM OF THE SENATE

I have argued that *Reference re Senate Reform* makes it more difficult to know what future reforms of the Senate are possible to effect without provincial consent. Yet the preceding analysis suggests that it is possible to engage in informal changes to the Senate so long as they do not alter the institution's essential functioning or role. As noted in Chapter 2, Andrew Heard writes that there are significant strides the Senate itself can make, through changes to its rules, to ensure that it fulfills an in-creasingly useful role and also to constrain the use of its own formal powers.[9] Moreover, Parliament is free to enact changes to the *Parliament of Canada Act* to ensure the equitable distribution of resources and the smooth functioning of the renewed Senate as it moves away from the traditional government-versus-opposition partisan dynamic. Such changes would be consistent with the reform to the appointments process and the continued evolution of an independent chamber of sober second thought.

Nevertheless, not all changes that might enhance the sober second thought role of the Senate could be enacted by Parliament alone. Some might simply be too sweeping to effect under the informal discretionary ambit of the prime minister's appointing power. An interesting proposal to reconstitute the Senate as a randomly selected citizen assembly, for example, would almost certainly require provincial consent, as such a system of appointment would remove entirely any plausible discretion on the part of the prime minister in the selection process.[10]

Even proposals to entrench in law the appointments process estab-lished in 2016, articulated as recently as the summer of 2019 by the Government Representative in the Senate, Peter Harder, collide head-on with the constitutional objections described above.[11] An attempt to formalize the change via statute triggers the "method of selection" requirement for provincial consent as laid out in section 42(1)(b) of the *Constitution Act, 1982*.

What is pretty remarkable about *Reference re Senate Reform* is that the Supreme Court's opinion does not even make clear the permissibility of issues directly relevant to the questions asked of it. Recall the electoral processes established by Alberta for the Senate. A handful of the winners of those elections were subsequently appointed (one by Brian Mulroney in 1990, and four more by Stephen Harper from 2007 to 2013). The court's opinion makes no comment on the constitutionality of these appointments, and while its analysis of the consultative elections pro-posal clearly prevents Parliament from establishing an elections process by itself or in concert with the provinces, it is not clear that provinces are somehow prohibited from holding nominee elections of their own volition, or that prime ministers would be prohibited from appointing the winners of those as Mulroney and Harper did in the past.

Finally, and most fundamentally, *Reference re Senate Reform* makes it highly unlikely that critics of the Senate in its present, appointive form will ever be satisfied. Democratization of the Senate via elections, abolition of the upper house entirely, or even a fundamental shift to give provinces more direct input into senatorial selection are all off the table given the demands of the amending formula and a political culture that is, to put it mildly, antagonistic to the very thought of intergovernmental negotiations on major constitutional reform.

The dim prospects of achieving formal constitutional amendment have prompted patently unconstitutional proposals from opponents of the Senate. As noted in Chapter 2, the Co-operative Commonwealth Federation (CCF) and its successor party, the NDP, have advanced failed motions in Parliament to simply starve the Senate of its funding. This occurred as recently as 2011 under the leadership of Thomas Mulcair.[12] But of course starving the Senate of its funding is not a legitimate or workable path to abolition, the NDP's preferred position. The outcome of such a tactic, even if not challenged on constitutional grounds, would simply be to stop the functioning of Parliament and its ability to pass any legislation.

Another proposed tactic is to refuse to make appointments to the Senate at all. The idea of letting the Senate die by "atrophy" attracted bipartisan support in the aftermath of the Senate expenses scandal, and was adopted by Prime Minister Harper, promised by Mulcair in the event he became prime minister, and endorsed by Brad Wall, then-premier of Saskatchewan. Historically, there have been serious delays in filling certain Senate seats in certain contexts, particularly as prime ministers seek to take advantage of exercising the patronage function the appointing power has traditionally offered them. But a policy of non-appointment is distinct from isolated and haphazard delays. The Harper policy of non-appointment was even challenged in litigation by Vancouver lawyer Aniz Alani, but the case was dismissed as moot following the decision by Trudeau to implement the new appointments process.[13] Alani's case rested in part on section 32 of the *Constitution Act, 1867,* which states that "[w]hen a Vacancy happens in the Senate by Resignation, Death, or otherwise, the Governor General shall by Summons to a fit and qualified Person fill the Vacancy." The "shall" language specifically lends credence to the view that non-appointment is not a valid option.

Despite this relative textual clarity, the legal challenge likely faced an uphill battle. First, courts may have been timid about making a finding of unconstitutionality simply for the reason that the only practicable remedy – an order that a prime minister provide the necessary advice to the governor general to make an appointment – would have been relatively unprecedented, and therefore potentially politically explosive. Second, and more germane to the law itself, is that section 32 puts the onus on the governor general, not the prime minister. The prime minister's role in appointments, as Léonid Sirota points out, is conventional rather than explicitly set out in the constitutional text.[14] Although the Supreme Court has taken it upon itself to comment on matters of convention – most notably in the 1981 *Patriation Reference*[15] – and conventions are obviously implicated in considerations about the constitutional architecture as reflected in *Reference re Senate Reform,* it has thus far not attempted to enforce them. It is possible to regard the constitutional requirement here as informed, rather than constituted, by the conventional role of the prime minister. In other words, by articulating a formal policy of non-appointment, the prime minister makes it impossible for the governor general to fulfill her legal requirement to make appointments, and thus the policy is unconstitutional for that reason alone.

Regardless of this complexity, *Reference re Senate Reform* offers us a distinct reason that a policy of non-appointment is likely unconstitutional: if kept in place for a sufficient period of time, it would damage, if not completely impair, the Senate's ability to function. Indeed, in 2014 the Senate speaker, the late Pierre Claude Nolin, spoke out about the impact of Harper's refusal to make appointments and its deleterious effects on the Senate's functioning, especially its capacity to properly represent the various regions.[16] At that time there were sixteen vacancies.

As an intentional change to the Senate's core functioning, a formal policy of non-appointment is unconstitutional by virtue of the court's reference opinion logic. Moreover, even if the constitutional validity of such a policy were upheld by the courts, the effect would be to injure Parliament's capacity to pass legislation, not, as its proponents seem to suggest, to forge an indirect path to abolishing the upper house.

BROADER CONSTITUTIONAL REFORM

I have argued that the Supreme Court's appeal to constitutional architecture, together with its general antipathy towards indirect methods of amending the Constitution, threatens to exacerbate Canada's constitutional stasis. A central implication of *Reference re Senate Reform* is that it may inhibit even informal changes to the Constitution. Dennis Baker and Mark Jarvis write that, in contrast to formal constitutional amendments, informal methods of constitutional change include judicial amendments through interpretation, the evolution of constitutional conventions, and, "perhaps most controversially, constitutional change through ordinary statutory enactment."[17] Not all such attempts at constitutional change are necessarily illegitimate, and the examples Baker and Jarvis cite include the *Clarity Act,* setting out the role of the House of Commons in determining whether a future referendum question was sufficiently clear and whether the results were sufficient to initiate negotiations around secession; fixed-date elections legislation; and the federal regional veto law, which effectively grants the various regions of the country a veto over any major constitutional amendments.

Yet under the court's logic, such legislative initiatives might not be possible, especially if they stand as changes to the constitutional architecture. Baker and Jarvis rightly point out that as a result of *Reference re Senate Reform,* "the meta-rule seems to be whether the Court deems a change to be mere 'housekeeping' or a 'fundamental' change. Here 'context' is likely to collapse into whether a change is desirable or not: a change that is consistent with one's understanding of the underlying principles is more likely to be 'housekeeping' and a change – no matter how minor – that runs contrary to that understanding is likely to be seen as part of a 'fundamental' shift."[18]

Consistent with this interpretation of the implications of *Reference re Senate Reform,* Warren Newman writes about the use of "organic legislation" that "enhances, rather transforms ... central institutions or that otherwise implements and advances structural constitutional principles."[19] In his view, even after *Reference re Senate Reform,* such enhancements to the Constitution are possible to effect via statute by virtue of the fact they do not alter the constitutional architecture. Examples he cites include not only statutes such as the *Multiculturalism Act* and the *Official Languages Act* but also the regional veto law.

Yet the court's rationale might have implications for the constitutionality of statutes like the regional veto act. Following the 1995 Quebec secession referendum, the federal government enacted *An Act Respecting Constitutional Amendments* to effectively provide Quebec (and, by design, Canada's other regions) with a veto over most major amendments. The act prohibits government ministers from proposing constitutional resolutions unless consent is first obtained from Ontario, Quebec, British Columbia, at least two Atlantic provinces representing at least 50 percent of the Atlantic populations, and at least two Prairie provinces representing at least 50 percent of the Prairie population (in effect, giving Alberta its own veto). The act effectively uses the federal government's inherent veto under most of the amending procedures to establish a system of regional vetoes for constitutional amendment.[20] The act was passed to fulfill the government's commitment to Quebec federalists but, by giving Ontario, British Columbia, and (in effect) Alberta a veto, it makes future constitutional reform – including reform desired by Quebec federalists – considerably more difficult.[21]

It is worth noting that the constitutionality of the regional veto law was heavily debated from the outset.[22] Importantly, the Supreme Court's general rationale regarding the ability of Parliament to implement changes to the Constitution without the consent of the provinces would seem to apply to the regional veto law, which in practice acts as a unilateral amendment to the amending formula itself. From the perspective of the basic architecture of the Constitution, the law compels the federal government to restrict the legitimate exercise of the amending formula without the consent of provinces. Moreover, it goes beyond a political decision by an individual government about whether to support a resolution because it binds future governments in law. If Parliament is not free to implement changes to the method of selecting senators or to impose term limits without provincial consent, it would be inconsistent with the court's approach to interpreting the amending formula to permit such disregard for the basic constitutional architecture, which includes the foundational agreement about the structure of the amending formula itself.

Similarly, the federal *Fixed Date Election Act* was explicitly premised on the idea that it did not formally constrain or alter the governor general's power to dissolve Parliament. Indeed, any such change would clearly require the unanimous consent of the provinces under the amending formula.[23] Yet as an indirect constraint on formal practice it seems to parallel the notion of whether consultative elections for the Senate actually fettered the prime minister's discretion over appointments. In fact, when Prime Minister Harper did not adhere to the law and asked the governor general for dissolution and an election in 2008, his decision to do so was challenged in court by Duff Conacher, the head of Democracy Watch. This particular challenge was, in my view, doomed to fail. The law explicitly preserved the governor general's discretion and powers to accept advice on dissolution. Harper did not so much exercise a hidden loophole as simply walk through the open door provided by the law. Recognizing this, Conacher's challenge asserted that the law sought to create a binding convention preventing prime ministers from calling snap elections, which Harper failed to follow.[24]

The challenge sought to have the Federal Court not only recognize this alleged new convention but also *enforce* it, and thus can only be characterized as a long shot, if not an outright misunderstanding of the proper role of the judiciary as it relates to conventions. As Baker and Jarvis write, "ironically, the federal government's nonadherence to the Fixed Date Election Act actually might be its best constitutional defence!"[25] By demonstrating that neither the prime minister nor the governor general is bound to adhere to fixed election dates, the circumstances of 2008 prove that the law does not formally alter the powers of the Crown.

From a broader perspective, the court's approach to interpreting the amending formula might also be evaluated on the basis of the balance between flexibility and rigidity that animates the constitutional design. If the Constitution represents the fundamental rules and structure for the country's governing system, then the amending formula determines who gets to write those rules. A good formula provides enough flexibility for change to occur when it is needed or where there is sufficiently deep and broad consensus, but ensures enough rigidity so that fundamental changes can be accomplished only where consensus warrants. Debate during constitutional negotiations over the design of the formula recognized this tension.[26] The 1982 agreement resulted in a complex set of procedures designed to accommodate the need for consensus over fundamental change while ensuring the flexibility to prevent constitutional stasis.

Judicial interpretation of these various procedures that expands the application of some over others risks imbalance, the result of which is to either lower the threshold for constitutional change to the point of disregarding the need for consensus or raising it so high as to invite constitutional stasis. *Reference re Senate Reform* arguably contributes to an imbalance in the direction of stasis. In Baker and Jarvis's view, the "uncertainty introduced by the Court is likely to 'chill' future debates on institutional reform in Canada."[27] Examining the court's privileging of federalism as the core of the amending formula, Carissima Mathen writes that the court's approach "runs the risk of reifying the federal principle at the expense of other values."[28]

Others are less concerned. Dwight Newman, for example, thinks there remains some flexibility in the amending formula, pointing to the bilateral amending procedure as something that may hold great promise because it can effect changes on matters relating to only one or more, but not all, provinces.[29] Still, even those observers who are not particularly critical of the court's approach to the amending formula acknowledge that a major impact of the opinion is the increased likelihood that "future attempts at formal constitutional amendment will be steered by the courts, whether directly or indirectly."[30] This simple fact itself may contribute to the chilling effect Baker and Jarvis warn us about.

Even changes to regular election law might be implicated by *Reference re Senate Reform.* According to Michael Pal, the court's opinion clouds the issue of whether federal electoral reform is feasible without provincial consent.[31] Elsewhere I have argued that Parliament should generally be free to implement most mainstream electoral systems in Canada under the unilateral amending procedure of section 44 of the *Constitution Act, 1982.*[32] Nonetheless, Pal raises an important point. If Parliament's ability to implement changes under section 44 is limited to mere "housekeeping" matters, then electoral reform might constitute a fundamental change to the Constitution's architecture, thus necessitating provincial consent.

The threat of constitutional stasis represented by *Reference re Senate Reform*'s logic is compounded by what might be considered its sister reference, *Reference re Supreme Court Act.*[33] That reference, released mere weeks before *Reference re Senate Reform,* concerned the validity of the appointment of Marc Nadon, a supernumerary judge of the Federal Court of Appeal, to the Supreme Court. The statutory issue involved whether the specific eligibility requirements under sections 5 and 6 of the *Supreme Court Act* prevented the appointment of a Federal Court judge to one of the three "Quebec seats." The constitutional issue, and the one relevant for this discussion, involved whether Parliament was free to unilaterally amend the eligibility requirements to clarify or change them. On that issue, a majority of the Supreme Court of Canada determined that the eligibility requirements were part of the "composition" of the court and thus changes to them required the unanimous consent of the provinces under section 41(d) of the amending formula. The majority found that the references to the Supreme Court in the amending formula effectively entrenched its essential features in the Constitution (more controversially, part of the court's analysis implies that this entrenchment, and the court as "a key matter of interest to both Parliament and the provinces,"[34] happened as early as 1949, when it became the final court of appeal with the abolition of appeals to the Judicial Committee of the Privy Council in London).

Prior to the court's reference opinion, adding additional eligibility requirements under the *Supreme Court Act,* such as mandating bilingualism for Supreme Court appointees – a policy supported by the Liberal Party and New Democratic Party – was not thought by many to have required constitutional amendment. The decision now renders any such formal changes extremely unlikely, and indeed, may constitute an unintended consequence of the court's logic. There has never been an amendment successfully ratified under the Constitution's unanimity procedure and the current political climate is such that this is unlikely to change.[35]

Hugo Cyr argues that it would be "absurd to deny Parliament the capacity to require a working knowledge of the language in which the judge will be called to adjudicate"[36] – and indeed, it is an absurdity, but it is an absurdity that flows directly from the Supreme Court's decision. Cyr's general argument about functional bilingualism constituting a bona fide work requirement can be subject to debate, but it is not something that has ever been required in law, and in fact there are many examples of judges appointed to the top court lacking that ability. Adding such a requirement to the *Supreme Court Act* is clearly a substantive addition requiring provincial consent, and an addition cannot be meaningfully distinguished from a subtraction or alteration of existing requirements. As Paul Daly writes, adding to the eligibility requirements "interferes much more with constitutional form than does streamlining the process for Senate appointments."[37] Kate Glover Berger argues that the effects of a mandatory bilingualism requirement "would be transformative to the composition of the Court" – not just because it stands as an addition to the eligibility requirements but because it would have a "substantive effect on the conception of the composition of the Court" by introducing "a new marker of identity that all judges of the Court must possess."[38]

Reference re Supreme Court Act thus raises the prospect that any number of ordinary statutes might someday be elevated to entrenched constitutional status by judicial fiat. In some ways, this may seem like a contradictory problem in relation to the one presented by *Reference re Senate Reform,* where statutory or informal changes to the Constitution might be deemed unconstitutional. Whether the issue becomes entrenchment or unconstitutionality, the fundamental problem amounts to two sides of the same coin: a considerable increase in constitutional rigidity, under a Constitution that is already described as possibly the most difficult to amend in the world.[39]

CONSTITUTIONAL CONVENTIONS: PART OF THE CONSTITUTIONAL ARCHITECTURE?

The Supreme Court's articulation of the constitutional architecture concept also raises questions of when informal changes impact, or are viewed as an attempt to create, constitutional conventions. Recall that the court stated that the underlying architecture of the government extends beyond the discrete textual provisions of the Constitution to include the structure of government and the assumptions underlying the text. This would seem to implicate not only unwritten constitutional principles that the court has elaborated upon in other references[40] but also constitutional conventions that animate how the governing structure operates in practice.

As noted, the proposed consultative elections for the Senate arguably sought what Albert describes as constitutional amendment by stealth precisely because they (illegitimately, in his view) would impose a new binding convention to override existing law. Similarly, the fixed-date election law was perceived by some (incorrectly, in my view) as establishing a new convention governing the prime minister's advice to the governor general on dissolution. Whether the implementation of informal constitutional change through the creation of a new convention is possible thus depends on the specifics of the proposed change, perhaps, but at a more fundamental level is further complicated by an existing debate over how conventions form or solidify. For example, the famous "Jennings test" for the existence of conventions, laid out by Sir Ivor Jennings, demands the existence of at least one precedent, consensus among the relevant actors that they are bound by a rule, and a reason for the rule.[41] Yet other commentators, including Andrew Heard, do not believe a precedent is necessary so long as there is express agreement among the relevant political actors.[42]

Others have correctly pointed out that neither approach to identifying conventions is free of challenges. Peter Aucoin, Mark Jarvis, and Lori Turnbull note that despite the Jennings test, there are examples of widely regarded conventions that include no existing precedents, such as the notion that upon losing confidence of the House a prime minister has the option of simply resigning and allowing the Opposition an opportunity to govern. In practice, prime ministers have always requested dissolution and an election instead. By contrast, the notion of express agreement among the relevant actors is less than ideal because it can be extremely difficult to identify the relevant actors (for example, are they limited to those in government, or do they include opposition leaders?).[43] As Philippe Lagassé points out, further complicating this aspect of the debate about convention formation is the fact that conventions "are too often conflated with other types of rules, notably practices, customs, and norms."[44]

Lagassé's typology is useful for characterizing the 2016 reform to the Senate appointments process. He describes practices as rules that may become conventions but are not quite there yet, either because the relevant actors do not agree they are bound by the rule or there are inconsistent precedents. Like conventions, there are reasons for the rules, and as a result certain practices can solidify into conventions over time. Customs are rules that are adhered to but they are either antiquated conventions whose reasons no longer apply or "simply reflect the established ways of doing things" with no connection to a rule that rose to the level of convention. The key distinction here is that reasons for the custom are either no longer relevant or never existed. Finally, norms are effectively rules of fairness or ethics, and so are not just about the letter of the Constitution but also about its spirit. Unlike conventions, norms are often contested and the precedents attached to them are not always clear.[45] As this typology relates to the new Senate appointments process, I have already argued that it is not (at least not yet) a convention, as there is clear evidence that not all relevant actors – in this case, the extant opposition leaders who would be most likely to replace Trudeau as prime minister – feel bound to adhere to the new process. Yet there is a clear reason for merit-based, non-partisan selection, and so the process established in 2016 is best characterized as a new practice, one that may or may not mature into convention.

As it relates to attempts to bring about informal constitutional change, the added complexity around convention formation will include a consideration not only of whether rule-based changes in political practices, customs, or norms stand as an attempt to create a convention but also of whether the change is one that amounts to a change in the Constitution's architecture or the essential features of the relevant institution. As the examples above demonstrate, this is rarely going to be a clear-cut analysis.

Informal reforms can also implicate constitutional conventions in other, perhaps unintended ways. The outcome of the 2019 federal election, resulting in a Liberal minority government, saw the governing party unable to capture a single seat in Alberta or Saskatchewan. This left the government in a quandary regarding Cabinet representation, where representation in the Cabinet from each region, or even from each province, is widely regarded as an important convention (this convention has almost always been adhered to with the occasional exception of Prince Edward Island).[46] Historically, such a problem would normally be resolved by appointing either a senator or two from the affected provinces to Cabinet or by appointing a non-parliamentarian with the expectation that they would seek a by-election (reflecting another important convention that Cabinet members in Canada be sitting parliamentarians).

Yet the prime minister was faced with a political problem: Senator Yuen Pau Woo, the facilitator of the Independent Senators Group, argued that appointing a senator to Cabinet in the post-2016 context would run counter to the idea of senatorial independence. He stated that doing so "would be a departure from what the prime minister has said was his plan for the Senate, i.e., that senators are independent, that they do not represent the government, [that] they are not part of the government."[47] It is doubtful the appointment of one or two independent senators would affect the independence of the renewed Senate. Nonetheless, the government appeared to take the caution seriously, and it refrained from making any appointment. As a result, the Cabinet sworn in on 20 November 2019 broke with convention and lacked any representation from Alberta or Saskatchewan.

The Supreme Court's constitutional architecture logic, if pushed to its natural end, might also mean that abandoning certain conventions may be interpreted as an unconstitutional attempt at constitutional change. For example, regional representation on the Supreme Court is guaranteed in part by convention. Aside from the statutory guarantee (now entrenched in the Constitution due to *Reference re Supreme Court Act*) of three members from Quebec, appointments to the top court are appointed by convention on a regional basis, with three from Ontario, two from the western provinces, and one from the Atlantic region. It is not clear that a prime minister can depart from this convention if conventions are indeed part of the constitutional architecture, or if the "composition of the Court" as outlined in section 41(d) of the *Constitution Act, 1982* includes regional considerations.

The implications of *Reference re Senate Reform* as it relates to the legal status of conventions is also unclear, and interpretations of what the constitutional architecture concept means for conventions diverge wildly. Christa Scholtz, for example, argues that the court's logic dramatically reduces the role of conventions, even casting them as "saboteurs of a unified constitutional design."[48] By contrast, Sirota suggests the court's decision actually "has the effect – perhaps the deliberate effect – of entrenching at least some, although possibly not all, of the conventions of the Canadian constitution," effectively erasing a core distinction between conventions and judicially enforceable law.[49] These are radically different, if not diametrically opposed, understandings of the impact the Supreme Court's reasoning may have on constitutional conventions, their legal status, and their future evolution. And there is a third possibility: it may simply not have occurred to the justices that their logic had any relevance for political conventions at all. None of these options is particularly desirable. The court has likely set itself up to confront a quandary of its own making at some future date. One must hope that it will abandon or dramatically prune the application of the architecture concept when it does.

CONCLUSION

Reference re Senate Reform set the stage for the most significant reform to Parliament's upper chamber in Canadian history. Yet this was far from an inevitable development, especially when considering the confusion and complexity the Supreme Court's reference opinion introduces for future constitutional change in Canada. The reform to the Senate's appointments process is constitutional for two reasons: first, it is a product of the prime minister's discretion, not a formal change in law that would bind future prime ministers; and second, it is a change to the culture of appointments that is consistent with, rather than a change to, the Senate's primary roles.

Yet not all constitutional changes, however minor, are possible to effect in this manner. *Reference re Senate Reform* makes it difficult to know what potential changes – particularly those that might have been thought possible to effect by Parliament alone – might now stand as constitutionally dubious. From electoral reform to changes to constitutional convention, anything that might be implicated as important to the constitutional "architecture" is now possibly frozen in the nebulous amber of the court's interpretation of the amending formula. Further to this, important laws, from the regional veto law to the *Clarity Act,* should perhaps now be considered constitutionally suspect. When it comes to the future prospects of constitutional change, the legacy of *Reference re Senate Reform* is that it raises more questions than it clarifies.

CONCLUSION

The Future of the Senate, Parliament, and Constitutional Reform

*R*EFERENCE RE SENATE REFORM ultimately played a key role in the most significant reform of the Senate, perhaps of Parliament itself, in Canadian history. It is no small irony that the decision also ensures, in the short term at least, that the reform may prove fragile, even easily overturned (although many of those appointed under the new system will be in the Senate for decades). The implications also continue to play out as the renewed Senate adjusts to the reality of its non-partisan membership. We do not know what the Senate might look like in as little as five or ten years. Yet that uncertainty is a feature connected to the other primary impact of *Reference re Senate Reform:* a profound lack of clarity over the permissibility and possibility of future constitutional change, not merely in relation to Parliament itself but also across the entire gamut of structures, rules, and processes that embody the Constitution.

The story of *Reference re Senate Reform* as it relates to the Senate is one about the roles the upper house is meant to fulfill, and whether changes to the appointments process designed to eliminate aspects that are not necessarily integral to that role – such as patronage and partisanship – have altered the institution's functioning in a way not contemplated by the Supreme Court of Canada. The court wielded its power as one of the pre-eminent veto players in Canada's governance structure when it ruled that Parliament alone could not implement consultative elections or term limits for senators. Its decision did not open a door for future reform so much as force creative solutions to addressing the status quo. Indeed, it foreclosed major reform to such an extent that the leaders of two of the three largest national political parties proposed the (unconstitutional) policy of not making appointments to the Senate at all, rather than try to accomplish constructive reform. The Liberals, meanwhile, decided that the next best alternative to major changes like electoral reform or abolition was to improve the appointments process. It is quite possible that doing so resulted in bigger changes than they expected.

The story of *Reference re Senate Reform* as it relates to constitutional change is about the dividing lines between the amending formula's various procedures. The Supreme Court's reasoning clouds, rather than clarifies, when Parliament can effect changes to itself or to a wide variety of institutions and rules that might implicate written or unwritten components of the Constitution. In a country with a rigorous written amending formula and a political culture around intergovernmental negotiations that makes discussions of major constitutional reform almost impossible (what Richard Albert describes as "constructive unamendability"[1]), the court has arguably managed to make the prospects of constitutional stasis even worse. It has added a jurisprudential hurdle based on the amorphous concept of the constitutional architecture, a concept premised on the Supreme Court itself correctly identifying the fundamental features of the various institutions and processes in the Constitution. The approach is based on a presumption that the court will get this analysis right – a dubious proposition given its relatively simplistic depiction of the role of the Senate. It also invites the judges to rely on their normative preconceptions, as they do regularly in constitutional law,[2] by raising the likelihood that more and more initiatives to enact institutional change will be brought to court for adjudication. This increases the risk that relatively minor changes get recast into foundational ones as the basic test is transformed into a question of whether a given change is desirable.

The reform to the Senate has resulted in media attention typically focusing on the rise in amendment activity and its internal organizational debates. Yet the reform also raises fundamental institutional questions that hark back to the various roles of the Senate explored in Chapter 1, and the very meaning of senatorial independence. An examination of the critiques of the reform, with the objective of elucidating the Senate's proper role, is warranted. I will then revisit the issue of constitutional change in Canada. The successful reform of the Senate may present an exemplar for governments pursuing reform initiatives in other areas, but this carries with it potential risks. I will briefly conclude with thoughts on such future prospects.

THE SENATE, SENATORIAL INDEPENDENCE, AND CRITICS NEW AND OLD

In the 42nd Parliament, the difficulties the Senate faced in procedural terms as it adjusted to the lack of a government caucus caused much confusion and consternation. Lines of communication between the government and senators grew complicated in the absence of a joint caucus. With regard to some government bills, the work of public servants expanded as they held an increasing number of briefings with dispersed groups of (or even individual) senators. The new senators were also adjusting to their role.

Even as these behind-the-scenes difficulties emerged, the increase in the Senate's amendment activity in relation to government legislation drew most of the media attention. Critics connected the increase directly to the new appointments process, decrying the upper house's new activism and even suggesting that the legislative activity constituted a crisis in the making.[3] Yet to some extent the activity of the Conservative opposition, responsible for many amendments, was overlooked. The vestiges of partisanship in the Senate contributed, in the case of many of the bills affected, to the perception of chaos and the delays towards the end of the 42nd Parliament. Such delays are hardly unprecedented. More importantly, the Senate was not, in fact, obstructionist. Whatever difficulties arose in the context of certain bills, the government's overall legislative agenda proceeded largely unimpeded, and the House and the government accepted many of the Senate's amendments, arguably resulting in improved legislation.

In this conclusion my task is not to rehash this particular argument but to examine more broadly how this new senatorial independence is properly conceived. One issue is the perception that many, if not all, of the senators appointed under the new process are Liberals in all but name. This criticism stems from the fact that members of the Independent Senators Group (ISG) were more likely than all other Senate caucuses or groups to vote in favour of government legislation. It is difficult to attribute this to any partisan affinity on the part of the independent senators, however. The voting patterns may simply reflect a fidelity among the independents to the upper house as a complementary rather than competitive body. In short, the new senators may have a conception of their role that while they may propose amendments it is not their role to block legislation emanating from the elected chamber. The real test of this will be when there is a change in government, and whether the independent senators adhere to this understanding of their role when a different party's legislative agenda is at stake.

A more fundamental criticism of the new senatorial independence arises in contexts where certain behaviours on the part of senators are viewed as somehow impairing their independence, or even as hypocritical in light of the government's reform objectives. Much of this is misapplied and some of it even comes from the senators themselves. For example, the unwillingness of certain members of the ISG in the last Parliament to meet with Cabinet ministers about specific bills for fear that being "lobbied" by them would impair their independence misconstrues the nature of individual independence. Hearing out substantive arguments from the very people setting the legislative agenda does not impair one's ability to decide. Indeed, the appointments process itself and the protections of tenure until retirement ensure that a Cabinet minister has no real power to apply inappropriate pressure to impair a senator's independence. Independence at this level cannot possibly mean that senators be immunized from argument or attempts at moral suasion! This is equally true of the absurd argument that senators who agree to sponsor a bill are somehow co-opted by doing so.[4]

Another context where these fears have arisen is in relation to Cabinet formation. The results of the 2019 federal election, leaving the governing Liberals without a seat in Alberta or Saskatchewan, would normally be settled by having representation for those provinces come from the Senate. Yet immediate criticism came from ISG facilitator Senator Yuen Pau Woo that appointing independent senators to Cabinet would impair their independence and run contrary to the government's objectives when it implemented Senate reform.[5] Undoubtedly an individual senator appointed to Cabinet is no longer independent from the government of the day. A senator subject to Cabinet solidarity would be expected to vote in lockstep with the government. But we should be cautious about embedding certain assumptions in the analysis of how the nature of independence is affected in this context.

First, it is important to remember that the individual independence of each senator is distinct from the independence of the upper house as an institution within Parliament. The appointment of one or two senators to Cabinet – a long-standing practice – cannot impair the independence of the entire body. Second, the merit-based, non-partisan appointments process is designed to eliminate patronage and partisanship as explicit considerations for senatorial selection. The process does not stem from a prohibition on partisanship altogether. Moreover, non-partisanship at the individual level is distinct from independence from the government. There is nothing in the parliamentary tradition that requires a Cabinet to be composed solely of the members of a single party, even though this has been the normal practice in Canada. Thus, while an independent senator appointed to Cabinet becomes, in practice, a member of the government, that individual does not necessarily become a partisan. Upon leaving the Cabinet and resuming life as an "ordinary" senator, there is no reason to view the individual's independence as permanently tainted, either in the partisan sense or in the sense that the senator remains loyal to the government of the day.

Instead, it may be more appropriate to view a senator's appointment to Cabinet as an exception to a general practice of individual independence, much like the role of the Government Representative in the Senate. It is an overstatement to suggest, as Woo does, that such an appointment would undermine the objectives of senatorial independence *generally*.

Other criticisms about the nature of independence in the renewed Senate are based on what are essentially false premises. Senator Serge Joyal writes in a deeply critical fashion about the new appointments process, arguing that it came with unintended consequences, including undermining of "the very relevance of political parties in our democratic system by eliminating the effort at compromise upon which they are necessarily built."[6] He adds that the independent senators now face the threat of meeting Cabinet ministers behind the scenes, worrying that "this type of exchange is not conducted on equal footing. An 'independent' senator is more vulnerable to individual pressure, whereas a group discussion has the merit or benefit of opening up debate and cushioning the unequal nature of the relationship."[7]

Yet it is not clear why the lack of partisan caucuses inhibits compromise or why individuals in a deliberative body like the Senate would be less capable of engaging in that sort of debate. Indeed, the Senate process at the end of the 42nd Parliament ensured the passage of virtually all of the government bills that had passed the House – evidence of the very compromise that Joyal worries a non-partisan body might lack. Moreover, Joyal provides no evidence for his assertion that individual senators are somehow vulnerable to pressure from Cabinet ministers. As noted above, there are no institutional or procedural reasons why someone with functional life tenure would be susceptible to undue influence.

Joyal's critique also gets a number of facts wrong. He claims that under the new appointments process "future senators would be required to pledge that they have no particular political affiliation."[8] This is not true. He also states that the "selection criteria screened out all individuals who had previous parliamentary experience or who had recently worked for a political party."[9] This is only partially true, to the extent that it was an outcome of the existing advisory board's deliberations. As a matter of the formal requirements, the selection criteria as they relate to non-partisanship merely require that individuals "demonstrate to the Advisory Board that they have the ability to bring a perspective and contribution to the work of the Senate that is independent and non-partisan." Although there is a disclosure requirement for past political service, the criteria explicitly state that "past political activities would not disqualify an applicant."[10]

Joyal's perspective on independence is, to be blunt, confusing. He asks, "is anyone absolutely independent who presses no allegiance to a line of thinking identified with a given political party?" He answers this question by noting that "[i]ndependent senators cannot claim to be as independent or objective as judges, who must be wholly impartial when conducting hearings or making decisions. Senators have a more qualified independence. A senator who does not have a stated allegiance to a political party is presumed to adopt a position *de novo* on each new issue as it arises."[11] This is a disingenuous analogy wrapped in a straw man. Notwithstanding the fact that judges do carry with them the baggage of ideology and policy preferences, and that these do have influence on their decisions, at least in constitutional law,[12] no one has argued that senators selected under the non-partisan process come to the upper house without political views. In fact, they are often selected on the basis of having expertise or having engaged in public service, things that often carry a normative perspective on a variety of policy issues.

Independence is not synonymous with objectivity or impartiality in the political sense, and it would be naive to expect the latter even if the Senate is meant to be the body of sober second thought. Joyal asks whether a former activist engaged in Indigenous or women's issues is "more or less independent in this regard" than one with a partisan affiliation, and in doing so he unwittingly reveals a key distinction about the nature of independence as he understands it and how it ought to be understood in this context. Independence is *not* about an apolitical impartiality on political issues; rather, it is about functional independence *from the government of the day.* The removal of patronage, the rejection of Senate appointments as reward for partisan service, is the central factor that improves senatorial independence. Evidence that senators appointed under the new process still have political views or even identity-based or representational commitments such as advocacy for Indigenous rights is quite irrelevant to that, and there may be distinct reasons to desire a Senate composed of a diversity of such commitments but not partisan ones.

None of this is to deny that one key problem with the new appointments process is that it has arguably produced an ideologically homogeneous group. Most of the senators appointed since 2016 appear to be people who could comfortably sit on the centre-left part of the political spectrum. If there is a lack of ideological diversity – whether it results from a self-selection bias among those applying to the process, the advisory board's shortlisting process, or the prime minister's final selection – it is a legitimate object of concern. And it raises the prospect that the Senate might become obstructionist in the face of a more conservative government, something that will threaten its legitimacy if it begins defeating or unduly delaying legislation on ideological grounds. This might be resolved by abandoning the self-application process and requiring the advisory board to *seek out* qualified senators as it did in the initial transitional phase of the reform. Yet this concern is distinct from the ones often articulated by the renewed Senate's critics – ones that often mischaracterize the nature of institutional and individual senatorial independence in order to leverage an accusation of hypocrisy or decry the break from the past.

If the new Senate critics are sometimes basing their concerns on a disregard for the facts or misconstrual of what independence means, the old Senate critics remain alarmed at the fact that the 2016 reform does little to improve the Senate's legitimacy from a purely democratic perspective. To the extent the reform improves the Senate's legitimacy in other ways, the fact that it remains an appointed body is all the more alarming to these critics: armed with its enhanced legitimacy it threatens to become an even more powerful and important unelected body. There is only one response to this (valid) complaint, and that is to say that if an unelected institution with the formal powers it enjoys by virtue of the Constitution is to remain in place – and *Reference re Senate Reform* almost guarantees it – better that it be filled with those from a variety of backgrounds who make good faith efforts to operate as a complementary body of advice, a useful institution, and, hopefully, one that avoids the occasional partisan flare-ups Parliament has witnessed in the past.

Looking back at the primary roles of the Senate examined in Chapter 1, there is also good reason to see the renewed Senate as more capable of fulfilling them. As it relates to the Senate as a body of sober second thought, the increased amendment activity in the upper house in the 42nd Parliament is best seen as a feature, not a bug, of the 2016 reform. The Senate may be taking an opportunity to make itself an even more useful organ of Parliament, particularly as it relates to improving legislation.

Moreover, the Senate might also become more effective at protecting minority rights. Commentators like Hayden King have noted in relation to the 42nd Parliament, for example, that "[t]he (independent) Senate was basically the only layer of accountability in Parliament on Indigenous legislation. If not for them, a lot of the Indigenous-specific bills would have been much worse."[13] Indigenous representation in the Senate is important in this regard and, as I have written elsewhere, the upper house may become an increasingly important vehicle for the representation of Indigenous interests.[14] Similar arguments have been made with regard to the representation of women.[15]

Finally, the role of the Senate as a vehicle for regional representation is arguably all the more important in the wake of two recent developments following the 2019 federal election. First, the formation of the Canadian Senators Group, which includes former Conservative, Liberal, and ISG members, is designed in part to focus more explicitly on regional interests. Second, the lack of Cabinet representation for Alberta and Saskatchewan may elevate the relevance and voice of senators from those provinces. Much remains in flux in the Senate, but the recent reforms grant it a unique opportunity to strengthen its traditional roles.

CREATIVE CONSTITUTIONAL CHANGE?

The Supreme Court's emphasis on changes to the "constitutional architecture" risks abrogating reforms if they are interpreted as affecting the essential features of an institution or government process without recourse to the formal amending formula. My analysis has painted a relatively bleak portrait of the effects *Reference re Senate Reform* may have on preventing both formal constitutional amendment and informal constitutional reform in the future. Given the significant uncertainty created by the court's approach, however, it is conceivable that informal constitutional reform is nonetheless possible in a number of situations.

One type of reform involves changes to a political process, such as appointments, if those changes are brought about under the two conditions explored in Chapter 6. First, informal changes can be made only within the ambit of discretionary authority held by relevant decision makers, such as the prime minister. Efforts to entrench certain changes in law, with the effect of binding future decision makers, may by virtue of their formality trigger relevant amending procedures that require provincial consent. Second, the change cannot alter the essential features of the relevant constitutional process or institution such that provincial input may be required.

An example of this, aside from the 2016 Senate reform, is the decision by Prime Minister Justin Trudeau to limit appointments to the Supreme Court to candidates fluent in both official languages. If such a change were put into law, it would undoubtedly constitute a formal change to the eligibility requirements under the *Supreme Court Act,* and thus require unanimous provincial consent as an amendment to the composition of the Supreme Court under section 41(d) of the *Constitution Act, 1982.*[16] Because the prime minister imposes this condition as a matter of his discretion under the appointing power, even as a potential effort to create a new convention surrounding appointments to the court, it is likely a constitutional act.

The question of establishing new conventions or altering old ones is a challenging one to consider in light of the Supreme Court's *Reference re Senate Reform* logic. Core parts of Canada's constitutional architecture are composed of unwritten conventional rules of practice, ranging from the very lynchpin of the modern parliamentary tradition – responsible government – to specific conventions surrounding institutional processes and appointments. For example, the regional convention concerning the composition of the Supreme Court dictates that, in addition to the statutory (now constitutionally entrenched) guarantee of three Quebec seats, three justices are appointed from Ontario, two from the West, and one from the Atlantic region. Would departing from this convention constitute a change to the constitutional architecture? If regional representation is viewed as part of the composition of the court, then conceivably a rupture with normal practice might require provincial consent. In tension with this possibility, however, is the fact that conventions are not legally enforceable by courts.

The Supreme Court's reference opinion is silent about the place of conventions within the constitutional architecture, but it does state that amendments are not limited to textual changes, and that changes to the architecture that modify the meaning of constitutional text trigger the requirements of the amending formula.[17] Arguably, abandoning the regional convention of appointments to the Supreme Court alters the "composition of the Court" as entrenched in section 41(d) of the *Constitution Act, 1982.*

Constitutional conventions are also implicated by other informal reforms. As noted, Trudeau arguably broke with convention by not appointing any members from Alberta or Saskatchewan to form his new Cabinet after the 2019 federal election. In the period before the reform to the Senate appointments process, the lack of MPs from those provinces would have been offset by appointing a senator or two to Cabinet. Apparent concern over senatorial independence precluded this solution, but it reduced a fairly solid convention to mere political practice as a result.

Other types of informal constitutional reform may include formal changes to law that are not explicitly contemplated by the amending formula and do not create a fundamental change to the essential features of the Constitution. Warren Newman argues persuasively that changes to "organic" or quasi-constitutional statutes in this vein should be possible for Parliament alone to implement.[18] Yet by his own account, the legitimacy of such statutes depends on their enhancing, rather than fundamentally altering, existing constitutional values. Among the examples Newman cites are the *Official Languages Act* and the *Clarity Act,* laws that augment or enhance established constitutional values or unwritten principles (at least in terms of how they are characterized by the Supreme Court). Because certain laws risk running afoul of the amending formula if they are seen as modifying or adding to aspects of the constitutional architecture, it becomes difficult to explain how they stand as legitimate or constitutional in light of the court's architecture logic. The federal regional veto law, which effectively puts additional constraints on the amending formula itself, may be an example of this.

Perhaps the least analyzed context where constitutional reforms, or at least changes in constitutional practice, are likely to occur involves changes in political culture within institutions themselves. The Senate has a lot of capacity as an independent body within Parliament to effect changes to its own rules and behaviour. Similarly, the Supreme Court, which effectively entrenched its own essential features in the Constitution in *Reference re Supreme Court Act,*[19] has the capacity to initiate reform of itself and of the broader Constitution through interpretation. Indeed, *judicial amendment* of the Constitution, through decisions that depart from the traditions of mere interpretation but effectively add to or radically alter the Constitution, might be one of the most viable methods of constitutional change in the future.[20] This comes with heavy normative, institutional, and democratic implications, and might be criticized as a function of the Supreme Court's very approach to the amending formula. By constraining the ability of elected actors to make constitutional amendments, the court arguably further empowers itself to do so.

A more optimistic conclusion might follow from the events witnessed since 2014. By further cementing Canada's formal constitutional stasis, the Supreme Court may have encouraged political actors to seek creative, informal solutions to spur constitutional change. Yet this too may raise potential problems, subjecting reform efforts to serious uncertainty or raising the spectre of the boundaries of legitimacy being pushed too far. The 2016 Senate reform may be an outlier, in terms of both its apparent success and its legitimacy. Attempts to replicate this sort of informal change in other contexts may not be so desirable or permissible.

We are potentially left on the thin edge of the wedge between a static, immutable Constitution that resembles too closely the values and institutions of the nineteenth century and a scenario where decision makers evade the formal requirements of the Constitution to enact informal changes with dubious legitimacy and unintended consequences. If political norms or even constitutional conventions are eroded by an inability to achieve legitimate constitutional change, then the Supreme Court may have unwittingly contributed to the very thing its decision explicitly forbade. Avoiding this predicament will take the injection of a heretofore unseen maturity into Canada's constitutional culture, or the clarification and introduction of a more coherent interpretation of the amending rules themselves.

THE LEGACY OF A LANDMARK DECISION

Some landmark cases achieve that designation by virtue of their long-standing historical significance.[21] *Reference re Senate Reform,* decided so recently, achieves its status as a landmark case in part because of its groundbreaking nature. Along with its sister case, *Reference re Supreme Court Act,*[22] the spring 2014 decision was the first comprehensive elaboration of the constitutional amending formula by the Supreme Court of Canada. Moreover, it had an immediate impact: the court acted as a powerful veto player by preventing the Conservative government from enacting consultative elections or term limits for senators. It is noteworthy that this is one of only a handful of times the Supreme Court has ever blocked or invalidated policies that were promised in a sitting government's election campaign platform.[23]

The decision thus directly influenced the eventual reform to the Senate appointments process, a change that, as this study reveals, has thus far had a hugely significant impact on the relationships between the Senate and the government, and the Senate and the House of Commons. *Reference re Senate Reform* effectively shut the door on formal amendments that would establish an elected upper house or abolish it altogether, at least in the current, long-standing political climate where intergovernmental negotiations over the Constitution remain radioactive. This constraint led directly to the only plausible alternative: an attempt to improve the standing of the institution through an informal change to the selection of senators. That reform will perhaps stand as the most significant reform to Parliament in modern history.

While *Reference re Senate Reform* stands as a landmark case, its long-term impact as it relates to the Senate remains uncertain. The flexibility provided by informal change may be a virtue, but it often means that the reform can be easily undone. In the medium term, the Senate's membership, and therefore its operation, will constitute a dramatic departure from the past. Senators appointed under the new process, if they remain until mandatory retirement, will be present until as late as the 2040s. And that does not include senators who will be appointed in the 43rd Parliament (and possibly future ones). The longer the new appointments process remains in place, the more likely the changes will endure, particularly if changes to the Rules of the Senate or to the *Parliament of Canada Act* help facilitate a fully non-partisan character and organization.

If the legacy of the reference for the Senate itself may prove positive, its legacy with respect to constitutional change is arguably the opposite. Indeed, uncertainty is itself a potential legacy of the reference. Until the Supreme Court of Canada is given more opportunities to elaborate on the dividing lines between the Constitution's different amending procedures, we are left with a lot of guesswork in any attempt to apply the constitutional architecture metaphor to proposed reforms (or even existing legislation) across an array of areas and institutions. What is clear is that the court has reduced Parliament's formal authority to make changes in relation to the House of Commons, the Senate, and the executive to virtual obsolescence. Even within the confines of the matters before it in 2014, the court created confusion. Parliament can effect a mandatory retirement age but not a lengthy non-renewable term limit, on the implausible logic that the latter reform threatens to change the Senate's essential features but the former does not. The court has established a standard such that all "important" changes require provincial consent, and what is deemed important may ultimately be left to a series of future cases, giving judges alone the power to decide what they consider desirable or not. *Reference re Senate Reform* thus deserves its status as a landmark case, but if it stands as the last word on the amending formula and its limits, it may ultimately be to the detriment of constitutional evolution in Canada.

Notes

INTRODUCTION:
THE MAKING OF A LANDMARK CASE

1 Emmett Macfarlane, "'You Can't Always Get What You Want': Regime Politics, the Harper Government, and the Supreme Court of Canada" (2018) 51:1 Canadian Journal of Political Science 1.

2 Robert Schertzer, *The Judicial Role in a Diverse Federation: Lessons from the Supreme Court of Canada* (Toronto: University of Toronto Press, 2016).

3 Richard Albert, "The Difficulty of Constitutional Amendment in Canada" (2015) 53:1 Alta L Rev 85; Emmett Macfarlane, "The Future of Constitutional Change in Canada: Examining Our Legal, Political, and Jurisprudential Straitjacket" in Richard Albert, Paul Daly, and Vanessa MacDonnell, eds, *The Canadian Constitution in Transition* (Toronto: University of Toronto Press, 2019).

4 Sir George Ross, *The Senate of Canada: Its Constitution, Powers and Duties Historically Considered* (Toronto: Copp, Clark Company, 1914); Robert A. Mackay, *The Unreformed Senate of Canada,* revised ed (Toronto: McClelland and Stewart, 1963); F.A. Kunz, *The Modern Senate of Canada 1925–1963: A Re-appraisal* (Toronto: University of Toronto Press, 1965); Colin Campbell, *The Canadian Senate: A Lobby from Within* (Toronto: Macmillan of Canada, 1978).

5 David E. Smith, *The Canadian Senate in Bicameral Perspective* (Toronto: University of Toronto Press, 2003); Serge Joyal, ed, *Protecting Canadian Democracy: The Senate You Never Knew* (Montreal and Kingston: McGill-Queen's University Press, 2003); Jennifer Smith, ed, *The Democratic Dilemma: Reforming the Canadian Senate* (Montreal and Kingston: McGill-Queen's University Press, 2009); J. Patrick Boyer, *Our Scandalous Senate* (Toronto: Dundurn, 2014); Helen Forsey, *A People's Senate for Canada: Not a Pipe Dream!* (Black Point, NS: Fernwood Publishing, 2015); James T. McHugh, *The Senate and the People of Canada: A Counterintuitive Approach to Reform of the Senate of Canada* (New York: Lexington Books, 2017); Serge Joyal and Judith Seidman, eds, *Reflecting on Our Past and Embracing Our*

Future: A Senate Initiative for Canada (Montreal and Kingston: McGill-Queen's University Press, 2018).

6 Carissima Mathen, *Courts without Cases: The Law and Politics of Advisory Opinions* (Oxford: Hart Publishing, 2019); Kate Puddister, *Seeking the Court's Advice: The Politics of the Canadian Reference Power* (Vancouver: UBC Press, 2019).

7 Mathen, *supra* note 6 at 228.

8 Emmett Macfarlane, *Governing from the Bench: The Supreme Court of Canada and the Judicial Role* (Vancouver: UBC Press, 2013) at 89.

9 *Re: Resolution to amend the Constitution,* [1981] 1 SCR 753.

10 *Reference re Secession of Quebec,* [1998] 2 SCR 217.

11 *Re B.C. Motor Vehicle Act,* [1985] 2 SCR 486; *Reference re Same-Sex Marriage,* [2004] 3 SCR 698, 2004 SCC 79; *Reference re Assisted Human Reproduction Act,* 2010 SCC 61, [2010] 3 SCR 457; *Reference re Securities Act,* 2011 SCC 66, [2011] 3 SCR 837; *Attorney-General for Manitoba v Manitoba Egg and Poultry Association et al.,* [1971] SCR 689.

12 Puddister, *supra* note 6 at 111.

13 *Ibid* at 124–32.

14 Mathen, *supra* note 6 at 158.

15 *Ibid* at 163.

CHAPTER 1:
THE SENATE'S (UNFULFILLED) ROLES

1 David E. Smith, *The Canadian Senate in Bicameral Perspective* (Toronto: University of Toronto Press, 2003) at 16–17.

2 Janet Ajzenstat, "Bicameralism and Canada's Founders: The Origins of the Canadian Senate" in Serge Joyal, ed, *Protecting Canadian Democracy: The Senate You Never Knew* (Montreal and Kingston: McGill-Queen's University Press, 2003) at 6.

3 Sir George Ross, *The Senate of Canada: Its Constitution, Powers and Duties Historically Considered* (Toronto: Copp, Clark Company, 1914) at 54–55.

4 *Ibid* at 55.

5 F.A. Kunz, *The Modern Senate of Canada 1925–1963: A Re-appraisal* (Toronto: University of Toronto Press, 1965) at 6.

6 *Ibid* at 10.

7 Ross, *supra* note 3 at xv.

8 James T. McHugh, *The Senate and the People of Canada: A Counterintuitive Approach to Reform of the Senate of Canada* (New York: Lexington Books, 2017) at 21.

9   Robert A. Mackay, *The Unreformed Senate of Canada,* revised ed (Toronto: McClelland and Stewart, 1963) at 31.

10   *Ibid* at 42.

11   Smith, *The Canadian Senate in Bicameral Perspective, supra* note 1 at 79.

12   Ross, *supra* note 3 at 54–55.

13   *Ibid* at 70.

14   Mackay, *supra* note 9 at 87.

15   Colin Campbell, *The Canadian Senate: A Lobby from Within* (Toronto: Macmillan of Canada, 1978) at 6.

16   Mackay, *supra* note 9 at 95.

17   Campbell, *supra* note 15 at 6.

18   Andrew Heard, *Canadian Constitutional Conventions: The Marriage of Law and Politics,* 2d ed (Oxford: Oxford University Press, 2014) at 144.

19   Ross, *supra* note 3 at 77.

20   Kunz, *supra* note 5 at 176.

21   Heard, *supra* note 18 at 145. From 1963 to 2014, of 110 bills amended by the Senate 81 "were promptly accepted by the Commons."

22   Smith, *The Canadian Senate in Bicameral Perspective, supra* note 1 at 117.

23   *Ibid* at 188, n 26.

24   C.E.S. Franks, *The Parliament of Canada* (Toronto: University of Toronto Press, 1987) at 189–90.

25   Gil Rémillard, "Senate Reform: Back to Basics" in Joyal, *supra* note 2, at 115–16.

26   Andrea Lawlor and Erin Crandall, "Committee Performance in the Senate of Canada: Some Sobering Analysis for the Chamber of 'Sober Second Thought'" (2013) 51:34 Commonwealth and Comparative Politics 549 at 550.

27   *Ibid.*

28   Mackay, *supra* note 9 at 156.

29   *Ibid.*

30   Jean-François Godbout, *Lost on Division: Party Unity in the Canadian Parliament* (Toronto: University of Toronto Press, 2020) at 219.

31   *Ibid.*

32   Kunz, *supra* note 5 at 93.

33   *Ibid.*

34   *Ibid.*

35   *Ibid* at 95, citing Arthur Meighen, "The Canadian Senate," *Queen's Quarterly* (1937) 159–60.

36   Smith, *The Canadian Senate in Bicameral Perspective, supra* note 1 at 153.

37   Godbout, *supra* note 30 at 220.

38 *Ibid.*

39 C.E.S. Franks, "The Canadian Senate in Modern Times" in Joyal, *supra* note 2, at 155.

40 *Ibid,* 156–58.

41 *Ibid* at 163.

42 *Ibid* at 153.

43 Campbell, *supra* note 15 at 8; Franks, *The Parliament of Canada, supra* note 24 at 188.

44 Norman Ward, *Dawson's The Government of Canada,* 6th ed (Toronto: University of Toronto Press, 1987) at 155.

45 Heard, *supra* note 18 at 148.

46 Donald J. Savoie, *Democracy in Canada: The Disintegration of Our Institutions* (Montreal and Kingston: McGill-Queen's University Press, 2019) at 50–52.

47 Ward, *supra* note 44 at 154.

48 *Ibid.*

49 Peter H. Russell, *Constitutional Odyssey: Can Canadians Become a Sovereign People?* 3d ed (Toronto: University of Toronto Press, 2004) at 25.

50 Ross, *supra* note 3 at 50.

51 David E. Smith, "The Improvement of the Senate by Nonconstitutional Means" in Joyal, *supra* note 2, at 239. See also Helen Forsey, *A People's Senate for Canada: Not a Pipe Dream!* (Black Point, NS: Fernwood Publishing, 2015) at 17 (quoting Eugene Forsey).

52 Mackay, *supra* note 9 at 37.

53 *Ibid* at 43.

54 *Ibid* at 38 [emphasis in original].

55 *Ibid* at 44.

56 Kunz, *supra* note 5 at 317.

57 *Ibid* at 319.

58 Campbell, *supra* note 15 at 5.

59 Donald V. Smiley, *The Federal Condition in Canada* (Toronto: McGraw-Hill Ryerson, 1987) at 113; Campbell, *supra* note 15 at 6–7; Franks, *The Parliament of Canada, supra* note 24 at 194; Smith, *The Canadian Senate in Bicameral Perspective, supra* note 1 at 11.

60 Mackay, *supra* note 9 at 59; Ajzenstat, *supra* note 2 at 17.

61 *Ibid* at 113.

62 *Ibid* at 121.

63 Russell, *supra* note 49 at 50.

64 Ronald L. Watts, "Bicameralism in Federal Parliamentary Systems" in Joyal, *supra* note 2, at 71.

65 Phillip Buckner, "The Maritimes and the Debate Over Confederation" in Daniel Heidt, ed, *Reconsidering Confederation: Canada's Founding Debates 1864–1999* (Calgary: University of Calgary Press, 2018) at 107–8.

66 Savoie, *supra* note 46 at 52.

67 Kunz, *supra* note 5 at 336.

68 *Ibid.*

69 Paul G. Thomas, "Comparing the Lawmaking Roles of the Senate and the House of Commons" in Joyal, *supra* note 2, at 208–9.

70 Paula Simons, "No, I Haven't Broken the Senate," *Maclean's* (21 May 2019), online: <https://www.macleans.ca/politics/ottawa/no-i-havent-broken-the -senate/>.

71 Emily Mertz, "Kenney Says Bills C-48, C-69 'Prejudicial Attack on Alberta'; Bring Referendum on Equalization Closer," *Global News* (21 June 2019), online: <https://globalnews.ca/news/5418579/alberta-kenney-senate-bills-referendum -equalization-pipelines/>.

72 BC Ministry of Environment and Climate Change Strategy, News Release, "Minister's Statement on Federal Tanker Ban" (16 April 2019), online: <https:// news.gov.bc.ca/releases/2019ENV0014-000693>.

73 David E. Smith, *Federalism and the Constitution of Canada* (Toronto: University of Toronto Press, 2010) at 79.

74 Mackay, *supra* note 9 at 49.

75 Ajzenstat, *supra* note 2 at 10.

76 *Ibid* at 11.

77 Campbell, *supra* note 15 at 2.

78 Kunz, *supra* note 5 at 281–82.

79 *Ibid* at 293.

80 Franks, *The Parliament of Canada, supra* note 24 at 194.

81 Forsey, *supra* note 51 at 18.

82 Alexander Alvaro, "Why Property Rights Were Excluded from the Canadian Charter of Rights and Freedoms" (1991) 24:2 Canadian Journal of Political Science 309 at 315.

83 *Re: Authority of Parliament in relation to the Upper House,* [1980] 1 SCR 54 at 76.

84 Kunz, *supra* note 5 at 47.

85 Emmett Macfarlane, "The Senate May Become an Increasingly Important Site for Indigenous Activism," *CBC News* (15 October 2018), online: <https:// www.cbc.ca/news/opinion/supreme-court-decision-1.4862275>.

86 Mackay, *supra* note 9 at 128.

87 Franks, *The Parliament of Canada, supra* note 24 at 194.

88 Kunz, *supra* note 5 at 316.

89 Smith, *The Canadian Senate in Bicameral Perspective, supra* note 1 at 87.

90 Heard, *supra* note 18 at 147–48.

91 Smith, *The Canadian Senate in Bicameral Perspective, supra* note 1 at 85–87.

92 *Ibid* at 145.

93 Franks, *The Parliament of Canada, supra* note 24 at 194, citing Dawson, *The Government of Canada*, 331.

94 J. Gareth Morley, "Dead Hands, Living Trees, Historic Compromises: The Senate Reform and Supreme Court Act References Bring the Originalism Debate to Canada" (2016) 53 Osgoode Hall LJ 745; Léonid Sirota and Benjamin Oliphant, "Originalist Reasoning in Canadian Constitutional Jurisprudence" (2017) 50:2 UBC L Rev 505.

CHAPTER 2:
A BRIEF HISTORY OF SENATE REFORM

1 Donald J. Savoie, *Democracy in Canada: The Disintegration of Our Institutions* (Montreal and Kingston: McGill-Queen's University Press, 2019) at 101.

2 David C. Docherty, "The Canadian Senate: Chamber of Sober Reflection or Loony Cousin Best Not Talked About" (2002) 8:3 Journal of Legislative Studies 27 at 46.

3 Sir George Ross, *The Senate of Canada: Its Constitution, Powers and Duties Historically Considered* (Toronto: Copp, Clark Company, 1914) at 91.

4 *Ibid* at 92–93.

5 *Ibid* at 94–95.

6 *Ibid* at 93–94.

7 Colin Campbell, *The Canadian Senate: A Lobby from Within* (Toronto: Macmillan of Canada, 1978) at 28–29.

8 *Ibid* at 29.

9 *Ibid* at 30.

10 *Ibid* at 27.

11 C.E.S. Franks, *The Parliament of Canada* (Toronto: University of Toronto Press, 1987) at 194.

12 Jack Stillborn, "Forty Years of Not Reforming the Senate" in Serge Joyal, ed, *Protecting Canadian Democracy: The Senate You Never Knew* (Montreal and Kingston: McGill-Queen's University Press, 2003) at 32. See also James T. McHugh, *The Senate and the People of Canada: A Counterintuitive Approach to Reform of the Senate of Canada* (New York: Lexington Books, 2017).

13 David E. Smith, *The Canadian Senate in Bicameral Perspective* (Toronto: University of Toronto Press, 2003) at 4. See also Dale Smith, *The Unbroken Machine: Canada's Democracy in Action* (Toronto: Dundurn, 2017).

14 McHugh, *supra* note 12 at 6–7.

15 Robert A. Mackay, *The Unreformed Senate of Canada,* revised ed (Toronto: McClelland and Stewart, 1963) at 59.

16 Smith, *The Canadian Senate in Bicameral Perspective, supra* note 13 at 4.

17 C.E.S. Franks, "The Canadian Senate in Modern Times" in Joyal, *supra* note 12, at 183, citing Dawson, *The Government of Canada*, 279.

18 Helen Forsey, *A People's Senate for Canada: Not a Pipe Dream!* (Black Point, NS: Fernwood Publishing, 2015) at 59–60.

19 Ronald L. Watts, "Bicameralism in Federal Parliamentary Systems" in Joyal, *supra* note 12, at 87.

20 Smith, *The Canadian Senate in Bicameral Perspective, supra* note 13 at 52–53.

21 *Ibid* at 7.

22 *Ibid* at 18.

23 Keith G. Banting, *The Welfare State and Canadian Federalism,* 2d ed (Montreal and Kingston: McGill-Queen's University Press, 1987) at 152.

24 Smith, *The Canadian Senate in Bicameral Perspective, supra* note 13 at 18.

25 Franks, *The Parliament of Canada, supra* note 11 at 197–98.

26 *Ibid* at 199.

27 Stillborn, *supra* note 12 at 58.

28 McHugh, *supra* note 12 at 5.

29 Peter H. Russell, *Constitutional Odyssey: Can Canadians Become a Sovereign People?* 3d ed (Toronto: University of Toronto Press, 2004) at 106.

30 *Ibid.*

31 Smith, *The Canadian Senate in Bicameral Perspective, supra* note 13 at 54.

32 Stillborn, *supra* note 12 at 33.

33 Peter McCormick, Ernest C. Manning, and Gordon Gibson, *Regional Representation: The Canadian Partnership* (Calgary: Canada West Foundation, 1981) at 27.

34 *Ibid* at 28.

35 *Ibid* at 29.

36 McHugh, *supra* note 12 at 5.

37 Watts, *supra* note 19 at 96.

38 Forsey, *supra* note 18 at 69.

39 Smith, *The Canadian Senate in Bicameral Perspective, supra* note 13 at 6.

40 McHugh, *supra* note 12 at 185–86.

41 Stillborn, *supra* note 12 at 33.

42 *Ibid* at 34.

43 David E. Smith, *Federalism and the Constitution of Canada* (Toronto: University of Toronto Press, 2010) at 81.

44 Russell, *supra* note 29 at 205.

45 McHugh, *supra* note 12 at 9.

46 Franks, 201.

47 F.A. Kunz, *The Modern Senate of Canada 1925–1963: A Re-appraisal* (Toronto: University of Toronto Press, 1965) at 370.

48 Smith, *The Canadian Senate in Bicameral Perspective, supra* note 13 at 58–59.

49 Emmett Macfarlane, *Governing from the Bench: The Supreme Court of Canada and the Judicial Role* (Vancouver: UBC Press, 2013).

50 Gwyneth Bergman and Emmett Macfarlane, "The Impact and Role of Officers of Parliament: Canada's Conflict of Interest and Ethics Commissioner" (2018) 61:1 Canadian Public Administration 5.

51 Jonathan Craft, *Backrooms and Beyond: Partisan Advisers and the Politics of Policy Work in Canada* (Toronto: University of Toronto Press, 2016).

52 Donald J. Savoie, *Breaking the Bargain: Public Servants, Ministers, and Parliament* (Toronto: University of Toronto Press, 2003).

53 F.L. Morton and Rainer Knopff, *The Charter Revolution and the Court Party* (Toronto: University of Toronto Press, 2000); Kent Roach, *The Supreme Court on Trial: Judicial Activism or Democratic Dialogue,* revised ed (Toronto: Irwin Law, 2016); Emmett Macfarlane, "Dialogue or Compliance? Measuring Legislatures' Policy Responses to Court Rulings on Rights" (2013) 34 International Political Science Review 39.

54 David E. Smith, "The Improvement of the Senate by Nonconstitutional Means" in Joyal, *supra* note 12, at 249.

55 Russell, *supra* note 29 at 206.

56 *Ibid* at 209–10.

57 *Ibid* at 210.

58 *Ibid* at 215.

59 Watts, *supra* note 19 at 99. Stan Waters was appointed by Mulroney in 1990.

60 Bert Brown (2007), Betty Unger (2012), Doug Black (2013), and Scott Tannas (2013).

61 Smith, *The Canadian Senate in Bicameral Perspective, supra* note 13 at 55.

62 Campbell, *supra* note 7 at 2–3.

63 *Ibid* at 31.

64 Smith, *The Canadian Senate in Bicameral Perspective, supra* note 13 at 58.

65 Watts, *supra* note 19 at 87.

66 Janet Ajzenstat, "Bicameralism and Canada's Founders: The Origins of the Canadian Senate" in Joyal, *supra* note 12, at 8.

67 Smith, *The Canadian Senate in Bicameral Perspective, supra* note 13 at 98.

68 Meagan Fitzpatrick, "NDP Says Senate Should Be Starved of Funds," *CBC News* (22 June 2011), online: <https://www.cbc.ca/news/politics/ndp-says-senate-should-be-starved-of-funds-1.976912>.

69 Section 32 reads: "When a Vacancy happens in the Senate by Resignation, Death, or otherwise, the Governor General shall by Summons to a fit and qualified Person fill the Vacancy."

70 Stillborn, *supra* note 12 at 57.

71 Smith, *The Canadian Senate in Bicameral Perspective, supra* note 13 at 155.

72 *Ibid.*

73 Emmett Macfarlane, ed, *Constitutional Amendment in Canada* (Toronto: University of Toronto Press, 2016).

74 Russell, *supra* note 29 at 270; Docherty, *supra* note 2.

75 Andrew Heard, "Tapping the Potential of Senate-Driven Reform: Proposals to Limit the Powers of the Senate" (2015) 24:2 Const Forum Const 47 at 48.

76 *Ibid* at 49.

77 *Ibid* at 51.

78 *Ibid.*

79 *Ibid.*

80 *Ibid* at 52.

81 *Ibid* at 50.

82 Smith, "The Improvement of the Senate by Nonconstitutional Means," *supra* note 54 at 252–56.

83 McHugh, *supra* note 12 at 235.

84 Smith, "The Improvement of the Senate by Nonconstitutional Means," *supra* note 54 at 258.

85 *Ibid;* see also Forsey, *supra* note 18 at 96; McHugh, *supra* note 12 at 8.

86 Gil Rémillard, "Senate Reform: Back to Basics" in Joyal, *supra* note 12, at 122.

87 McHugh, *supra* note 12 at 176–77; Smith, "The Improvement of the Senate by Nonconstitutional Means," *supra* note 54 at 262.

88 Smith, "The Improvement of the Senate by Nonconstitutional Means," *supra* note 54 at 262.

89 Norman Ward, *Dawson's The Government of Canada,* 6th ed (Toronto: University of Toronto Press, 1987) at 157.

90 Kunz, *supra* note 47 at 372.

91 J.A. Corry and J.E. Hodgetts, *Democratic Government and Politics,* 3d ed, revised (Toronto: University of Toronto Press, 1959) at 182–83.

92 Forsey, *supra* note 18 at 32–33.

CHAPTER 3:
IF AT FIRST YOU DON'T SUCCEED

1 Jonathan Malloy, "More Than a Terrain of Struggle: Parliament as Ideological Instrument and Objective under Conservatism" in J.P. Lewis and Joanna Everitt, eds, *The Blueprint: Conservative Parties and Their Impact on Canadian Politics* (Toronto: University of Toronto Press, 2017) at 250.

2 *Ibid* at 250–51.

3 Reform Party of Canada, *A Fresh Start for Canadians* (1997) at 23.

4 Canadian Alliance, *A Time for Change: An Agenda of Respect for All Canadians* (2000) at 20.

5 See also Adam Dodek, "The Politics of the *Senate Reform Reference:* Fidelity, Frustration, and Federal Unilateralism" (2015) 60:4 McGill LJ 623.

6 Peter H. Russell, *Constitutional Odyssey: Can Canadians Become a Sovereign People?* 3d ed (Toronto: University of Toronto Press, 2004).

7 Peter Aucoin, Mark D. Jarvis, and Lori Turnbull, *Democratizing the Constitution: Reforming Responsible Government* (Toronto: Emond Montgomery, 2011) at 226.

8 Janyce McGregor, "'We Are Not Opening the Constitution': Trudeau Pans Quebec's Plans," *CBC News* (1 June 2017), online: <https://www.cbc.ca/news/politics/trudeau-constituion-opening-thursday-1.4140989>.

9 Emmett Macfarlane, "The Future of Constitutional Change in Canada: Examining Our Legal, Political, and Jurisprudential Straitjacket" in Richard Albert, Paul Daly, and Vanessa MacDonnell, eds, *The Canadian Constitution in Transition* (Toronto: University of Toronto Press, 2019).

10 Anna Esselment, "Federal Feet and Provincial Pools: The Conservatives and Federalism in Canada" in Lewis and Everitt, *supra* note 1. For a different take on this point, see Nadia Verrelli, "Harper's Senate Reform: An Example of Open Federalism?" in Jennifer Smith, ed, *The Democratic Dilemma: Reforming the Canadian Senate* (Montreal and Kingston: McGill-Queen's University Press, 2009).

11 Richard Albert, for example, has described the government's proposals as amounting to "constitutional amendment by stealth." Richard Albert, "Constitutional Amendment by Stealth" (2015) 60:4 McGill LJ 673.

12 Conservative Party of Canada, *Stand Up for Canada* (2006) at 44.

13 Senate, *Proceedings of the Special Senate Committee on Senate Reform,* Issue 2 – Evidence (7 September 2006) (The Right Honourable Stephen Harper).

14 *Ibid.*

15 Senate, *Proceedings of the Special Senate Committee on Senate Reform,* Issue 2 – Evidence (7 September 2006) (Warren J. Newman, General Counsel, Constitutional and Administrative Law Section, Department of Justice Canada).

16 Senate, Special Senate Committee on Senate Reform, "Report on the Subject-Matter of Bill S-4, *An Act to amend the Constitution Act, 1867* (Senate Tenure)" (October 2006) ["Report on the Subject-Matter of Bill S-4"].

17 Senate, *Proceedings of the Special Senate Committee on Senate Reform, supra* note 13.

18 *Re: Authority of Parliament in relation to the Upper House,* [1980] 1 SCR 54 [*Upper House Reference*].

19 Senate, Special Senate Committee on Senate Reform, *supra* note 16.

20 *House of Commons Debates,* 39th Parl, 1st Sess (7 May 2007) at 12:05p.m. (Scott Reid).

21 Section 42(b) of Part V of the *Constitution Act, 1982,* being Schedule B to the *Canada Act 1982* (UK), 1982, c 11.

22 *House of Commons Debates, supra* note 20.

23 *Ibid.*

24 Conservative Party of Canada, *The True North Strong and Free: Stephen Harper's Plan for Canadians* (2008) at 24.

25 Conservative Party of Canada, *Here for Canada: Stephen Harper's Low-Tax Plan for Jobs and Economic Growth* (2011) at 62.

26 Aaron Wherry, "How to Spend a Year Not Doing Anything on Senate Reform, While Demanding Change," *Maclean's* (27 February 2013), online: <https://www.macleans.ca/politics/ottawa/how-to-spend-a-year-not-doing -anything-on-senate-reform-while-demanding-change/>.

27 Laura Payton and Meagan Fitzpatrick, "Auditor General Finds Contracting Problems in House, Senate," *CBC News* (13 June 2012), online: <https://www. cbc.ca/news/politics/auditor-general-finds-contracting-problems-in-house -senate-1.1177039>.

28 "A Chronology of the Senate Expenses Scandal," *CBC News* (13 July 2016), online: <https://www.cbc.ca/news/politics/senate-expense-scandal-timeline -1.3677457>.

29 "Read the Senate Expense Audits and Reports," *CBC News* (9 May 2013), online: <https://www.cbc.ca/news/politics/read-the-senate-expense-audits-and -reports-1.1343327>.

30 Leslie MacKinnon, "Nigel Wright Has 'Full Confidence' of PM after Duffy Cheque," *CBC News* (16 May 2013), online: <https://www.cbc.ca/news/politics/ nigel-wright-has-full-confidence-of-pm-after-duffy-cheque-1.1333044>.

31 "A Chronology of the Senate Expenses Scandal," *supra* note 28.

32 James T. McHugh, *The Senate and the People of Canada: A Counterintuitive Approach to Reform of the Senate of Canada* (New York: Lexington Books, 2017) at 212.

33 Office of the Auditor General of Canada, *Report of the Auditor General of Canada to the Senate of Canada: Senators' Expenses* (June 2015).

34 Jordan Press, "Auditor General Michael Ferguson Breaks Down $23M Cost of Senate Audit," *CBC News* (10 June 2015), online: <https://www.cbc.ca/news/politics/auditor-general-michael-ferguson-breaks-down-23m-cost-of-senate-audit-1.3108276>.

35 Ian Binnie, *Report of the Special Arbitrator on the Expense Claims Identified by the Auditor General in His Report Dated June 4, 2015* (2015) at 27.

36 John Paul Tasker, "Justice Ian Binnie Cuts Senators' Expenses Owed in 10 of 14 Cases," *CBC News* (21 March 2016), online: <https://www.cbc.ca/news/politics/justice-binnie-senate-arbitrator-1.3500650>.

37 Joseph Brean, "Majority of Canadians Support Either Abolished or Reformed Senate: Poll," *National Post* (7 April 2015), online: <https://nationalpost.com/news/politics/majority-of-canadians-support-either-abolished-or-reformed-senate-poll>.

38 Laura Stone, "Conservative Senator Nancy Ruth: Airplane Food Is 'Ice Cold Camembert and Broken Crackers," *Global News* (1 April 2015), online: <https://globalnews.ca/news/1916681/conservative-senator-nancy-ruth-airplane-food-is-ice-cold-camembert-and-broken-crackers/>.

39 McHugh, *supra* note 32 at 217.

40 J. Patrick Boyer, *Our Scandalous Senate* (Toronto: Dundurn, 2014).

41 Carissima Mathen, *Courts without Cases: The Law and Politics of Advisory Opinions* (Oxford: Hart Publishing, 2019); Kate Puddister, *Seeking the Court's Advice: The Politics of the Canadian Reference Power* (Vancouver: UBC Press, 2019).

42 *Projet de loi fédéral relatif au Sénat (Re)*, 2013 QCCA 1807 at para 61.

43 *Ibid* at para 56.

44 *Ibid* at para 66 [author's translation].

45 *Ibid* at para 79.

46 *Ibid* at para 81, citing *Upper House Reference, supra* note 18 at 76–77.

47 *Ibid* at para 84.

48 Christopher P. Manfredi, *An Expert Opinion on the Possible Effects of Bill C-7* (June 2013).

49 *Upper House Reference, supra* note 18 at 65.

50 *Ibid* at 66.

51 Ronald L. Watts, "Bill C-20: Faulty Procedure and Inadequate Solution (Testimony before the Legislative Committee on Bill C-20, House of Commons,

7 May 2008" in Smith, *The Democratic Dilemma, supra* note 10; John D. Whyte, "Senate Reform: What Does the Constitution Say?" in Smith, *The Democratic Dilemma, supra* note 10; Mark D. Walters, "The Constitutional Form and Reform of the Senate: Thoughts on the Constitutionality of Bill C-7" (2013) 7 Journal of Parliamentary and Political Law 37.

52 Andrew Heard, "Constitutional Doubts about Bill C-20 and Senatorial Elections" in Smith, *The Democratic Dilemma, supra* note 10.

53 But see Don Desserud, "Whither 91.1? The Constitutionality of Bill C-19: An Act to Limit Senate Tenure" in Smith, *The Democratic Dilemma, supra* note 10.

54 *Reference re Supreme Court Act, ss. 5 and 6,* 2014 SCC 21, [2014] 1 SCR 433 at para 74.

55 *Constitution Act, 1982, supra* note 21, s 41(d).

56 For a comprehensive examination of the *Supreme Court Act* reference and the events surrounding it, see Carissima Mathen and Michael Plaxton, *The Tenth Justice: Judicial Appointments, Marc Nadon, and the Supreme Court Act Reference* (Vancouver: UBC Press, 2020).

CHAPTER 4: THE DECISION

1 *Reference re Senate Reform,* 2014 SCC 32 at para 14 [*Senate Reform*].

2 *Ibid* at para 15.

3 *Ibid* at para 17.

4 Léonid Sirota and Benjamin Oliphant, "Originalist Reasoning in Canadian Constitutional Jurisprudence" (2017) 50:2 UBC L Rev 505 at 525–26.

5 *Senate Reform, supra* note 1 at para 16.

6 *Reference re Secession of Quebec,* [1998] 2 SCR 217, 161 DLR (4th) 385 [*Secession Reference*].

7 *Senate Reform, supra* note 1 at para 25, citing *Secession Reference, ibid* at para 32.

8 *Ibid.*

9 Patrick J. Monahan, "The Public Policy Role of the Supreme Court of Canada in the *Secession Reference*" (2000) 11 NJCL 65.

10 See *Secession Reference, supra* note 6 at para 50; *OPSEU v Ontario (AG),* [1987] 2 SCR 2 at 57, 41 DLR (4th) 1 [*OPSEU*].

11 *Secession Reference, supra* note 6 at para 50.

12 *OPSEU, supra* note 10 at 57.

13 *Senate Reform, supra* note 1 at para 26.

14 *Ibid* at para 27.

15 *Ibid* at para 29.

16 Peter H. Russell, *Constitutional Odyssey: Can Canadians Become a Sovereign People?* 3d ed (Toronto: University of Toronto Press, 2004) at 50.

17 *Ibid* at 66; James Ross Hurley, *Amending Canada's Constitution: History, Processes, Problems and Prospects* (Ottawa: Minister of Supply and Services Canada, 1996) at 30; B.L. Strayer, "Saskatchewan and the Amendment of the Canadian Constitution" (1966) 12 McGill LJ 443 at 466.

18 Paul Gérin-Lajoie, *Constitutional Amendment in Canada* (Toronto: University of Toronto Press, 1950) at xiv–xix.

19 *Ibid.*

20 *Senate Reform, supra* note 1 at para 5.

21 *Ibid* at para 62.

22 *Ibid.*

23 *Ibid* at para 52.

24 *Ibid* at para 57.

25. *Ibid* at para 58 [emphasis in original].

26 *Ibid* at para 59.

27 (UK), 30 & 31 Vict, c 3, reprinted in RSC 1985, Appendix II, No 5 [*Constitution Act, 1867*].

28 See Paul G. Thomas, "Comparing the Lawmaking Roles of the Senate and the House of Commons" in Serge Joyal, ed, *Protecting Canadian Democracy: The Senate You Never Knew* (Montreal and Kingston: McGill-Queen's University Press, 2003) at 189; David E. Smith, *The Canadian Senate in Bicameral Perspective* (Toronto: University of Toronto Press, 2003) at 114.

29 For two recent studies on the reference or "advisory" context, see Kate Puddister, *Seeking the Court's Advice: The Politics of the Canadian Reference Power* (Vancouver: UBC Press, 2019); Carissima Mathen, *Courts without Cases: The Law and Politics of Advisory Opinions* (London: Hart Publishing, 2019).

30 *Senate Reform, supra* note 1 at para 52.

31 See, for example, Aaron Wherry, "Justin Trudeau's Unilateral Senate Reform," *Maclean's* (29 January 2014), online: <https://www.macleans.ca/uncategorized/justin-trudeaus-unilateral-senate-reform/>.

32 *Senate Reform, supra* note 1 at para 65.

33 Emmett Macfarlane, "Unsteady Architecture: Ambiguity, the Senate Reference, and the Future of Constitutional Amendment in Canada" (2015) 60:4 McGill LJ 883 at 892–93.

34 *Senate Reform, supra* note 1 at para 5.

35 Plans by the Government of New Brunswick to hold Senate elections were described as being "in limbo" following the Supreme Court's decision. See Jacques Poitras, "David Alward's Senate Reform Plans in Legal Limbo," *CBC News* (30

April 2014), online: <https://www.cbc.ca/news/canada/new-brunswick/david
-alward-s-senate-reform-plans-in-legal-limbo-1.2625938>.

36 *Senate Reform, supra* note 1 at para 5.

37 Nonetheless, it was clear that an amendment would be required given that senatorial tenure is listed in s 29(2) of the *Constitution Act, 1867,* which states: "A Senator who is summoned to the Senate ... shall ... hold his place in the Senate until he attains the age of seventy-five years."

38 *Senate Reference, supra* note 1 at para 78.

39 *Ibid* at para 74.

40 (UK), 13 Geo VI, c 81, s 1.

41 See Patrick J. Monahan and Byron Shaw, *Constitutional Law,* 4th ed (Toronto: Irwin Law, 2013) at 169–73.

42 *Ibid* at 171.

43 See *Senate Reform, supra* note 1 at para 75.

44 Gérin-Lajoie, *supra* note 18 at xxx.

45 *Ibid* at xxxi.

46 *Ibid* at xxii.

47 *Senate Reform, supra* note 1 at para 79, citing *Re: Authority of Parliament in relation to the Upper House,* [1980] 1 SCR 54 at 76 [*Upper House Reference*].

48 *Upper House Reference, supra* note 47 at 77.

49 Monahan and Shaw, *supra* note 41 at 213–14.

50 *Senate Reference, supra* note 1 at para 81.

51 Christopher P. Manfredi, *An Expert Opinion on the Possible Effects of Bill C-7* (June 2013) at para 50.

52 *Ibid* at para 34.

53 Andrew Heard, however, argues that term limits as short as eight years might have an effect on a senator's performance and attitudes. See Andrew Heard, "Assessing Senate Reform through Bill C-19: The Effects of Limited Terms of Senators" in Jennifer Smith, ed, *The Democratic Dilemma: Reforming the Canadian Senate* (Montreal and Kingston: McGill-Queen's University Press, 2009).

54 *Senate Reform, supra* note 1 at paras 85–86.

55 *Ibid* at para 88.

56 *Senate Reform, supra* note 1 at para 5.

57 Teresa Wright, "Scrapping the Senate Bad for P.E.I., Local Politicians Argue," *The Guardian* (Charlottetown) (28 May 2013), online: <https://www.pressreader. com/canada/the-guardian-charlottetown/20130528/textview>.

58 *Constitution Act, 1982,* s 41(b).

59 *Ibid,* s 47(1):

(1) An amendment to the Constitution of Canada made by proclamation under section 38, 41, 42 or 43 may be made without a
resolution of the Senate authorizing the issue of the proclamation
if, within one hundred and eighty days after the adoption by the
House of Commons of a resolution authorizing its issue, the Senate
has not adopted such a resolution and if, at any time after the expiration of that period, the House of Commons again adopts the
resolution and if, at any time after the expiration of that period, the
House of Commons again adopts the resolution.

(2) Any period when Parliament is prorogued or dissolved shall not be
counted in computing the one hundred and eighty day period
referred to in subsection (1).

60 *1987 Constitutional Accord* (Ottawa: Library of Parliament, 3 June 1987)
[Meech Lake Accord].

61 See Russell, *supra* note 16 at 142–48.

62 *Senate Reform, supra* note 1 at para 106.

CHAPTER 5: INFORMAL REFORM
AND A NEW APPOINTMENTS PROCESS

1 Government of Canada, "The Mandate Letter Tracker and the Results and
Delivery Approach" (29 November 2018), online: <https://www.canada.ca/en/
privy-council/services/results-delivery-unit.html#toc2>.

2 James Cudmore, "Justin Trudeau Removes Senators from Liberal Caucus,"
CBC News (29 January 2014), online: <https://www.cbc.ca/news/politics/
justin-trudeau-removes-senators-from-liberal-caucus-1.2515273>.

3 *Ibid.*

4 *Ibid.*

5 *Ibid.*

6 *Ibid.*

7 F.A. Kunz, *The Modern Senate of Canada 1925–1963: A Re-appraisal*
(Toronto: University of Toronto Press, 1965) at 91.

8 Norman Ward, *Dawson's The Government of Canada,* 6th ed (Toronto:
University of Toronto Press, 1987) at 161.

9 Justin Trudeau, Prime Minister of Canada, News Release, "New Process for
Judicial Appointments to the Supreme Court of Canada" (2 August 2016), online:
<https://pm.gc.ca/eng/news/2016/08/02/new-process-judicial-appointments
-supreme-court-canada>.

10 Independent Advisory Board for Senate Appointments, *Transitional Process Report* (31 March 2016), online: <https://www.canada.ca/content/dam/di-id/images/transition/transitional-phase-report.pdf>.

11 Canada, Independent Advisory Board for Senate Appointments, "Assessment Criteria" (8 January 2018), online: <https://www.canada.ca/en/campaign/independent-advisory-board-for-senate-appointments/assessment-criteria.html>.

12 Donald J. Savoie, *Democracy in Canada: The Disintegration of Our Institutions* (Montreal and Kingston: McGill-Queen's University Press, 2019) at 209.

13 Canada, Independent Advisory Board for Senate Appointments, *supra* note 11.

14 Savoie, *supra* note 12 at 209.

15 Canadian Press, "Christy Clark Says Trudeau Legitimizing Unaccountable Senate, B.C. Under-Representation," *CBC News* (6 December 2015), online: <http://www.cbc.ca/news/politics/clark-trudeau-senate-reform-1.3353128>; Adam Dodek, "Maybe Purging Parties from the Senate Isn't Such a Hot Idea, Mr. Trudeau," *iPolitics* (30 December 2015), online: <http://ipolitics.ca/2015/12/30/maybe-purging-parties-from-the-senate-isnt-such-a-hot-idea-mr-trudeau/>; Andrew Coyne, "New Senate Activism Undermines the Very Principle of Democracy," *National Post* (9 June 2016), online: <http://news.nationalpost.com/full-comment/andrew-coyne-new-senate-activism-undermines-the-very-principle-of-democracy>.

16 *Ibid.*

17 *Ibid.*

18 Peter O'Neil, "Justin Trudeau's Senate Reform 'Dangerous' for B.C.: Experts," *Vancouver Sun* (22 January 2017), online: <http://vancouversun.com/news/local-news/justin-trudeaus-senate-reform-dangerous-for-b-c-experts>.

19 Emmett Macfarlane, "The Perils and Paranoia of Senate Reform: Does Senate Independence Threaten Canadian Democracy?" in Elizabeth Goodyear-Grant and Kyle Hanniman, *Canada: State of the Federation 2017 – Canada at 150: Federalism and Democratic Renewal* (Montreal and Kingston: McGill-Queen's University Press, 2019). See also the study that was the basis for this analysis: Emmett Macfarlane, *The Renewed Canadian Senate: Organizational Challenges and Relations with the Government,* IRPP Study 71 (Montreal: Institute for Research on Public Policy, 2019).

20 Paul G. Thomas, *Moving toward a New and Improved Senate,* IRPP Study 70 (Montreal: Institute for Research on Public Policy, 2019) at 24.

21 Government Representative Office in the Senate, *Towards an Independent Senate: A Progress Report to Canadians* (22 August 2019) at 7–8.

22 In relation to Bill C-49, the Senate returned the legislation to the House with eighteen amendments. The House accepted two amendments, modified three

others, and rejected the rest. The Senate Conservatives and a handful of independent senators insisted on sending the bill with two further amendments to the House a second time, something the upper house had not done since 2006. The House rejected the amendments and the Senate then passed the bill. See Canadian Press, "Senators Bow to Will of Elected Government on Transport Modernization Bill," *CBC News* (23 May 2018), online: <https://www.cbc.ca/news/politics/transportation-bill-passes-1.4674077>.

23 For context, see Institute for Research on Public Policy, *Renewal of the Canadian Senate: Where to from Here?* IRPP Report (Montreal: Institute for Research on Public Policy, 2019).

24 Interview with public servant.

25 Interviews with various senators.

26 Interview with public servant.

27 Madeleine Blais-Morin and Peter Zimonjic, "Conservative Senators Travel to Washington to Talk Marijuana with Jeff Sessions," *CBC News* (4 April 2018), online: <https://www.cbc.ca/news/politics/batters-pot-sessions-carignan-boisvenu-1.4605443>.

28 Peter Zimonjic, "Senate Passes Pot Bill, Paving Way for Legal Cannabis in 8 to 12 Weeks," *CBC News* (19 June 2018), online: <https://www.cbc.ca/news/politics/senate-passes-government-pot-bill-1.4713222>.

29 Interviews.

30 Zimonjic, *supra* note 28. The comments from Senator Pratte are interesting because they came after a speech he made during debates on the second version of the bill, in which he spoke in opposition to another vote against the bill. See Thomas, *supra* note 20 at 26–27. In other words, although Pratte was unhappy with the substantive decision of the government to refuse certain amendments, he did not believe the Senate's role was to obstruct the will of the House.

31 Interviews.

32 Canada, Crown-Indigenous Relations and Northern Affairs Canada, "Collaborative Process on Indian Registration, Band Membership and First Nation Citizenship: Report to Parliament June 2019" (8 July 2019), online: <https://www.rcaanc-cirnac.gc.ca/eng/1560878580290/1568897675238>.

33 Maura Forrest, "Law Means Thousands Can Get Indian Status, but Government Hasn't Provided Any Forms to Fill Out," *National Post* (22 December 2017), online: <https://nationalpost.com/news/politics/law-means-thousands-can-get-indian-status-but-government-hasnt-provided-any-forms-to-fill-out>.

34 Interviews.

35 Marie-Danielle Smith, "Six-Fold Increase in Senate Lobbying under Trudeau, with Independents Taking Most Meetings," *National Post* (22 January 2018),

online: <https://nationalpost.com/news/politics/six-fold-increase-in-senate-lobbying-under-trudeau-with-independents-taking-most-meetings>.

36 Institute for Research on Public Policy, *supra* note 23.

37 *Ibid* at 11.

38 Aengus Bridgman, "A Nonpartisan Legislative Chamber: The Influence of the Canadian Senate," online: (April 2020) Party Politics, <https://doi.org/10.1177/1354068820911345>.

39 Independent Senators Group, *Charter of the Independent Senators Group (ISG)* (Ottawa: Senate of Canada, 2018).

40 *Ibid.*

41 Interview with Senator Joseph A. Day.

42 Interview with Senator Peter Harder.

43 Interview with Senator Yonah Martin.

44 Interview with Senator Yuen Pau Woo.

45 For more detail on proposed future changes, see Thomas, *supra* note 20.

46 Interview with public servant.

47 Jesse Snyder, "Senate Drops Deadlines to Pass Controversial Legislation, Including Bill C-69 and Oil Tanker Ban," *National Post* (5 April 2019), online: <https://nationalpost.com/news/senate-drops-deadlines-to-pass-controversial-legislation-including-bill-c-69-and-oil-tanker-ban>.

48 Interview.

49 Emily Mertz, "Kenney Says Bills C-48, C-69 'Prejudicial Attack on Alberta'; Bring Referendum on Equalization Closer," *Global News* (21 June 2019), online: <https://globalnews.ca/news/5418579/alberta-kenney-senate-bills-referendum-equalization-pipelines/>.

50 John Paul Tasker, "Federal Government Accepts Dozens of Amendments to Environmental Review Bill, Rejects Most of the Tory Ones," *CBC News* (12 June 2019), online: <https://www.cbc.ca/news/politics/c69-environmental-assessment-senate-1.5171913>.

51 Janice Dickson, "How Conservative Senator Plett Slows Down the Liberal Agenda; If There Is Any Legislation Backed Up in the Senate – You Might Blame the Country's Most High Profile Plumber," *Globe and Mail* (11 June 2019), online: <https://www.theglobeandmail.com/politics/article-how-conservative-senator-plett-slows-down-the-liberal-agenda/>.

52 Interview with Senator Peter Harder.

53 Interview with Senator Joseph A. Day.

54 A similar point was made by Senator Leo Housakos on the 18 March 2019 episode of TVO's "The Agenda."

55 Events since this interview was conducted might call this point into question.

56 Christian Paas-Lang, "Bills Now Taking More Than Twice as Long to Get through Canada's Senate," *Global News* (30 June 2019), online: <https://globalnews. ca/news/5447756/bills-senate-delays/>.

57 Andrew Coyne, "Our Unelected Senate Doesn't Even Have to Actually Defeat a Bill to Kill It," *National Post* (26 June 2019), online: <https://nationalpost.com/ opinion/andrew-coyne-our-unelected-senate-doesnt-even-have-to-actually-defeat -a-bill-to-kill-it>.

58 Special Senate Committee on Senate Modernization, *Senate Modernization: Moving Forward: Report of the Special Senate Committee on Senate Modernization – Part 1* (Ottawa: Senate of Canada, October 2016). The second major interim report of the committee was released in April 2018. That report, drawing from expert witness testimony, took a broad examination of what principles were required in a Westminster system: Special Senate Committee on Senate Modernization, *Senate Modernization: Moving Forward: Interim Report of the Special Senate Committee on Senate Modernization – Part II* (Ottawa: Senate of Canada, April 2018).

59 Michael Kirby and Hugh Segal, *A House Undivided: Making Senate Independence Work* (Ottawa: Public Policy Forum, 2016).

60 Michael Kirby and Hugh Segal, "Take Senate Reform Back to Basics: Regional Representation," *Globe and Mail* (21 September 2016), online: <https:// www.theglobeandmail.com/opinion/take-senate-reform-back-to-basics-regional -representation/article31993257/>.

61 *Ibid.*

62 Kirby and Segal, *A House Undivided, supra* note 59.

63 André Pratte, "Why Regional Representation Is the Wrong Basis for Senate Reform," *Globe and Mail* (26 September 2016), online: <https://www.theglobeand mail.com/opinion/why-regional-representation-is-the-wrong-basis-for-senate -reform/article32037411/>.

64 Interview with Senator Peter Harder.

65 Interviews with public servants.

66 RSC 1985, c P-1.

67 Jordan Press, "With Eye to Election, Senators Push Trudeau to Fulfill Promise of Non-Partisan Senate," *Globe and Mail* (24 October 2018), online: <https:// www.theglobeandmail.com/politics/article-with-eye-to-election-senators-push -trudeau-to-fulfill-promise-of-non/>.

68 Olivia Stefanovich, "Canadian Senators Group Forms to Focus on Regional Interests," *CBC News* (4 November 2019), online: <https://www.cbc.ca/news/ politics/stefanovich-new-senate-group-1.5346470>.

69 John Paul Tasker, "There's Another New Faction in the Senate: The Progressive Senate Group," *CBC News* (14 November 2019), online: <https://www.cbc.ca/ news/politics/new-faction-progressive-senate-group-1.5358269?cmp=rss>.

70 Press, *supra* note 67.

71 Interview with Senator Yuen Pau Woo.

72 Emmett Macfarlane, "The Senate May Become an Increasingly Important Site for Indigenous Activism," *CBC News* (15 October 2018), online: <https://www.cbc.ca/news/opinion/supreme-court-decision-1.4862275>.

73 Elizabeth McCallion, "Feminist Senators Are Critical Actors in Women's Representation," *Policy Options* (11 November 2019), online: <https://policyoptions.irpp.org/magazines/november-2019/feminist-senators-are-critical-actors-in-womens-representation/>.

74 Charelle Evelyn and Samantha Wright Allen, "Independent Senators Still Most Likely to Vote with Government, but Less and Less," *Hill Times* (25 July 2018), online: <https://www.hilltimes.com/2018/07/25/independent-senator-voting-shifts-away-liberal-rep-isg-still-likely-allies-152033-152033/152033>; see also J.F. Godbout, "Partisanship in the Senate" (Paper delivered at the "Renewal of the Canadian Senate: Where to from Here?" conference of the Institute for Research on Public Policy, Ottawa, 27 September 2018).

75 Dale Smith, "Can the ISG Survive the Next Election?" *Loonie Politics* (30 July 2019), online: <https://looniepolitics.com/can-the-isg-survive-the-next-election/>.

76 *Ibid.*

77 Emmett Macfarlane, *Governing from the Bench: The Supreme Court of Canada and the Judicial Role* (Vancouver: UBC Press, 2013); Emmett Macfarlane, "Consensus and Unanimity at the Supreme Court of Canada" (2010) 52 Sup Ct L Rev 379.

78 Lawrence Baum, *Judges and Their Audiences: A Perspective on Judicial Behaviour* (Princeton, NJ: Princeton University Press, 2006).

CHAPTER 6:
A CONSTITUTION IN STASIS?

1 *Reference re Senate Reform,* 2014 SCC 32 at para 65 [*Senate Reform*].

2 Emmett Macfarlane, "The Perils and Paranoia of Senate Reform: Does Senate Independence Threaten Canadian Democracy?" in Elizabeth Goodyear-Grant and Kyle Hanniman, eds, *Canada: The State of the Federation 2017 – Canada at 150: Federalism and Democratic Renewal* (Montreal and Kingston: McGill-Queen's University Press, 2019).

3 *Senate Reform, supra* note 1 at para 57 [emphasis added].

4 Richard Albert, "Constitutional Amendment by Stealth" (2015) 60:4 McGill LJ 673.

5 *Ibid* at 709.

6 *Ibid* at 710.

7 Joan Bryden, "Scheer Stands by Vow to Return to Partisan Senate, Make Patronage Appointments," *Global News* (29 September 2019), online: <https://globalnews.ca/news/5966549/scheer-senate-trudeau-partisan-appointments/>.

8 Senate Government Representative Office, "Canadians Back New Independent Senate Appointment Process: Poll" (17 April 2019), online: <https://senate-gro.ca/senate-renewal/appointment-poll/>.

9 Andrew Heard, "Tapping the Potential of Senate-Driven Reform: Proposals to Limit the Powers of the Senate" (2015) 24:2 Const Forum Const 47.

10 Arash Abizadeh, "Representation, Bicameralism, Political Equality, and Sortition: Reconstituting the Second Chamber as a Randomly Selected Assembly," Perspectives on Politics (forthcoming).

11 Joanna Smith, "Senate's New Independence So Good It Should Be Enshrined in Law: Harder," *CTV News* (23 August 2019), online: <https://www.ctvnews.ca/politics/senate-s-new-independence-so-good-it-should-be-enshrined-in-law-harder-1.4562552>.

12 Meagan Fitzpatrick, "NDP Says Senate Should Be Starved of Funds," *CBC News* (22 June 2011), online: <https://www.cbc.ca/news/politics/ndp-says-senate-should-be-starved-of-funds-1.976912>.

13 "Stephen Harper's Unappointed Senate Seats Unconstitutional, Vancouver Lawyer Says," *CBC News* (15 December 2014), online: <https://www.cbc.ca/news/canada/british-columbia/stephen-harper-s-unappointed-senate-seats-unconstitutional-vancouver-lawyer-says-1.2873629>.

14 Léonid Sirota, "Please Advise" (7 January 2015), *Double Aspect* (blog), online: <https://doubleaspect.blog/2015/01/07/please-advise/>.

15 *Re: Resolution to amend the Constitution,* [1981] 1 SCR 753.

16 Joanna Smith, "Stephen Harper in No Rush to Fill Senate Vacancies," *The Star* (4 December 2014), online: <https://www.thestar.com/news/canada/2014/12/04/stephen_harper_in_no_rush_to_fill_senate_vacancies.html>.

17 Dennis Baker and Mark D. Jarvis, "The End of Informal Constitutional Change in Canada?" in Emmett Macfarlane, ed, *Constitutional Amendment in Canada* (Toronto: University of Toronto Press, 2016) at 188.

18 *Ibid* at 195.

19 Warren Newman, "Constitutional Amendment by Legislation" in Macfarlane, *Constitutional Amendment in Canada, supra* note 17, at 117.

20 It would not appear to apply to certain amendments under section 38 where provinces can opt out, and presumably not to those that only require the federal government acting alone. See Patrick J. Monahan and Byron Shaw, *Constitutional Law,* 4th ed (Toronto: Irwin Law, 2013) at 217.

21 *Ibid* at 216–17.

22 Rainer Knopff, "U2: Unanimity versus Unilateralism in Canada's Politics of Constitutional Amendment" in Macfarlane, *Constitutional Amendment in Canada, supra* note 17, at 132–37.

23 Philippe Lagassé and Patrick Baud, "The Crown and Constitutional Amendment after the Senate Reform and Supreme Court References" in Macfarlane, *Constitutional Amendment in Canada, supra* note 17, at 256–57.

24 Knopff, *supra* note 22 at 139.

25 Baker and Jarvis, *supra* note 17 at 198.

26 See Howard Leeson, *The Patriation Minutes* (Edmonton: Centre for Constitutional Studies, 2011); Barry L. Strayer, *Canada's Constitutional Revolution* (Edmonton: University of Alberta Press, 2013); Peter H. Russell, *Constitutional Odyssey: Can Canadians Become a Sovereign People?* 3d ed (Toronto: University of Toronto Press, 2004) at 121, 141; "Premiers' Conference, Ottawa, Ontario, April 16, 1981" in Anne F. Bayefsky, ed, *Canada's Constitution Act 1982 & Amendments: A Documentary History,* vol 2 (Toronto: McGraw-Hill Ryerson, 1989) 804 at 804.

27 Baker and Jarvis, *supra* note 17 at 200.

28 Carissima Mathen, "The Federal Principle: Constitutional Amendment and Intergovernmental Relations" in Macfarlane, *Constitutional Amendment in Canada, supra* note 17, at 75.

29 Dwight Newman, "Understanding the Section 43 Bilateral Amending Formula" in Macfarlane, *Constitutional Amendment in Canada, supra* note 17.

30 Kate Glover, "Structure, Substance and Spirit: Lessons in Constitutional Architecture from the Senate Reform Reference" (2014) 67 Sup Ct L Rev 221 at 254.

31 Michael Pal, "Constitutional Amendment after the *Senate Reference* and the Prospects for Electoral Reform" (2016) 76 Sup Ct L Rev 377.

32 Emmett Macfarlane, "Constitutional Constraints on Electoral Reform in Canada: Why Parliament Is (Mostly) Free to Implement a New Voting System" (2016) 76 Sup Ct L Rev 399.

33 *Reference re Supreme Court Act, ss. 5 and 6,* 2014 SCC 21, [2014] 1 SCR 433.

34 *Ibid* at para 85.

35 This may not have been an unintended feature of the Supreme Court's opinion: it is in the court's institutional interest to read section 41(d) as broadly as possible and thereby immunize it from a host of changes by Parliament.

36 Hugo Cyr, "The Bungling of Justice Nadon's Appointment to the Supreme Court of Canada" (2014) 67 Sup Ct L Rev 73 at 106.

37 Paul Daly, "Administering Constitutional Change: The Case of Bilingual Supreme Court Judges" (16 November 2015), *Administrative Law Matters* (blog),

online: <https://www.administrativelawmatters.com/blog/2015/11/16/administering
-constitutional-change-the-case-of-bilingual-supreme-court-judges/>.

38 Kate Glover, "Hard Amendment Cases in Canada" in Richard Albert, Xenophon Contiades, and Alkmene Fotiadou, eds, *Foundations and Traditions of Constitutional Amendment* (Oxford: Hart Publishing, 2017) at 289.

39 Richard Albert, "The Difficulty of Constitutional Amendment in Canada" (2015) 53:1 Alta L Rev 85.

40 For the most prominent example, see *Reference re Secession of Quebec,* [1998] 2 SCR 217.

41 Peter Aucoin, Mark D. Jarvis, and Lori Turnbull, *Democratizing the Constitution: Reforming Responsible Government* (Toronto: Emond Montgomery, 2011) at 80.

42 Andrew Heard, *Canadian Constitutional Conventions: The Marriage of Law and Politics,* 2d ed (Oxford: Oxford University Press, 2014).

43 Aucoin, Jarvis, and Turnbull, *supra* note 41 at 80–81.

44 Philippe Lagassé, "The Crown and Government Formation: Conventions, Practices, Customs, and Norms" (2019) 28:3 Const Forum Const 1 at 1.

45 *Ibid* at 1–4.

46 Christopher Cochrane, Kelly Blidook, and Rand Dyck, *Canadian Politics: Critical Approaches,* 8th ed (Toronto: Nelson Education, 2017) at 524.

47 Peter Zimonjic, "Trudeau Has Options to Ponder for Bringing Alta., Sask. Interests to the Cabinet Table," *CBC News* (24 October 2019), online: <https://www.cbc.ca/news/politics/trudeau-alberta-saskatchewan-cabinet-1.5333069>.

48 Christa Scholtz, "The Architectural Metaphor and the Decline of Political Conventions in the Supreme Court of Canada's Senate Reform Reference" (2018) 68 UTLJ 661.

49 Léonid Sirota, "Immuring Dicey's Ghost: The Senate Reform Reference and Constitutional Conventions" (2020) 51:2 Ottawa L Rev 313–60.

CONCLUSION: THE FUTURE OF THE SENATE, PARLIAMENT, AND CONSTITUTIONAL REFORM

1 Richard Albert, "Constructive Unamendability in Canada and the United States" (2014) 67 Sup Ct L Rev 181.

2 Emmett Macfarlane, *Governing from the Bench: The Supreme Court of Canada and the Judicial Role* (Vancouver: UBC Press, 2013).

3 Peter O'Neil, "Justin Trudeau's Senate Reform 'Dangerous' for B.C.: Experts," *Vancouver Sun* (22 January 2017), online: <http://vancouversun.com/news/local-news/justin-trudeaus-senate-reform-dangerous-for-b-c-experts>.

4 Dale Smith, "Can the ISG Survive the Next Election?" *Loonie Politics* (9 August 2019), online: <https://looniepolitics.com/can-the-isg-survive-the -next-election/>.

5 Peter Zimonjic, "Trudeau Has Options to Ponder for Bringing Alta., Sask. Interests to the Cabinet Table," *CBC News* (24 October 2019), online: <https:// www.cbc.ca/news/politics/trudeau-alberta-saskatchewan-cabinet-1.5333069>.

6 Serge Joyal, Introduction to "The Senate – Better Protecting the Federal Principle" in Serge Joyal and Judith Seidman, eds, *Reflecting on Our Past and Embracing Our Future: A Senate Initiative for Canada* (Montreal and Kingston: McGill-Queen's University Press, 2018) at 474.

7 *Ibid* at 475–76.

8 *Ibid* at 473.

9 *Ibid.*

10 Canada, Independent Advisory Board for Senate Appointments, "Assessment Criteria" (8 January 2018), online: <https://www.canada.ca/en/campaign/independent -advisory-board-for-senate-appointments/assessment-criteria.html>.

11 Joyal, *supra* note 6 at 478.

12 See Macfarlane, *Governing from the Bench, supra* note 2.

13 Hayden King, "The (independent) Senate was basically the only layer of accountability in Parliament on Indigenous legislation. If not for them, a lot of the Indigenous-specific bills would have been much worse" (15 October 2019 at 11:30a.m.), online: Twitter <https://twitter.com/Hayden_King/status/ 1184176999457329154>.

14 Emmett Macfarlane, "The Senate May Become an Increasingly Important Site for Indigenous Activism," *CBC News* (15 October 2018), online: <https:// www.cbc.ca/news/opinion/supreme-court-decision-1.4862275>.

15 Elizabeth McCallion, "Feminist Senators Are Critical Actors in Women's Representation," *Policy Options* (11 November 2019), online: <https://policyoptions. irpp.org/magazines/november-2019/feminist-senators-are-critical-actors-in -womens-representation/>.

16 *Reference re Supreme Court Act, ss. 5 and 6,* 2014 SCC 21, [2014] 1 SCR 433 [*Reference re Supreme Court Act*].

17 *Reference re Senate Reform,* 2014 SCC 32 at paras 26–27 [*Senate Reform*].

18 Warren Newman, "Constitutional Amendment by Legislation" in Emmett Macfarlane, ed, *Constitutional Amendment in Canada* (Toronto: University of Toronto Press, 2016).

19 *Reference re Supreme Court Act, supra* note 16.

20 Emmett Macfarlane, "Judicial Amendment of the Constitution," International Journal of Constitutional Law (forthcoming). The decision to impose on the partners of Confederation a "duty to negotiate" the secession of a province is

arguably an example of judicial amendment of the Constitution, whereby the Supreme Court effectively added a rule/process to the amending formula not through interpretation of the clear text of the Constitution but by articulating "unwritten principles" and applying them. See *Reference re Secession of Quebec,* [1998] 2 SCR 217.

21 Kent McNeil, *Flawed Precedent: The St. Catherine's Case and Aboriginal Title* (Vancouver: UBC Press, 2019).

22 *Reference re Supreme Court Act, supra* note 16.

23 Emmett Macfarlane, "'You Can't Always Get What You Want': Regime Politics, the Harper Government, and the Supreme Court of Canada" (2018) 51:1 Canadian Journal of Political Science 1.

Selected Bibliography

JURISPRUDENCE

Attorney-General for Manitoba v Manitoba Egg and Poultry Association et al., [1971] SCR 689.

OPSEU v Ontario (AG), [1987] 2 SCR 2, 41 DLR (4th) 1.

Re: Authority of Parliament in relation to the Upper House, [1980] 1 SCR 54.

Re B.C. Motor Vehicle Act, [1985] 2 SCR 486.

Re: Resolution to amend the Constitution, [1981] 1 SCR 753.

Reference re Assisted Human Reproduction Act, 2010 SCC 61, [2010] 3 SCR 457.

Reference re Same-Sex Marriage, [2004] 3 SCR 698, 2004 SCC 79.

Reference re Secession of Quebec, [1998] 2 SCR 217, 161 DLR (4th) 385.

Reference re Securities Act, 2011 SCC 66, [2011] 3 SCR 837.

Reference re Senate Reform, 2014 SCC 32.

Reference re Supreme Court Act, ss. 5 and 6, 2014 SCC 21, [2014] 1 SCR 433.

OTHER SOURCES

Abizadeh, Arash. "Representation, Bicameralism, Political Equality, and Sortition: Reconstituting the Second Chamber as a Randomly Selected Assembly," Perspectives on Politics (forthcoming).

Ajzenstat, Janet. "Bicameralism and Canada's Founders: The Origins of the Canadian Senate" in Serge Joyal, ed, *Protecting Canadian Democracy: The Senate You Never Knew* (Montreal and Kingston: McGill-Queen's University Press, 2003).

Albert, Richard. "Constitutional Amendment by Stealth" (2015) 60:4 McGill LJ 673.

–. "Constructive Unamendability in Canada and the United States" (2014) 67 Sup Ct L Rev 181.

–. "The Difficulty of Constitutional Amendment in Canada" (2015) 53:1 Alta L Rev 85.

Alvaro, Alexander. "Why Property Rights Were Excluded from the Canadian Charter of Rights and Freedoms" (1991) 24:2 Canadian Journal of Political Science 309.

Aucoin, Peter, Mark D. Jarvis, and Lori Turnbull. *Democratizing the Constitution: Reforming Responsible Government* (Toronto: Emond Montgomery, 2011).

Baker, Dennis, and Mark D. Jarvis. "The End of Informal Constitutional Change in Canada?" in Emmett Macfarlane, ed, *Constitutional Amendment in Canada* (Toronto: University of Toronto Press, 2016).

Banting, Keith G. *The Welfare State and Canadian Federalism,* 2d ed (Montreal and Kingston: McGill-Queen's University Press, 1987).

Baum, Lawrence. *Judges and Their Audiences: A Perspective on Judicial Behaviour* (Princeton, NJ: Princeton University Press, 2006).

Bergman, Gwyneth, and Emmett Macfarlane. "The Impact and Role of Officers of Parliament: Canada's Conflict of Interest and Ethics Commissioner" (2018) 61:1 Canadian Public Administration 5.

Boyer, J. Patrick. *Our Scandalous Senate* (Toronto: Dundurn, 2014).

Bridgman, Aengus. "A Nonpartisan Legislative Chamber: The Influence of the Canadian Senate," online: (August 2020) Party Politics, <https://doi.org/10.1177/1354068820911345>.

Buckner, Phillip. "The Maritimes and the Debate Over Confederation" in Daniel Heidt, ed, *Reconsidering Confederation: Canada's Founding Debates 1864–1999* (Calgary: University of Calgary Press, 2018).

Campbell, Colin. *The Canadian Senate: A Lobby from Within* (Toronto: Macmillan of Canada, 1978).

Corry, J.A., and J.E. Hodgetts, *Democratic Government and Politics,* 3d ed, revised (Toronto: University of Toronto Press, 1959).

Craft, Jonathan. *Backrooms and Beyond: Partisan Advisers and the Politics of Policy Work in Canada* (Toronto: University of Toronto Press, 2016).

Cyr, Hugo. "The Bungling of Justice Nadon's Appointment to the Supreme Court of Canada" (2014) 67 Sup Ct L Rev 73.

Desserud, Don. "Whither 91.1? The Constitutionality of Bill C-19: An Act to Limit Senate Tenure" in Jennifer Smith, ed, *The Democratic Dilemma: Reforming the Canadian Senate* (Montreal and Kingston: McGill-Queen's University Press, 2009).

Docherty, David C. "The Canadian Senate: Chamber of Sober Reflection or Loony Cousin Best Not Talked About" (2002) 8:3 Journal of Legislative Studies 27.

Dodek, Adam. "The Politics of the *Senate Reform Reference:* Fidelity, Frustration, and Federal Unilateralism" (2015) 60:4 McGill LJ 623.

Esselment, Anna. "Federal Feet and Provincial Pools: The Conservatives and Federalism in Canada" in J.P. Lewis and Joanna Everitt, eds, *The Blueprint:*

Conservative Parties and Their Impact on Canadian Politics (Toronto: University of Toronto Press, 2017).

Forsey, Helen. *A People's Senate for Canada: Not a Pipe Dream!* (Black Point, NS: Fernwood Publishing, 2015).

Franks, C.E.S. *The Parliament of Canada* (Toronto: University of Toronto Press, 1987).

Gérin-Lajoie, Paul. *Constitutional Amendment in Canada* (Toronto: University of Toronto Press, 1950).

Glover, Kate. "Hard Amendment Cases in Canada" in Richard Albert, Xenophon Contiades, and Alkmene Fotiadou, eds, *Foundations and Traditions of Constitutional Amendment* (Oxford: Hart Publishing, 2017).

—. "Structure, Substance and Spirit: Lessons in Constitutional Architecture from the Senate Reform Reference" (2014) 67 Sup Ct L Rev 221.

Godbout, Jean-François. *Lost on Division: Party Unity in the Canadian Parliament* (Toronto: University of Toronto Press, 2020).

Heard, Andrew. *Canadian Constitutional Conventions: The Marriage of Law and Politics,* 2d ed (Oxford: Oxford University Press, 2014).

—. "Constitutional Doubts about Bill C-20 and Senatorial Elections" in Jennifer Smith, ed, *The Democratic Dilemma: Reforming the Canadian Senate* (Montreal and Kingston: McGill-Queen's University Press, 2009).

—. "Tapping the Potential of Senate-Driven Reform: Proposals to Limit the Powers of the Senate" (2015) 24:2 Const Forum Const 47.

Hurley, James Ross. *Amending Canada's Constitution: History, Processes, Problems and Prospects* (Ottawa: Minister of Supply and Services Canada, 1996).

Institute for Research on Public Policy. *Renewal of the Canadian Senate: Where to from Here?* IRPP Report (Montreal: Institute for Research on Public Policy, 2019).

Joyal, Serge. Introduction to "The Senate – Better Protecting the Federal Principle" in Serge Joyal and Judith Seidman, eds, *Reflecting on Our Past and Embracing Our Future: A Senate Initiative for Canada* (Montreal and Kingston: McGill-Queen's University Press, 2018).

—, ed. *Protecting Canadian Democracy: The Senate You Never Knew* (Montreal and Kingston: McGill-Queen's University Press, 2003).

Joyal, Serge, and Judith Seidman, eds. *Reflecting on Our Past and Embracing Our Future: A Senate Initiative for Canada* (Montreal and Kingston: McGill-Queen's University Press, 2018).

Kirby, Michael, and Hugh Segal. *A House Undivided: Making Senate Independence Work* (Ottawa: Public Policy Forum, 2016).

Knopff, Rainer. "U2: Unanimity versus Unilateralism in Canada's Politics of Constitutional Amendment" in Emmett Macfarlane, ed, *Constitutional Amendment in Canada* (Toronto: University of Toronto Press, 2016).

Kunz, F.A. *The Modern Senate of Canada 1925–1963: A Re-appraisal* (Toronto: University of Toronto Press, 1965).

Lagassé, Philippe. "The Crown and Government Formation: Conventions, Practices, Customs, and Norms" (2019) 28:3 Const Forum Const 1.

Lagassé, Philippe, and Patrick Baud. "The Crown and Constitutional Amendment after the Senate Reform and Supreme Court References" in Emmett Macfarlane, ed, *Constitutional Amendment in Canada* (Toronto: University of Toronto Press, 2016).

Lawlor, Andrea, and Erin Crandall. "Committee Performance in the Senate of Canada: Some Sobering Analysis for the Chamber of 'Sober Second Thought'" (2013) 51:34 Commonwealth and Comparative Politics 549.

Leeson, Howard. *The Patriation Minutes* (Edmonton: Centre for Constitutional Studies, 2011).

Macfarlane, Emmett. "Consensus and Unanimity at the Supreme Court of Canada" (2010) 52 Sup Ct L Rev 379.

–, ed. *Constitutional Amendment in Canada* (Toronto: University of Toronto Press, 2016).

–. "Constitutional Constraints on Electoral Reform in Canada: Why Parliament Is (Mostly) Free to Implement a New Voting System" (2016) 76 Sup Ct L Rev 399.

–. "Dialogue or Compliance? Measuring Legislatures' Policy Responses to Court Rulings on Rights" (2013) 34 International Political Science Review 39.

–. "The Future of Constitutional Change in Canada: Examining Our Legal, Political, and Jurisprudential Straitjacket" in Richard Albert, Paul Daly, and Vanessa MacDonnell, eds, *The Canadian Constitution in Transition* (Toronto: University of Toronto Press, 2019).

–. *Governing from the Bench: The Supreme Court of Canada and the Judicial Role* (Vancouver: UBC Press, 2013).

–. "Judicial Amendment of the Constitution," International Journal of Constitutional Law (forthcoming).

–. "The Perils and Paranoia of Senate Reform: Does Senate Independence Threaten Canadian Democracy?" in Elizabeth Goodyear-Grant and Kyle Hanniman, eds, *Canada: State of the Federation 2017 – Canada at 150: Federalism and Democratic Renewal* (Kingston, ON: Institute of Intergovernmental Relations, 2019).

–. *The Renewed Canadian Senate: Organizational Challenges and Relations with the Government*. IRPP Study 71 (Montreal: Institute for Research on Public Policy, 2019).

–. "Unsteady Architecture: Ambiguity, the Senate Reference, and the Future of Constitutional Amendment in Canada" (2015) 60:4 McGill LJ 883.

–. "'You Can't Always Get What You Want': Regime Politics, the Harper Government, and the Supreme Court of Canada" (2018) 51:1 Canadian Journal of Political Science 1.

Mackay, Robert A. *The Unreformed Senate of Canada,* revised ed (Toronto: McClelland and Stewart, 1963).

Malloy, Jonathan. "More Than a Terrain of Struggle: Parliament as Ideological Instrument and Objective under Conservatism" in J.P. Lewis and Joanna Everitt, eds, *The Blueprint: Conservative Parties and Their Impact on Canadian Politics* (Toronto: University of Toronto Press, 2017).

Manfredi, Christopher P. *An Expert Opinion on the Possible Effects of Bill C-7* (June 2013).

Mathen, Carissima. *Courts without Cases: The Law and Politics of Advisory Opinions* (Oxford: Hart Publishing, 2019).

–. "The Federal Principle: Constitutional Amendment and Intergovernmental Relations" in Emmett Macfarlane, ed, *Constitutional Amendment in Canada* (Toronto: University of Toronto Press, 2016).

Mathen, Carissima, and Michael Plaxton. *The Tenth Justice: Judicial Appointments, Marc Nadon, and the Supreme Court Act Reference* (Vancouver: UBC Press, 2020).

McCallion, Elizabeth. "Feminist Senators Are Critical Actors in Women's Representation," *Policy Options* (11 November 2019), online: <https://policy options.irpp.org/magazines/november-2019/feminist-senators-are-critical -actors-in-womens-representation/>.

McCormick, Peter, Ernest C. Manning, and Gordon Gibson. *Regional Representation: The Canadian Partnership* (Calgary: Canada West Foundation, 1981).

McHugh, James T. *The Senate and the People of Canada: A Counterintuitive Approach to Reform of the Senate of Canada* (New York: Lexington Books, 2017).

McNeil, Kent. *Flawed Precedent: The St. Catherine's Case and Aboriginal Title* (Vancouver: UBC Press, 2019).

Monahan, Patrick J. "The Public Policy Role of the Supreme Court of Canada in the *Secession Reference*" (2000) 11 NJCL 65.

Monahan, Patrick J., and Byron Shaw. *Constitutional Law,* 4th ed (Toronto: Irwin Law, 2013).

Morley, J. Gareth. "Dead Hands, Living Trees, Historic Compromises: The Senate Reform and Supreme Court Act References Bring the Originalism Debate to Canada" (2016) 53 Osgoode Hall LJ 745.

Morton, F.L., and Rainer Knopff. *The Charter Revolution and the Court Party* (Toronto: University of Toronto Press, 2000).

Morton, Ted. *No Statecraft, Questionable Jurisprudence: How the Supreme Court Tried to Kill Senate Reform.* 8(21) The School of Public Policy: SPP Research Papers (University of Calgary, 2015).

Newman, Dwight. "Understanding the Section 43 Bilateral Amending Formula" in Emmett Macfarlane, ed, *Constitutional Amendment in Canada* (Toronto: University of Toronto Press, 2016).

Newman, Warren. "Constitutional Amendment by Legislation" in Emmett Macfarlane, ed, *Constitutional Amendment in Canada* (Toronto: University of Toronto Press, 2016).

Pal, Michael. "Constitutional Amendment after the *Senate Reference* and the Prospects for Electoral Reform" (2016) 76 Sup Ct L Rev 377.

Puddister, Kate. *Seeking the Court's Advice: The Politics of the Canadian Reference Power* (Vancouver: UBC Press, 2019).

Rémillard, Gil. "Senate Reform: Back to Basics" in Serge Joyal, ed, *Protecting Canadian Democracy: The Senate You Never Knew* (Montreal and Kingston: McGill-Queen's University Press, 2003).

Roach, Kent. *The Supreme Court on Trial: Judicial Activism or Democratic Dialogue*, revised ed (Toronto: Irwin Law, 2016).

Ross, Sir George. *The Senate of Canada: Its Constitution, Powers and Duties Historically Considered* (Toronto: Copp, Clark Company, 1914).

Russell, Peter H. *Constitutional Odyssey: Can Canadians Become a Sovereign People?* 3d ed (Toronto: University of Toronto Press, 2004).

Savoie, Donald J. *Breaking the Bargain: Public Servants, Ministers, and Parliament* (Toronto: University of Toronto Press, 2003).

–. *Democracy in Canada: The Disintegration of Our Institutions* (Montreal and Kingston: McGill-Queen's University Press, 2019).

Schertzer, Robert. *The Judicial Role in a Diverse Federation: Lessons from the Supreme Court of Canada* (Toronto: University of Toronto Press, 2016).

Scholtz, Christa. "The Architectural Metaphor and the Decline of Political Conventions in the Supreme Court of Canada's Senate Reform Reference" (2018) 68 UTLJ 661.

Sirota, Léonid. "Immuring Dicey's Ghost: The Senate Reform Reference and Constitutional Conventions" (2020) Ottawa L Rev 313.

Sirota, Léonid, and Benjamin Oliphant. "Originalist Reasoning in Canadian Constitutional Jurisprudence" (2017) 50:2 UBC L Rev 505.

Smiley, Donald V. *The Federal Condition in Canada* (Toronto: McGraw-Hill Ryerson, 1987).

Smith, Dale. *The Unbroken Machine: Canada's Democracy in Action* (Toronto: Dundurn, 2017).

Smith, David E. *The Canadian Senate in Bicameral Perspective* (Toronto: University of Toronto Press, 2003).

–. *Federalism and the Constitution of Canada* (Toronto: University of Toronto Press, 2010).

—. "The Improvement of the Senate by Nonconstitutional Means" in Serge Joyal, ed, *Protecting Canadian Democracy: The Senate You Never Knew* (Montreal and Kingston: McGill-Queen's University Press, 2003).

Smith, Jennifer, ed. *The Democratic Dilemma: Reforming the Canadian Senate* (Montreal and Kingston: McGill-Queen's University Press, 2009).

Stillborn, Jack. "Forty Years of Not Reforming the Senate" in Serge Joyal, ed, *Protecting Canadian Democracy: The Senate You Never Knew* (Montreal and Kingston: McGill-Queen's University Press, 2003).

Strayer, Barry L. *Canada's Constitutional Revolution* (Edmonton: University of Alberta Press, 2013).

—. "Saskatchewan and the Amendment of the Canadian Constitution" (1966) 12 McGill LJ 443.

Thomas, Paul G. "Comparing the Lawmaking Roles of the Senate and the House of Commons" in Serge Joyal, ed, *Protecting Canadian Democracy: The Senate You Never Knew* (Montreal and Kingston: McGill-Queen's University Press, 2003).

—. *Moving toward a New and Improved Senate.* IRPP Study 70 (Montreal: Institute for Research on Public Policy, 2019).

Verrelli, Nadia. "Harper's Senate Reform: An Example of Open Federalism?" in Jennifer Smith, ed, *The Democratic Dilemma: Reforming the Canadian Senate* (Montreal and Kingston: McGill-Queen's University Press, 2009).

Walters, Mark D. "The Constitutional Form and Reform of the Senate: Thoughts on the Constitutionality of Bill C-7" (2013) 7 Journal of Parliamentary and Political Law 37.

Ward, Norman. *Dawson's The Government of Canada,* 6th ed (Toronto: University of Toronto Press, 1987).

Watts, Ronald L. "Bicameralism in Federal Parliamentary Systems" in Serge Joyal, ed, *Protecting Canadian Democracy: The Senate You Never Knew* (Montreal and Kingston: McGill-Queen's University Press, 2003).

—. "Bill C-20: Faulty Procedure and Inadequate Solution (Testimony before the Legislative Committee on Bill C-20, House of Commons, 7 May 2008" in Jennifer Smith, ed, *The Democratic Dilemma: Reforming the Canadian Senate* (Montreal and Kingston: McGill-Queen's University Press, 2009).

Whyte, John D. "Senate Reform: What Does the Constitution Say?" in Jennifer Smith, ed, *The Democratic Dilemma: Reforming the Canadian Senate* (Montreal and Kingston: McGill-Queen's University Press, 2009).

Index of Cases

Index

abolition of the Senate: consequences of, 47–48, 50, 55; procedure to effect, 48, 94–96, 144, 146; proposals, 4, 8, 34–35, 37, 46–50, 55, 63, 69, 144; public opinion 3, 66; *Reference re Senate Reform*, 58, 69, 71–73, 76–77, 94–96, 170; reform as alternative to, 158; unlikelihood of, 5, 50, 55, 144, 146, 170; *Upper House reference*, 72–73, 89

Aboriginal self-government, 45. *See also* First Nations; Indigenous peoples

Acadians, 30

Ajzenstat, Janet, 13, 47

Alani, Aniz, 144–45

Albert, Richard, ix, 141, 152, 158

Alberta: constitutional amendment process, 147; environmental legislation, 27, 123; federal Cabinet representation, 154–55, 161, 165, 167; Senate elections, 46, 62, 86, 143; Senate reform, 41–42

amending formula: bilateral procedure, 149; Charlottetown Accord proposals, 45; complexity, 60; electoral reform, 150; entrench-ment, 36, 50, 71–72, 80; general procedure (7/50 rule), 62, 71, 73, 76, 81–82, 84–85, 87–89, 94–95, 97; House of Commons seats, 95; Parliament in, 28, 60, 77, 88–89, 97, 137, 147–48, 150; political culture surrounding, 59, 144, 158; provincial consent under, 8–9, 52, 74, 80, 87–90, 148, 166; purpose, 149; Quebec Court of Appeal, 68; reform of Senate, 10, 52, 60, 68, 73–74, 76–98, 137–40, 144; regional veto, 147–48, 168; Senate abolition, 94–96; Senate suspen-sive veto in, 96; Supreme Court appointments, 150, 167; Supreme Court's elaboration on, 3–4, 9–10, 75–98, 137–40, 149–50, 156, 158, 166–71, 196*n*20; unanimity pro-cedure, 68, 73–74, 76–77, 95–96, 148. *See also Constitution Act, 1982:* section 38; section 41; section 41(a); section 41(b), sec-tion 41(d); section 41(e); section 42(1)(b); section 44; section 45

Atlantic provinces, 27, 44, 50, 147, 155, 167

Aucoin, Peter, 153

auditor general, 44, 56, 64–66

Printed and bound in Canada by Friesens
Set in Garamond by Artegraphica Design Co. Ltd.
Copy editor: Frank Chow
Proofreader: Judith Earnshaw
Cover designer: Will Brown